Preparing
for the
Athletic Trainers' Certification Examination

Lorin Cartwright, MS, EMT, ATC
Pioneer High School, Ann Arbor, MI

Human Kinetics

Library of Congress Cataloging-in-Publication Data

Cartwright, Lorin, 1956-
  Preparing for the Athletic Trainers' certification examination / Lorin
Cartwright
      p. cm.
  Includes bibliographical references and index.
  ISBN 0-87322-504-X
  1. Personal trainers--Certification--Examinations--Study guides.
 I. Title.
  GV4287.C37 1995   94-29306
  613.7—dc20   CIP

ISBN: 0-87322-504-X

Acquisitions Editor: Richard A. Washburn, PhD; **Developmental Editor:** Mary Fowler; **Assistant Editor:** Henry Woolsey; **Copyeditor:** Tom Plummer; **Proofreader:** Sue Fetters; **Typesetter and Text Layout:** Yvonne Winsor; **Illustrations:** Tara Welsch; **Text Designer:** Judy Henderson; **Cover Designer:** Judy Henderson; **Printer:** United Graphics.

Printed in the United States of America

10 9 8 7 6 5 4 3 2 1

Human Kinetics
P.O. Box 5076, Champaign, IL 61825-5076
1-800-747-4457

Canada: Human Kinetics, Box 24040, Windsor, ON N8Y 4Y9
1-800-465-7301 (in Canada only)

Europe: Human Kinetics, P.O. Box IW14, Leeds LS16 6TR, England
(44) 532 781708

Australia: Human Kinetics, 2 Ingrid Street, Clapham 5062, South Australia
(08) 371 3755

New Zealand: Human Kinetics, P.O. Box 105-231, Auckland 1
(09) 309 2259

To all athletic training educators, for the blessing of passing on vast volumes of knowledge to future athletic trainers.

Contents

Preface

You know you're ready to become a certified athletic trainer. You have the education and hands-on-experience. But you might be uneasy about passing the National Athletic Trainers' Association (NATA) certification exam. You probably have several questions, ranging from what you need to know, to how to register for the test, to what your chances are for success. *Preparing for the Athletic Trainers' Certification Examination* can answer these questions and more. This easy-to-read text will put you at ease even before you go to the test site and it will give you a greater confidence in your ability.

You will find appropriate materials for review and help to assess your basic knowledge and skills in every area of athletic training. With this guide's help you can pinpoint weaknesses prior to examination day and use additional resources to strengthen these weaknesses. You will even have easy-to-understand guidelines for preparing and registering for the test.

This review guide is not intended to replace your 4-year athletic training curriculum or to be the sole preparation for the certification examination. However, it will provide you with valuable insights and strategies for successfully passing the NATA certification exam.

To help you get the most out of this book I've divided it into three parts. Part I provides all the information you need to pass the test on your first try, including useful information about procedures, scoring, and test structure and administration. You will learn what to expect on test day and suggestions for what to bring with you to the test. Information on receiving and interpreting your results is included, along with information on what to do when you receive test results. Additionally, Part I provides helpful hints to enhance your studying efficiency.

In Part II you'll find detailed information about each of the three parts of the certification examination: the written examination, the oral/practical test, and the written simulation. For each part of the test, I explain what it examines, how questions are presented, and how the part is administered. I also offer several test-taking strategies to help you succeed.

Part III presents the most complete, comprehensive list of study questions available. They will simulate taking the actual certification examination. Although these questions will not appear on the real exam, some may be similar to those you can expect to find. Answering these questions will not only prepare you to take and pass the exam, but also will provide you with an excellent studying opportunity.

For the written and oral/practical sections, questions appear in multiple choice and yes-no forms. The written simulation, which tests your decision-making skills in situations a certified athletic trainer faces daily, provides opening scenarios and asks you to select the best course of action from a list of possibilities. A complete answer key appears in Appendix A so you can easily check your answers and assess your ability to pass the exam. I've included the equivalent of four complete, fully referenced and documented written exams. By substantiating each question, I've made it easy for you to find additional information concerning a subject area, should you choose to do this.

Preparing for the Athletic Trainers' Certification Examination will help you develop strategies for remembering what you learned in college and for applying your knowledge while under rigorous testing pressure. This book gives you the valuable information you need to study, take, and pass the NATA certification exam. So relax and enjoy your review.

Acknowledgments

Special thanks to Barb Hansen, who has worked from start to finish typing the text. She graciously listened through the good and the bad.

Thanks also to my parents, the best teachers that life can provide. Thanks for your encouragement, support, motivation, and, most of all, for your love.

To Richard Ray, my friend and former NATA Board of Certification representative, who encouraged me to write a textbook (you're still one ahead of me). He, along with current NATA Board of Certification member Brad Sherman, assured me that the information in this text is up-to-date and correct.

To my colleagues who have read, typed, and scribbled their way through these pages on short notice: Linda Cartwright, Rowena Dansby, Joan Fitzgibbon, Suzy Heinzman, Gail Oljace, Bill Pitney, Ellen Taylor, and Robbie Vought.

To Bob Kisken, for the photographs taken on short notice.

To Diana Slowiejko, the most efficient research assistant with whom I've ever worked.

To Doug Woods—if you were not there when I needed a lift, I would not have become an athletic trainer.

And finally, to Brian Kohl, Rowena Dansby, and my student athletic trainers for holding down the fort while I was writing.

Taking the Certification Examination

I

1
CHAPTER

About the Examination

Athletic training goes back thousands of years, perhaps to the days when gladiators fought in the Colosseum. After a gladiator had fallen, several people ran out with a stretcher to carry off the dead man. In a sense, the groundwork was laid in ancient times for what we now know as the athletic trainer. The more recent forerunners of today's athletic trainer had no formal educational training: Their knowledge was developed through practical, hands-on training. The skills that we use today can be traced to those experiences with athletes. These early trainers came from backgrounds in the armed forces and as parents, coaches, and managers. The varied backgrounds and lack of formal training resulted in inconsistent care of athletes.

Ancient times were usually more gruesome, but modern athletes nonetheless need people who can do much more than carry a stretcher. As the need for better care of athletes has grown, so has the need for athletic trainers to have formal education and basic, entry-level knowledge. This is where the process of certification begins.

The first examination for certified athletic trainer occurred in December 1969. By the next year a group of individuals formed the National Athletic Trainers' Association Board of Certification (BOC). The BOC generates a test, decides how to administer and score it, and decides who meets the criteria for becoming certified. The BOC is made up of 10 representatives and a chairperson. The representatives are elected from their respective districts (the National Athletic Trainers Association is divided nationally into 10 districts).

■ Test Structure and Administration

The original certification test had 150 written questions. An additional oral/practical portion consisted of five questions. The oral/practical test was administered by three certified athletic trainers and hand corrected, taking up to 3 months for scores to be completed. Today the certification examination has three parts, including a written section, an oral/practical one, and a written simulation.

The written examination and simulation are administered by a certified athletic trainer, referred to as the *proctor*. The proctor is responsible for checking your admission ticket and photo identification before you enter the examination room. You will not be allowed to take the test without a proper admission ticket having the correct date and time for the test and a photo identification. These two items are needed for both the morning and afternoon tests, so do not lose them. The BOC issues the admission ticket when you are accepted to take the examination. At the examination the proctor will guide you in filling out the computer forms with your personal information for all three sections of the test.

The oral/practical test and written examination are given concurrently. During the written examination your name will be called to take the oral/practical test. At one time it could be done off-site, and therefore the written examination and the oral/practical could be taken on different days. The off-site oral/practical test was administered one-on-one by a certified athletic trainer, but this did not seem fair to all candidates, and it created inconsistencies in the certification process. Now it is less time-consuming, having only four questions. All the examiners must be certified. There are three certified athletic trainers at the oral/practical test: a model and two examiners. Models have been certified a minimum of 1 year, and examiners a minimum of 2 years. Earlier, models had no requirements for qualification.

The written simulation was added to assure that protocols are used in a variety of basic situations. The BOC is one of only a few organizations to use this type of test.

The BOC generates a pool of test questions from which some are chosen randomly for each examination. Because of this random selection there may be several questions from one area or no questions from another area. Examinations are not reused.

■ Eligibility Criteria

To bring professionalism to the certification process, the BOC instituted necessary changes. First a professional preparation standardized for those desiring to take the certification examination was established. This assured that the same instruction was given at colleges and universities across the country. A group to monitor the preparation of the standardized education, the Professional Education Committee (PEC), was formed. Those people who had been working in the athletic training field and would not be able to meet the requirements of the PEC were grandfathered (i.e., not required to take the certification examination to receive the title of certified athletic trainer).

The PEC regulates two types of programs. The first is the curriculum program and the second is the internship program. The curriculum program is under close scrutiny. Two members of the PEC visit each institution involved in preparation every 5 years. For a curriculum program to be approved the strict PEC guidelines must be met. These were set to insure standardization of education at institutions around the country. Deficiencies in a curriculum program must be corrected to maintain eligibility status. Certain classes are required and certain therapeutic modalities must be available. There must be instructional aids (textbooks, models, audiovisual equipment) and a training room of adequate size. There must be equal opportunity for all students and strong instructors in all phases of the curriculum. Supplies for care and rehabilitation of injuries and a certified athletic trainer on staff as the program director are also required. Clinical experience of 800 hr is necessary in a curriculum program. The clinical hours are required to provide the hands-on experience that early athletic trainers used to gain valuable experience working with injured athletes, to prevent injury, and to cover events. Twenty-five percent of clinical hours must be with sport activities such as football, lacrosse, rugby, soccer, gymnastics, wrestling, basketball, hockey, or volleyball.

The internship program is designed for colleges or universities that do not meet all curriculum rquirements and do not wish, or cannot actively pursue, curriculum status. The PEC requires that a minimum core curriculum be available for those desiring to pursue certification through an apprenticeship program. This program requires 1,500 clinical experience hr, with 1,000 hr being in a traditional athletic setting. It is thought that the increased clinical hours help fill the void of requirements found only in a curriculum program.

To add more professionalism and credence to athletic training, the PEC pursued and received the accreditation of the American Medical Association's Committee on Allied Health Education and Accreditation (CAHEA). The accreditation of the CAHEA was highly regarded, as the committee determines the conduct of the allied health professions. CAHEA has since been disbanded and replaced by another group, the Joint Review Committee on Athletic Training (JRC-AT), for which NATA educational programs must now be accredited.

■ Scoring System

Next standardization of the test was needed to ensure basic, entry-level athletic training skills and knowledge. The National Athletic Trainers' Association was solely responsible for designing and administering the certification examination. To increase credibility of the test, the BOC became an agency outside the NATA. The BOC then gained rights to give the certification examination on behalf of the NATA. The BOC took an additional step when it contracted with a testing service. All the testing materials have computer-generated answer and scoring sheets. The testing service, Columbia Assessment Services (CAS), is used to correct the computer answer sheets. CAS also has the responsibility to calculate oral/practical examiners' interexaminer reliability. Examiners are rated based on how their scores compare to each other in examinations of the same candidate. Those examiners with the highest interexaminer reliability are the examiners used in future certification examinations. Turnaround time has improved dramatically with the testing service. Scoring results now take only 1 week.

Scoring for the written test is basic, one point per question. Answer all the questions, because any questions left unanswered are marked one point against you. Scoring for the oral/practical is again one point per positive response to the specific question asked; responses are marked by the examiners. For example, if the question asked you to tape a sprained proximal interphalangeal joint in 5 min, the examiners' score sheet might read

1. The finger is placed into 30° of flexion.

   ❏ Yes   ❏ No

2. The tape is wrinkle free.

   ❏ Yes   ❏ No

3. The tape is supportive.

   ❏ Yes   ❏ No

4. The task is completed in 5 min or less.

   ❏ Yes   ❏ No

If you do all four tasks the examiners would mark the boxes yes and you would receive all the points available for this question. But you are not given bonus points for doing an evaluation of the finger or for giving a brief explanation of rehabilitation, so stick to the question that was asked.

In the written simulation, each question has a different point total, and each answer is weighted. The weighting of the answer is based on the importance of the answer related to the question. The written simulation is a critical thinking/priority test, meaning things must be put into the proper sequence to be correct. For example, an athlete has been evaluated with an acute ankle sprain. What is your initial treatment?

Options given to you include:

give cardiopulmonary resuscitation

apply ice

apply heat

elevate lower extremity

apply compression

You need to be careful when selecting an answer during the written simulation, because once it is selected the "highlighter" makes erasing impossible.

If you were to select letters *b, d,* and *e* you would be given three points for each of those responses. You would have a total of nine points for this question. If you selected letter *c,* "apply heat," you would loose three points, and your total for that question would be six. If at any point you were to select letter *a,* "give cardiopulmonary resuscitation," you would lose all possible points for this question, as this is not part of care for an ankle. More importantly, it would likely result in great harm to the athlete. The weighted points are not listed on the test or answer sheet; these are kept secret by the BOC and CAS.

■ Test Sites

The BOC determines the sites needed for the certification examination. They determine sites and test dates based on the number of candidates in an area and access to the site. The test sites are supervised by trained test site administrators. These administrators are certified athletic trainers who have the responsibility of organizing the test site by obtaining the certified athletic trainers, proctors, and models, and assigning candidates to the oral/practical examiners. Test site administrators also explain the examination the day of the test to all the candidates and to the oral/practical examiners. Lastly, these administrators send the information to CAS for processing.

2
CHAPTER

Taking the Test

For many people, test taking can be stressful and nerve-racking. But just having an idea of what to expect can reduce your anxiety level tremendously and can help you perform your best on test day. This chapter helps you prepare for the test by knowing everything from how to register to what to expect before, during, and after exam day. Special study hints help you be as relaxed and ready as possible to take your exam.

■ *Who Can Take the Test?*

College graduates who have completed their course work and practical hours in the curriculum or internship programs are eligible to take the certification examination. Graduation candidates from either curriculum or internship programs who have completed their course work and practical hours and are in their final semester are, with proof of graduation, also eligible candidates. Graduation candidates need to pick the certification test date nearest their graduation. Graduation candidates should note that if you do pass the certification examination and do not show final proof of graduation, your certification will not be sent.

■ *Registering for the Test*

Give yourself at least 6 months' lead time to be assured you meet all the requirements to take the exam. Candidates who mail in their applications and complete their requirements are assigned to test sites on a first-come, first-served basis. During a recent certification exam there were 1,500 candidates. If you delay registering for the test you will have difficulty getting your first choice for a testing site. If you need support to accommodate a special need, such as having someone read the test (for dyslexia), notify the BOC when you register.

■ Obtaining an Application

Tests are given nationwide five times a year, and each test date has a deadline (usually 1 month prior to the testing date), by which your application must be received. Once you are ready to take the test and have a date and time selected, write or call:

> Columbia Assessment Services
> NATA BOC
> 3725 National Dr., Ste. 213
> Raleigh, NC 27612
> 919-787-2721

■ Test Requirements

Columbia Assessment Services then will send information about the eligibility requirements to take the test. You will want to gather information before receiving the application so that you are ready when it arrives. You will need these items:

1. The names and dates of all the colleges and universities you attended and the degrees you received as well as an official copy of all your grade transcripts.

2. A copy of your NATA student membership card, if you are a member. (If you are not a member of NATA, it will cost more to take the certification examination.)

3. A check or money order to take the test (for members of NATA, currently $260; for nonmembers, $310).

4. A copy of the university course description for the NATA-required classes: health, anatomy, physiology, basic and advanced classes in athletic training, exercise physiology, kinesiology, and psychology.

5. The number of hours you have worked in various sports.

6. A copy of your first aid and cardiopulmonary resuscitation (CPR) cards. (If you don't have these, ask your instructor to give you a copy of the course record, indicating you took and passed the class; proof of current EMT certification can be used in place of first aid and CPR cards.)

7. A good idea of where and when you want to take the certification examination. (Have alternative choices, in case your first choice is full by the time your application is sent; the test is given five times annually, but space may be limited.)

8. A nearby notary public to witness your sponsoring athletic trainer's signature.

9. The certification number of the sponsoring certified athletic trainer.
10. Your social security number.

■ Test Locations

These are held at regional sites, usually on college campuses. Test sites are assigned by the number of candidates in an area, the location of a test site administrator, and the size of the available facility. The test starts at 8:00 a.m. and continues until noon, with the second session from 1:30 p.m. until 4:30 p.m. This is an all-day affair. Do not plan for other activities that might force you to rush through the test. You will be given time for lunch, and you may want to bring a lunch with you or find a restaurant ahead of time.

■ Testing Frequency

The test is given five times a year. Candidates who fail one or two sections have only to retake those sections if they do so within one year. After that time they are required to again pay full test fees and take the three-section test. A candidate may attempt the test and two retakes. If the candidate does not pass all three sections after three attempts, the BOC recommends course work to enhance the areas of education the person is lacking. Anyone who fails three times must wait at least 6 months before another retake.

■ Changing Your Mind

If you are not ready, call or write the BOC and ask for a postponement until the next test date. You can receive a refund ($195 for NATA members or $232.50 for nonmembers) if you cancel 30 days before the exam date, but your request for postponement must be in writing. To reschedule a test, send the BOC an additional check of $25 plus the test fee, within 30 days of your original cancellation.

Do not postpone because of fear or anxiety, especially if you know the material. If you are unusually anxious about test taking, you should seek professional help. The proctor and examiners are aware of the anxiety that tests can generate, and special allowances have been made in the past for people with unusually high anxiety levels, especially for the oral/practical portion of the test. The usual procedure is to allow you to relax, perhaps get a drink of water, return to the room, and continue from where you left off.

Don't just give up. Even if you feel you are stumbling your way through it, keep going. By continuing, you learn valuable information for retaking the test. A model may take a very anxious person in the hallway, give him water, and try to help him relax. If you find yourself in that situation, use visualization and relaxation techniques.

■ Test-Day Procedures

On the day of the test you will be required to bring the admissions ticket, confirmation notification from the BOC, and your driver's license for identification. The identification number on your admissions ticket is required to be on all of your testing materials (answer sheets and oral/ practical cassette). All testing sheets for the exam are computerized and require a number 2 pencil. Bring two. The proctor will supply one if you forget yours. For the written simulation the highlighting pen will be provided. Do not bring any books or paper to the test, as they are not allowed in the testing area.

If an emergency arises on exam day notify the BOC at 919-787-2721. Do not be surprised if no one answers the phone. Leave a message describing your emergency, along with your identification number and test site.

After you have completed the test you are not allowed to discuss the content of this examination with anyone. If you are caught doing so you will be put before the BOC review board for disciplinary measures, usually resulting in dismissal, and you will never be a certified athletic trainer. One thing that is helpful to do after the test is to debrief. This is simply talking—about how you felt during the test, about funny little things that happened, about how successful you were, and about how glad you are it is over. The comment by most examiners after giving the test is "I remember how I felt after just completing the test." I guess you could say it is a feeling that stays with you the rest of your life.

■ Helpful Hints

Preparation is the key to a successful performance on exam day. You can take several steps before and during the test to help you do your best.

Studying for the Exam

To help you study for the exam, I suggest the following:

1. Do not wait until the last minute to start studying—give yourself at least 3 months' preparation time. Try to study a minimum of an hour a day. Every once in a while give yourself a break.

2. Read the references that are recommended in the bibliography of this textbook and make notes.

3. Look over past exams you have taken in your college courses (generally college exam questions will be more comprehensive than those on the NATA certification exam).

4. Make use of a study group to cut down the amount of time you have to spend in any one area (each person in the group can be responsible for a section of the body).

5. Use memory joggers to help you remember things. For example, SOAP (a method of clinical note taking) means:

S–subjective
O–objective
A–assessment
P–plan

6. Do not study while watching television, as this will keep you from focusing on the topic. Avoid distractions.

7. Avoid using nonprescribed medications that will make you tired or keep you awake (e.g., caffeine) just to study. The use of medications will interrupt rapid eye movement sleep and you will wake up unrefreshed. Use of medication will be harmful to your study time and create gaps in your memorization of facts.

8. Try to study in a room that simulates the test site, as this will make you more comfortable on the exam day.

9. Do not spend time studying an area where there is disagreement about how to treat an injury.

For example, if one textbook says it is appropriate to relocate a dislocated patella and another says it is not, then do not relocate the patella. Once you get into the field of athletic training you will be guided by a team physician who must decide how you will handle injuries.

Reducing Anxiety

To minimize any anxiety you may have concerning the testing room, go to the test site as soon as you are accepted as a candidate for the exam and look over all potential examination rooms. Sit down in a seat you would normally pick and try it out for comfort. If you do not like it, move. Find a seat that you will be comfortable sitting in for 4 hr. You will want to keep your shoulders and neck loose. A seat with arms or a high table is suitable for this. If possible, try taking a sample exam at that particular site. It is also good to get to the examination site at a time of day similar to the scheduled examination time. Try to simulate the test by taking the three sections, with the same number of questions and the same length of time. Notice if the room has any distractions, such as windows, loud noises, heat or cold, bells, loud-ticking clocks, aisleways, or poor lighting. Other students will probably want to ask the proctor questions in the front of the room. Will this be a distraction for you? You must also decide if your study group will sit together or apart. In some settings candidates are assigned seats. Try to meet the proctor of the exam while you are there checking out potential rooms. Walk around in potential oral/practical rooms too. Again, sit down in a chair and look for distractions.

If you cannot visit the site prior to the exam, you may want to spend the night in a hotel close to the site and go there extra early to get a look around. (Staying in a hotel the night before also may relieve some of your anxiety about getting lost in an unfamiliar city.)

About 1 week before the test you should practice some relaxation techniques. You may want to do some creative visualization or some deep breathing to help you relax. Silently tell yourself, "I will do well, I will relax, I will pass." The technique of creative visualization is helpful in calming fears. Creative visualization is simply closing your eyes and imagining yourself relaxed and confidently going through the test without any difficulty. Imagine this good feeling on completion of the test. This is the same technique used by athletes to help them through game-pressure situations, so why shouldn't you use it?

If you have difficiulty with sweaty palms, a useful technique is to use clear spray deodorant. Spray the deodorant on your hands for a week. This will help your hands to stay drier during the test. A handkerchief would be helpful for profuse brow sweating. If you sweat profusely you may want to bring a second set of clothes to change into after lunch or at the end of the examination, although you will not be allowed to change during the test.

There are many textbooks on studying techniques. Many college bookstores as well as college libraries carry a variety of studying references. The *Hawes Guide to Successful Study Skills*, by Hawes and Hawes, and *Improve Your Grades*, by Bautista, are references I recommend as study-guide textbooks.

General Tips for Exam Day

You can do several things to make your test day go smoothly. I've outlined a few here and provide a test-day checklist on page 15 to get you going.

The Night Before the Test. On the eve of the test, review areas you believe you need to repeat. Be sure to get a good night's rest. Do not drink any caffeine products, which may make you stay up all night, and forget about taking sleep medications. These may make you sleep through your alarm or make you too tired to concentrate on the test. If you are staying in a hotel, be sure you are in a room that is isolated, so it will be quiet all night. Consider setting more than one alarm clock to be sure you awake in enough time to get ready and arrive at the test on time.

Clothing. When deciding what to wear for the test, consider something that is comfortable and typical of what you would wear as a certified professional in the training room setting. Do not wear any clothing with your school or team insignia, as some examiners may be biased. Wear a watch to help you keep track of the time if you so desire.

During the Test. While taking the test keep your head, neck, and shoulders relaxed. You may wish to rotate your head, neck, and shoulders periodically to keep them loose. Also, take a deep breath and exhale slowly while thinking to yourself, "Relax!" Some people press their fingertips together or press their feet into the ground as a way of getting rid of tension. Do what you must to remain relaxed.

■ Test-Day Checklist ■

You will need to take:

- ✔ an admission ticket.
- ✔ photo identification.
- ✔ two sharpened number 2 pencils.
- ✔ a map to the test site.
- ✔ a map of the test site and local area.
- ✔ the test site telephone number.
- ✔ the BOC telephone number.
- ✔ lunch or restaurant location.

You will want to wear:

- ✔ clean, comfortable, professional-looking clothing.
- ✔ no insignia or school identification.
- ✔ clothing suitable for the weather and room temperature.
- ✔ deodorant.
- ✔ a watch with a timer (if you desire).

Do you want to sit:

- ✔ in a well lit part of the room?
- ✔ near friends?
- ✔ in the front or the back?
- ✔ where there are no distractions?
- ✔ where you can see the clock?
- ✔ in a comfortable chair?
- ✔ on a wobbly chair?
- ✔ near the aisleway?
- ✔ in a particular chair or are seats assigned?

For the oral/practical and the written rooms:

✔ where is the bathroom?

✔ where is the drinking fountain?

✔ is room temperature hot, cold, or just right?

✔ do they contain tape, wraps, or mannequins?

■ Results Notification and Interpretation

About 1 week after you take the exam, CAS will notify you by mail of the results. If you have not heard anything in 2 weeks, contact CAS.

It took 3 months to get my results back. When I got them I locked myself in the bathroom while my college roommates tried to get in. I could barely bring myself to open the envelope, but I opened it and unfolded the letter. It read, "We are pleased . . . ." I threw the letter up in the air and ran out of the bathroom. I figured they would not say "pleased" if I did not pass! To this day I don't know anything else the letter said.

Interpreting Your Score

When you received your letter from CAS, your results will be broken down into three sections: written exam, oral/practical test, and written simulation. One does not have to pass all three sections at the same time. However, you must eventually pass all three sections to become a certified athletic trainer. Each section of results will indicate how many points were available, your score, and the passing points needed. You will have to read and compare your score. If you have the passing points or more, you have passed that section. The passing-point range changes with each new certification examination, based on exam difficulty, as rated by the BOC and CAS. In general, a score above 70% will pass. A retake form will be included with your test results if you failed any portion of the examination. Questions on the certification examination that are consistently missed are reviewed by the BOC and CAS. If the BOC and CAS determine that a question is ambiguous or unreliable, it is replaced by another question. Replacement is an excellent way of refining the certification examination into a good assessment tool. When the BOC replaces a question, specifically in the oral/practical test or the written simulation, the total number of points available changes, thus changing the points needed for passing.

General Pass Rates

Based on official data (Dallas: NATA BOC spring 1993), it appears that candidates who received their college degrees in athletic training through curriculum programs score better on the certification exam (see Table 2.1).

Table 2.1
Exam Pass Rates

Test section	New candidates Pass rate	Retake candidates Pass rate
Written Examination		
Intern	45%	32%
Curriculum	50%	44%
Oral/Practical Test		
Intern	57%	60%
Curriculum	66%	64%
Written Simulation		
Intern	56%	46%
Curriculum	64%	55%

More than 4,000 candidates have taken one or more certification examination sections during a calendar year.

Retake Options and Procedures

You will be given a score for each section of the examination. You can fail three sections, two, or just one. If you have failed any section of the test you can ask for an appeal of those sections. Your appeal letter must include the appropriate fee and reasons why you would like your case to be reviewed. If the oral/practical portion was failed you can ask that the audio cassette tape be reviewed to help gain points an examiner may have overlooked. The BOC will notify you of the review of your tests, usually in 1 month.

You can ask CAS to send you a copy of a report about your strengths and weaknesses, helpful if you have to retake any portion.

If you do not retake the failed portions of the test within one year, you will be required to take the entire test over again. The cost is $200 to retake any two portions of the test and $150 to retake one section.

You are not required to stay the entire day if you are retaking a portion. For example, if the written simulation is what you retake, show up in the morning, take that portion, and go home. If you failed the oral/ practical you do not have to take the written again, even though they are run concurrently. If you are taking the oral/practical section you will be one of the first candidates tested so you will be able to leave.

If you fail any portion of the exam three times, your application will be reviewed before further retakes. It is likely the BOC will recommend additional course work or more supervision of hours before the next retake.

ABOUT THE TESTS

II

3

CHAPTER

Written Examination

The written examination is designed to assess your ability to remember facts and details. Six main areas are covered: prevention; recognition and evaluation of injuries; management, treatment, and disposition; rehabilitation; organization and administration; and education and counseling. The written examination is given concurrently with the oral/practical portion of the examination: You will be taken from the written examination for 30 min to do the oral/practical test.

■ *Format and Number of Questions*

The written examination consists of 150 multiple-choice questions (NATA, 1991), mostly testing your recognition and evaluation abilities or your management, treatment, and disposition abilities (see Figure 3.1).

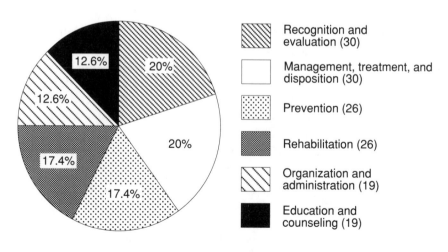

Figure 3.1 The approximate number of test questions in each category.

This portion of the examination is done in pencil and is scored by computer.

■ Time Limit

You will have 3 hr to take the written exam. Work at a fairly rapid pace. No question should take you longer than 1 min. You will need 30 min to take the oral/practical test.

The proctor will tell you when to begin and when to stop. Once you have completed the exam and are confident that you are finished, you may leave the testing area.

■ Scoring

There is only one correct answer to each question for the written examination, and all questions are worth the same points. You will lose 1 point for each question you do not complete or answer correctly. Do not skip, leave blank, or neglect to answer any questions.

■ Test-Taking Strategies

Here are some helpful hints for taking the multiple-choice test:

1. Read the questions carefully.

2. Before reading the possible answers try to determine the answer in your own mind. If the answer you think of is not listed, reread the question.

3. Eliminate answers right away to help narrow the possibilities.

4. If you are struggling with a question because you do not know a word in it, try to relate it to something else with which you are familiar or break the word down. For example, if you are unsure of the word *cardiopulmonary*, recall that *cardio-* means heart and *pulmonary* means lungs. Often you can discern the answer by selecting one that relates to what parts of the complete term mean.

5. If you cannot eliminate any of the potential answers, remember that test writers lean toward answer *b* more than any other.

6. Answers that use the terms *always, never, all,* and *none* often are incorrect. If you can think of any exception, that answer is not correct.

7. Test writers try to make sure the answer is grammatically correct with the stem statement of the question, so read carefully. Here is an example:

A laceration should be surgically stitched when

   a. profusely bleeds
   b. the multiple cuts are involved
   c. separated skin
   d. abraded skin
   e. the cut is half an inch or longer

Read the stem with what you think is the correct answer. Is it grammatically correct? The only correct answer is *e* because it makes grammatical sense with the sentence, whereas none of the other choices do. The sentence reads "A laceration should be surgically stitched when the cut is half an inch or longer."

8. If you can eliminate all but two answers you have a 50-50 chance.

9. Another technique is to visualize the page you studied that relates to a particular question. Visualize until you get to the needed information.

10. If you draw a blank and cannot relate anything to the question, skip it and go on to the next question. Leave it for last.

11. What do you do if you see two questions that are exactly the same except for one word? First, read them carefully. You will not see two identical questions on the certification examination. For example,

The elbow joint has a flexion range of motion of

   a. 90 degrees
   b. 75 degrees
   c. 0 to 5 degrees
   d. 135 degrees or more
   e. 60 degrees

The elbow joint has an extension range of motion of

   a. 90 degrees
   b. 75 degrees
   c. 0 to 5 degrees
   d. 135 degrees or more
   e. 60 degrees

The keys here are the words *flexion* and *extension*. Let's say you are sure that one of the ranges is 0 to 5 degrees. Great, but you cannot remember the difference. If you mark both answers with that range *c* you are assured of getting at least one right. If you mark one answer *c* and guess the other you may end up with two incorrect answers. (The correct answer to the first question is *d* and the second is *c*.)

12. Test writers try to avoid using *not*, as it is sometimes confusing. If *not* is used, generally it will be highlighted in some way, such as underlined, italicized, or in bold print. Read these questions carefully.

13. It is unlikely that you will see answer choices that say "all of the above" or "only *a* and *c*." These are avoided by test writers because they are too easy.

14. Sometimes test writers write the correct answer into another question of the test. You may want to recall those questions that relate to each other and answer those in combination. For example: The five open wound types are puncture, laceration, avulsion, amputation, and abrasion. Which wound is most likely to become infected?

   a. Puncture
   b. Laceration
   c. Avulsion
   d. Amputation
   e. Abrasion

Further along in the test is this question: Which of the following is an open wound?

   a. Contusion
   b. Stress fracture
   c. Internal injury
   d. Abrasion
   e. Spleen rupture

Here you can answer the second question by using a previous one. The first question recalls the five open wound types; the second question asks which is an open wound. By the way, the wound most likely to become infected is *a* (puncture).

15. If you are concerned you will forget some important fact, write the fact down on the test as soon as it is handed out. Do not write it on the desk, as this may be considered evidence of cheating.

Once you have completed the written test go back to the questions you skipped the first time through and answer them. Finally, review the entire test again and be sure you have not made any errors. You should only change answers if you know they are wrong or you read the question incorrectly. Many people change correct answers because they are unsure. Go through your answer sheet to erase any stray marks and to be sure all your answers correspond with the questions. Do not be concerned about others finishing before you—work at your own pace.

4
CHAPTER

Oral/Practical Test

You will be called for the oral/practical section of the exam while you are taking the written exam. Candidates taking the oral/practical test as a retake will be called first. After that names are called randomly. When the examiner calls your name, you will be escorted to the oral/practical room to complete this section of the exam. Bring the oral/practical answer sheets for the examiners. Feel free to go to the bathroom or get a drink to help you unwind from the written portion and get mentally ready to perform this section of the exam.

When you enter the oral/practical testing room, there are two examiners and a model (the person on whom you will demonstrate your skills). Give the oral/practical answer sheets to the examiners. They will check to see that your identification number and personal information are on the answer sheets.

In the room is a candidates' guide, which lists the questions for the oral/practical examination. You will be asked to follow along as each of the questions is read to you. Also in the room will be a table with supplies for your use. You may look over the supplies and think about what questions may be asked utilizing these materials. An audio cassette will record everything that is said in the oral/practical setting. In the event you do not pass this portion, you can ask for a review of the tape.

Once the examiner finishes reading your questions, you can reread the questions, relax, and think about what is required of you. The test begins once you begin working on the model. Be sure to do what is asked for in the questions. The model will not respond verbally to any questions. If the examiner stops you and rereads the question, it means you are on the wrong track or forgetting something. Pick up the guide if you have to and reread the question. If you forget something along the way and remember it later, go ahead and show it and explain it.

■ *Format and Number of Questions*

You will be asked four questions that allow you to exhibit your skills. Prepare yourself to answer questions in the following areas:

- Taping or wrapping technique
- Rehabilitation
- Evaluation
- Emergency technique (such as cardiopulmonary resuscitation)

■ Time Limit

Each question has a time limit depending on the skills the question is testing. The total oral/practical time will not exceed 30 min. You will be given 8 to 10 min for an evaluation, rehabilitation, and emergency technique. Taping or wrapping must be completed in 3 to 5 min.

More than ample time has been allotted to allow you time to finish all four questions. You might feel more at ease if you bring a watch with an alarm and set it to go off just before the end of the testing limits.

■ Scoring

Points are gained by answering the question. You will not be given points for being long winded, for quoting a page or a paragraph from a text, or for providing information on things outside the question. Get to the point.

You will lose one point if you do not complete the taping or wrapping techniques in the allotted time. (You will not have any points deducted for finishing early.) Generally, you will not lose points if you do things out of sequence, forget the name or a body part, or you refer to it incorrectly. (Exception: things that must be performed in sequence, such as with cardiopulmonary resuscitation.) What is most important is to

- cover the topic thoroughly,
- perform your testing bilaterally, and
- explain while you demonstrate a technique.

Failure to do these will result in a deduction of points.

You also are not required to perform every single test for evaluating a particular injury. Just perform a test that is accurate for identifying the injury. For example, to test for a tear in the anterior cruciate ligament, properly performing the anterior drawer test is sufficient to get the points. You do not also have to perform the crossover test, the pivotal shift, the anterior rotary instability test, and Lachman's test, although performing any one of these is sufficient to score the point. If you have time left over in a question, think the question over and mention anything else that specifically addresses that question.

■ Test-Taking Strategies

To be successful during the oral/practical section of the certification exam, you must be organized. To prepare properly it is important to avoid the most common errors candidates make. Things candidates fail to do during the test are:

1. Remaining calm
2. Knowing what the question asks you to do and performing only those things
3. Explaining while demonstrating what you are doing
4. Doing a thorough evaluation of the situation
5. Testing everything bilaterally
6. Referring your athlete to a physician

Your pretest preparation is crucial so you will not exceed the time limits. Learning and practicing the steps in wrapping an ankle, for example, will help you remember them when the pressure is on. The oral/practical should be practiced over and over, using different situations. Have your evaluations and rehabilitation protocols in the same sequence for all injuries. For example, do passive range-of-motion for each evaluation. Do not learn the elbow range-of-motion as active, passive, and active-resistive and the knee as passive, active, and active-resistive.

If you can test bilaterally at the same time, do so. An example of this is knee flexion and extension with hip adduction and abduction. This will conserve time and you will be less likely to forget the tests you have already done. Remember to test the nonaffected limb first, then the affected limb. If you do a specific test on a knee, for example, then upon completion of that test immediately test the other knee. This way you can do bilateral comparisons without forgetting.

General Evaluation Protocols

1. Observation of the Scene
   -Positioning of athlete
   -Safety of scene
2. Primary Survey
   -Airway
   -Breathing
   -Circulation
3. Get Permission to Treat
   -Check pulse and breathing rate, as applicable.
   -Check level of consciousness.
4. What Is the Complaint of this Athlete?
5. Secondary Survey
   -Observations (use throughout evaluation)
      a. Swelling
      b. Discoloration

    c. Deformities (distention, depressions, and rigidity)

    d. Bleeding or loss of fluids

    e. Skin color

    f. Unusual odors

    g. Sensitivity to pain

    h. Position of affected body part

-History (The following questions should be asked; there may be others, given the injury to the athlete.)

    a. What was the mechanism of the injury?

    b. Where was the pain initially?

    c. Did you hear a pop, snap, or crack?

    d. Were you able to use the body part immediately after the injury?

    e. Did you continue to play?

    f. Did the part feel unstable?

    g. Did the part swell up immediately or later?

    h. What treatment was applied immediately?

    i. Have you hurt this part before?

    j. Do you have any allergies or medical conditions?

    k. Do you take medication?

    l. Does anything else need care?

-Palpation

    a. Bony areas

    b. Soft tissues

    c. Skin temperature

    d. Circulation

-Active range of motion (More may need to be done, depending on the injury.)

    a. Flexion

    b. Extension

    c. Abduction

    d. Adduction

-Passive range of motion (More may need to be done, depending on the injury.)

    a. Flexion

    b. Extension

    c. Abduction

    d. Adduction

-Active-resistive range of motion (More ranges may need to be done, depending on the injury.)

    a. Flexion

    b. Extension

    c. Abduction

    d. Adduction

-Special Tests

-Neurological Testing

-Functional Testing

Explain and demonstrate all the things you are doing if the question asks for that. Just remember the model will not respond verbally. You are not expected to come to a conclusion on the injury—just treat, rehabilitate, and evaluate it.

5

CHAPTER

Written Simulation

This portion of the test is held in a large room, the same room that will be used for the written exam. The written simulation is the most interesting part of the certification test. It is designed to show how you would deal with real-life decision making, using a scenario. Each scenario will have different segments for you to prioritize the care of the athlete. When assessing the situation you will be asked to prioritize what should happen during each segment. In each segment you will receive more information about the scenario for you to again decide what should happen next. During the written simulation there is a problem guide, a separate answer guide, and a highlighting pen. The front of the answer guide will be completed under the guidance of the written simulation proctor.

The problem guide will give you the opening scenario and answers for each segment. In the answer guide you are to select the answers you feel are appropriate, given the scenario and priorities at that time. When you select an answer in the answer guide you will use the marker to highlight the area to the right of the number you have selected. When the double asterisks appear from highlighting, that is the end of the statement. After highlighting the area a brief statement will appear that gives you clues about the scenario. If given directions in the highlighted statement, follow them. Be careful—there are horror stories of candidates who laid their highlighting pen down and accidently marked several answers. Once an answer is selected it cannot be erased. Even a partially highlighted answer is considered a selected one. So a word of caution: Put the cap on the marker or do not place it near the answer guide when you are not marking. Select all answers that are appropriate to solving the scenario based on what you believe are priorities at the time. *Do not* complicate the written simulation by thinking of exceptions to the rule. For example, the scenario says: An athlete has an acute ankle sprain, diagnosed by the team physician. What is your initial treatment of this injury?

1. Apply heat
2. Apply compression
3. Apply ice
4. Elevate the ankle

The correct answer is 2, 3, and 4. But you may think, "Hey, I wouldn't apply ice. The athlete may have Raynaud's disease." If this athlete has this disorder it will be stated in the question. If you highlight an answer that tells you that the athlete's condition is changing, think about additional answers that may be necessary to assist in this athlete's care. As an example: An athlete has sustained a direct blow to the abdomen. What is your initial care of this athlete?

1. Palpate all abdominal quadrants. (The athlete has abdominal rigidity and pain with palpation.)
2. Apply ice.
3. Have the athlete stretch the abdominal muscles.
4. Take the athlete's blood pressure. (It is 90/60.)
5. Take the athlete's pulse. (It is 120 and weak.)
6. Call for ambulance. (It will arrive in 5 min.)

Your first priority is to determine the condition of the athlete or severity of injury. In this scenario, if you highlighted 1, 4, or 5, you have some clues as to the condition of the athlete. Once you have highlighted any of these answers you need to start thinking about what is causing the abdominal rigidity and pain. Is the blood pressure 90/60 normal, high, or low? A rapid and weak pulse indicates what? This question does not ask for a conclusive answer, but you had better call for an ambulance to get all the points possible! Also, selecting only response 6 as a way of superseding your evaluation will result in the loss of points. Although 6 is a correct selection, 1, 4, and 5 also must be selected to gain all available points for the scenario.

■ Format and Number of Questions

The written simulation has eight questions. It requires that you read a short scenario and then, using the numerous answers that are given, select all answers that aid you in the care of the patient. The scenario format includes

1. opening scene and initial question,
2. answers for the opening scene,
3. subsequent sections of the scenario asking different questions, and
4. "End of problem."

The answer guide is blank except for labeling the question and enumeration of answers, for example:

Problem I

1.
2.
3.

■ Time Limit

You will have 2.5 hr to complete this section of the test. Most recently, the written simulation has been administered in the morning.

■ Scoring

Points are gained by selecting all of the correct answers. Points are deducted for failing to select all of the correct answers and for selecting too many answers (answers that really would not be helpful or that are contraindicated in the given situation). It is best to determine the question's priorities to decide what protocol should be used. You should select answers in the order you would do them in an actual situation because this will make it easier for you to remember. You do not have to select answers in the correct order to gain points. If at the end of a problem you realize that you proceeded through a question using the incorrect protocol, do not go back and highlight more answers. Highlighting more answers in an attempt to make up for improper protocols results in more points against you.

Answers in this portion of the test are weighted. Some are worth more, and some can cost you more than others. For example, if an athlete you are treating dies, you will lose the points for that scenario.

■ Test-Taking Strategies

Select answers that expedite the scenario involved.

Be sure you have protocols set up for all sorts of situations. You should know what to do initially in an emergency situation, and you should know a progression for treatment. Select answers in the same order you would do them in an actual setting. For example, an athlete has an injured forearm. General protocol would be:

1. A, B, Cs–primary survey
2. Secondary survey
3. Splint the arm

The primary survey and secondary survey can be done rapidly in a conscious athlete who can respond. Although the athlete's arm is broken, you still follow the same protocols to be assured that the most serious injury is being cared for first. If you select to splint the arm first you may find out later that the athlete had no breathing or no heartbeat, so use your protocols to go step-by-step through a scenario.

Examination Study Questions

III

6
CHAPTER

Study Questions for the Written Examination

This portion of the text gives you the types of questions that could be found on the written examination. The questions are subdivided into sections on prevention; recognition and evaluation; treatment; rehabilitation; administration and education; and counseling.

I read everything listed in the bibliography and designed questions from my reading. Four complete, written exams are included in this chapter, totaling 600 questions. The certification test itself is 150 questions.

I have listed a passing-point score at the end of each section in Appendix A. The passing-point score is 70%. Your goal is to score equal to, or better than, the passing-point score. When reviewing your answers, if you fail to do well, in a particular section read the references listed in Appendix A for those questions missed. This will add to your knowledge.

■ *Prevention*

Directions—Each of the questions or incomplete statements here is followed by five suggested answers or completions. Select the *best* answer in each case.

1. **You are helping plan a new football stadium. What is your concern in the field setup to help prevent injuries?**
   a. orientation of the field to the sun's rays
   b. wind directions
   c. draining of the field
   d. grass versus turf
   e. outdoor lighting

2. **You must recommend a pair of eyeglass lenses for an athlete. Which should you recommend?**
   a. lens center 0.5 mm thick, CR 39 plastic or polycarbonate
   b. lens center 1 mm thick, CR 39 plastic or polycarbonate
   c. lens center 2 mm thick, CR 39 plastic or polycarbonate
   d. lens center 3 mm thick, glass
   e. lens center 3 mm thick, CR 39 plastic or polycarbonate

3. **An athlete who previously had a retinal detachment is cautioned to avoid participation in**
   a. any sport where a small ball is used
   b. jogging
   c. any sport where the lighting is poor
   d. any sport where the lighting is bright
   e. badminton

4. **Cantilever-type shoulder pads are worn by which group of football players?**
   a. quarterbacks
   b. wide receivers
   c. linebackers and linemen
   d. kickers
   e. running backs

5. **What will help an athlete resist heat and keep the body cool?**
   a. a cold shower before a workout
   b. taking calcium tablets
   c. a polyester jersey
   d. an electrolyte drink with 10% glucose
   e. working out in rubberized clothing

6. **Who is most susceptible to heat disorder?**
   a. athletes recovering from allergic reactions
   b. athletes with high blood pressure
   c. athletes with a previous history of cold illness or hypersensitivity
   d. thin athletes
   e. obese athletes or athletes with a previous history of heat illness

7. **Artificial turf can be watered to reduce injuries. What injury is likely to increase with high humidity?**
   a. asthmatic attacks
   b. sprains
   c. heat illness
   d. cold exposure
   e. strains

8. **Temperature regulation of the body is controlled by the**
    a. pituitary
    b. hypothalamus
    c. adrenal gland
    d. lymphatic system
    e. epidermis

9. **Plyometrics enhance what anatomical area?**
    a. energy stores
    b. neuromuscular mechanisms
    c. mitochondria
    d. endurance
    e. lactic acid

10. **Periodization, or cycle training, allows for year-round strengthening of the athlete through stages. These are**
    a. preseason, in season, and off-season
    b. five phases that increase 5% each week for 10 weeks
    c. foundation, preparation, precompetition, in-season maintenance, and active rest
    d. conditioning, flexibility, hypertrophy, and maintenance
    e. fitness base, short-term goals, long-term goals, and maintenance

11. **Doing free weight lifting or the Olympic press is likely to cause low-back hyperextension. This can lead to**
    a. a ruptured disk
    b. sacroiliac joint dysfunction
    c. nerve root impingement
    d. spondylolysis and spondylolisthesis
    e. muscular spasms

12. **A target heart rate or aerobic training should be between**
    a. 80% and 100% of maximum heart rate
    b. 60% and 80% of maximum heart rate
    c. 80% and 90% of maximum heart rate
    d. 70% and 85% of maximum heart rate
    e. 25% and 40% of maximum heart rate

13. **It is important to treat hemarthrosis promptly, as it will destroy**
    a. articular cartilage
    b. ligaments
    c. the joint capsule
    d. bone
    e. adipose tissue

14. **Blood pressure for a child under age 10 should not be higher than**
    a. 120/80 mmHg
    b. 140/80 mmHg
    c. 80/60 mmHg
    d. 90/60 mmHg
    e. 130/75 mmHg

15. **A Q angle of the patellar is considered excessive if it is**
    a. 20 degrees or greater
    b. 20 degrees or less
    c. 15 degrees
    d. 10 degrees
    e. anything greater than 0 degrees

16. **The American College of Sports Medicine (ACSM) recommends road races be rescheduled based on what wet-bulb globe temperature?**
    a. 32 °F
    b. 75 °F
    c. 50 °F
    d. 82 °F
    e. 63 °F

17. **To prevent prickly heat it is best to**
    a. wear a hat and stay out of the sun
    b. wear a sunscreen of SPF 15 or less
    c. wear loose fitting clothes and avoiding heavy sweating
    d. wear a sunscreen of SPF 30 or more
    e. drink plenty of fluids

18. **The American College of Sports Medicine (ACSM) recommends distance running should take place during what time(s) of the day during the summer?**
    a. between noon and 1:00 in the afternoon
    b. between 2:00 and 3:00 in the afternoon
    c. before 8:00 in the morning or after 6:00 in the evening
    d. no preference
    e. before 10:00 in the morning or after 3:00 in the afternoon

19. **The American College of Sports Medicine (ACSM) recommends use of what wet-bulb globe temperature equation?**
    a. WBGT = (0.7 Twb) + (0.2 Tg) + (0.1 Tdb)
    b. WBGT = (0.5 Twb) × (0.2 Tg) × (0.3 Tdb)
    c. WBGT = (0.7 Twb) + (0.2 Tg) − (0.8 Tdb)
    d. WBGT = (0.7 Twb) × (0.2 Tg) − (0.6 Tdb)
    e. WBGT = (0.7 Twb) + (0.2 Tg) + (0.5 Tdb)

20. **An athlete had a patella removed because of a previous injury. What does the knee need protection to prevent?**
    a. anterior cruciate tears
    b. posterior cruciate tears
    c. meniscus injury
    d. injury to femoral condyles
    e. quadricep strains

21. **The recommended amount of sleep per night for an athlete is**
    a. no recommendation—you will sleep if you're tired
    b. 6 hr
    c. 8 hr
    d. 9 hr
    e. 12 hr

22. **Which of the following is an illegal pad in football?**
    a. rib protectors
    b. bicep pad
    c. prophylactic knee braces
    d. a plastic splint made to protect a metacarpal
    e. plastic ankle stirrups

23. **The mass physical examination, compared to a personal physical examination, is**
    a. better because it is done by the team physician
    b. more effective because the coaching staff helps
    c. very personal
    d. less thorough than one given by a personal physician
    e. more thorough than one given by a personal physician

24. **The personal-physician physical examination**
    a. is less thorough than a mass examination
    b. is not necessary if a preparticipation fitness exam is done
    c. is the best examination and more thorough
    d. is the only physical examination an athlete needs
    e. may not be sport-specific enough to find predisposing conditions

25. **When lifting weights, which exercise requires a flat back to avoid injury?**
    a. military press
    b. bench press
    c. back rows
    d. leg press
    e. shoulder shrugs

26. **A weight lifter's belt is used to prevent**
    a. lumbar spine hyperextension
    b. inguinal hernia

    c. abdominal hernia

    d. trunk rotation

    e. lumbar spine flexion

27. **A football helmet that is certified by the National Operating Committee on Standards for Athletic Equipment (NOCSAE) means**

    a. the athlete is completely safe while wearing it

    b. the athlete is safe as long as it is not misused

    c. the helmet doesn't need maintenance until season's end

    d. the helmet doesn't protect the athlete from head and neck injuries

    e. the helmet passes NOCSAE standards, but still may fail

28. **Manual resistance for prevention of neck injuries**

    a. need not be done if a neck roll is used

    b. need not be done if athlete has full range of motion

    c. should not be done during the in season

    d. is not necessary for short-necked athletes

    e. should not be done just before collision-sport activities

29. **What is the most appropriate cleated shoe to prevent knee injuries in collision-sport activity?**

    a. soccer-style short-cleated shoes

    b. soccer-style long-cleated shoes

    c. football-style long, screw-in-cleated shoes

    d. football-style short, screw-in-cleated shoes

    e. circular-bottom shoes

30. **You are in charge of setting up a preparticipation physical for 200 athletes. What part of the physical can a student athletic trainer be responsible to carry out?**

    a. individual history

    b. the physical

    c. auscultation of the chest and abdomen

    d. Snellen's test

    e. review of physical examination and implementation of rehabilitation plans if needed

31. **According to the American College of Sports Medicine (ACSM), distance race organizers need to disqualify runners if they**

    a. stop running

    b. are way behind the group

    c. sweat profusely

    d. refuse to drink water at each water station

    e. show signs of heat injury

32. **Which of the following is a station at a preparticipation physical examination?**
    a. referral to outside physician if any conditions are found
    b. AIDS test
    c. Snellen's test
    d. rehabilitation of weaknesses
    e. taping

33. **What is (are) the purpose(s) of a stretching program?**
    a. to decrease resistance of tight musculature and increase strength of antagonistic muscles
    b. to decrease strength of tight musculature and increase resistance of antagonistic muscles
    c. to decrease resistance of loose musculature
    d. to decrease strength of loose musculature
    e. to increase strength of agonist muscles

34. **Using the contract–relax proprioceptive neuromuscular facilitation training will stretch the**
    a. belly of the muscle
    b. I band
    c. red muscle fibers
    d. Golgi tendon
    e. Z line

35. **The four-way chin strap used with football helmets is helpful in reducing**
    a. rotation of the helmet
    b. lateral motion of the helmet
    c. forward and backward shifting of the helmet
    d. neck injuries caused by direct blows
    e. head injuries caused by direct blows

36. **An athlete is wearing a face guard, as in hockey, football, baseball, or softball. The space between the athlete's nose and the face guard must be**
    a. one finger width
    b. 3/4 in.
    c. no space
    d. 1 to 1 1/2 in.
    e. 2 in. or more

37. **Which type of mouth guard provides the best dental protection from injury?**
    a. mouth-formed guard
    b. ready-made guard

    c. commercial mouth guard

    d. double mouth guard

    e. custom-made mouth guard

38. **For which football player would you recommend prophylactic knee bracing because the risk of knee injury is greatest, according to the American Academy of Orthopaedic Surgeons (AAOS)?**

    a. all linemen

    b. linemen and tight ends

    c. none—prophylactic knee braces don't reduce the number of knee injuries

    d. linebackers, linemen, and quarterbacks

    e. running backs, linemen, and tight ends

39. **When designing a conditioning program remember to**

    a. have exercise done daily

    b. ensure the athlete is tired after conditioning

    c. increase the quantity of work over time

    d. always ice after conditioning

    e. gear conditioning toward sport-specific goals

40. **Why is it important to have an active cool-down time?**

    a. so lactic acid will decrease more rapidly

    b. so blood pressure returns to normal

    c. so muscles return to a regular resting state

    d. so adrenaline decreases more rapidly

    e. to improve conditioning of the heart

41. **Muscle hypertrophy can limit**

    a. muscle length

    b. joint range of motion

    c. ability to increase strength

    d. ability to increase isometric contractions

    e. muscular tightness

42. **Which mode of strengthening is the most sport specific and safe?**

    a. isometrics

    b. isotonics

    c. isokinetics

    d. plyometrics

    e. variable resistance

43. **Muscular soreness is most often caused by**

    a. isometric exercise

    b. isotonic exercise

    c. isokinetic exercise

    d. eccentric exercise

    e. concentric exercise

44. **How long of a warm-up is necessary to bring about physiological readiness (nerve impulse conduction, body temperature rise, blood sugar level changes)?**
    a. longer for younger athletes
    b. shorter for older athletes
    c. No warm-up is necessary, as physiology is always ready.
    d. a longer warm-up for those who lack conditioning
    e. 15 to 30 min, but this varies with age

45. **Which sport is most likely to result in improper weight loss?**
    a. body building
    b. track
    c. field hockey
    d. gymnastics
    e. wrestling

46. **When do most injuries to athletes occur?**
    a. at home contests
    b. at away contests
    c. at practice
    d. at scrimmage
    e. while on the sideline

47. **The most likely (indirect) cause of athlete death is**
    a. asthma
    b. cardiovascular disease
    c. diabetes
    d. heat strokes
    e. congenital conditions

48. **The most likely cause of death directly attributed to athletic competition is**
    a. abdominal trauma
    b. head trauma
    c. spinal trauma
    d. throat trauma
    e. chest trauma

49. **The station method of a preparticipation physical examination**
    a. can yield a detailed evaluation in a relatively short period of time
    b. can miss problems from previous injuries
    c. is the only physical an athlete needs
    d. is less thorough than a mass examination
    e. is less thorough than a personal-physician physical examination

50. **The orthopedic portion of the physical examination often includes the duck walk. This tests for**
    a. leg length
    b. knee and ankle motion
    c. knee effusion
    d. hamstring tightness
    e. quadriceps strength

51. **How often should a football player have clean practice clothing?**
    a. only if clothing looks dirty
    b. monthly
    c. every 2 days
    d. daily
    e. weekly

52. **Athletes from ages 12 to 18 should be placed on teams based on**
    a. age
    b. size
    c. ability
    d. maturity
    e. athletic desire

53. **When using resistance training to gain muscular strength, what percentage of a muscle's maximum strength is enough overload to produce strength improvement?**
    a. 100%
    b. 90%
    c. 60% to 80%
    d. 50%
    e. 10%

54. **When taking a sling psychrometer reading, you should**
    a. not need to take a reading unless temperature is above 90 °F
    b. take the reading on the actual playing surface
    c. not need to take a reading if you have access to NOAA weather information
    d. take a reading next to a building or asphalt
    e. take readings periodically during practice

55. **To test an athlete's flexibility while performing a preparticipation fitness examination, use**
    a. a step test
    b. jumping jacks
    c. a sit-and-reach examination
    d. sit-ups
    e. a vertical jump

56. **Athletes with heart murmurs should be referred to a cardiologist if**
    a. systolic and diastolic murmurs increase with Valsalva's maneuver
    b. systolic and diastolic murmurs decrease with Valsalva's maneuver
    c. systolic murmur decreases with Valsalva's maneuver
    d. diastolic murmur decreases with Valsalva's maneuver
    e. diastolic murmur increases with Valsalva's maneuver

57. **An athlete who indicates frequent headaches on their preparticipation fitness form should be evaluated further for**
    a. visual problems
    b. scalp musculature spasms
    c. hypertension
    d. temporomandibular joint dysfunction
    e. stress

58. **What is the best initial summer practice uniform for nonacclimatized athletes?**
    a. long socks and sweat clothes
    b. full in-season uniforms
    c. rubberized sweat suits
    d. lightweight pants and regular jerseys
    e. short sleeve T-shirts, shorts, and short socks

59. **Who is most likely to suffer hypothermia?**
    a. a thin, short runner running 8 mi/hr into a 10 mi/hr head wind
    b. a thin, short runner running 8 mi/hr with a 10 mi/hr tail wind
    c. a young person with lots of subcutaneous fat layers running 8 mi/hr with a 10 mi/hr tail wind
    d. a large, tall runner running 8 mi/hr into a 10 mi/hr head wind
    e. There is no significant difference among these individuals in their likelihood of suffering from hypothermia.

60. **Maturation levels are best determined by what component of a preparticipation physical examination?**
    a. Snellen's test
    b. Tanner age classification
    c. X rays
    d. skinfold testing
    e. checking age on the examination form

61. **A hard, unyielding obstacle that is close to a playing field should**
    a. be mentioned to athletes so they will avoid it
    b. be padded if it cannot be removed
    c. limit play in the area to less coordinated younger athletes
    d. limit play in the area to more coordinated older athletes
    e. be marked with a big orange cone to warn athletes of the danger

62. **Which athletes should not travel to high-altitude competitions?**
    a. diabetics
    b. asthmatics
    c. those with sickle-cell trait
    d. those with air pollution sensitivities
    e. tall athletes

63. **When maximum preventative taping is desired,**
    a. apply tape directly to the skin
    b. use more tape adherent
    c. use stretch tape
    d. use more pressure during application
    e. apply several layers of tape

64. **The majority of injuries among wheelchair athletes are**
    a. soft-tissue injuries
    b. thermoregulatory conditions
    c. blisters
    d. friction and pressure injuries
    e. abrasions

65. **How are decubitus areas prevented in wheelchair athletes?**
    a. application of powder to areas
    b. additional padding under pressure areas
    c. stretching before and after exercise
    d. preventative taping over possible areas of pressure
    e. wearing polyester clothing

66. **A shoulder harness used to prevent dislocation must restrict abduction to no more than**
    a. 15 degrees
    b. 30 degrees
    c. 45 degrees
    d. 90 degrees
    e. 180 degrees

67. **Neoprene knee sleeves provide what advantage over lateral-support prophylactic knee braces?**
    a. increased lateral and medial protection
    b. increased anterior posterior translation protection
    c. increased heat retention and increased compression of area
    d. decreased severity of blows to patella
    e. absorb all impacts about the knee

68. **An advantage to regular physical activity for an older athlete is**
    a. increased level of total cholesterol
    b. increased level of blood triglycerides

c. decreased muscular strength

d. decreased risk of cardiovascular disease

e. increased dependence on the medical system for health care needs.

69. **To prevent impingement syndrome of the shoulder in a swimmer, suggest that the swimmer**

a. avoid hand paddle usage and use the backstroke more often

b. use hand paddles and use the backstroke more often

c. use the butterfly and freestyle strokes more often

d. stretch the posterior shoulder musculature

e. strengthen the anterior chest

70. **An athlete with medial collateral laxity of +1 should be instructed to avoid which swim stroke because of the kick?**

a. butterfly

b. breaststroke

c. freestyle

d. backstroke

e. sidestroke

71. **To prevent otitis media, swimmers are taught to**

a. apply alcohol to the ear canal before swimming

b. apply alcohol to the ear canal after swimming

c. cough up any phlegm

d. put cotton in their ears during swimming

e. do Valsalva's maneuver

72. **What factor increases developing the risk of hypertension?**

a. age

b. sex

c. increased exercise

d. low-salt diet

e. race

73. **When a urine test for protein is positive, the examiner also should check**

a. blood in urine

b. blood pressure

c. cholesterol level

d. food intake

e. family history of protein in urine

74. **To prevent impetigo skin infections among wrestlers,**

a. take cultures from wrestling mats weekly

b. take cultures of all skin lesions on wrestlers

c. keep all wrestlers out that have skin lesions

d. have wrestlers wear sweat suits to cover body area

e. wash mats with antiseptic solution daily

75. **The preparticipation questionnaire asks if a parent has died suddenly before the age of 50. If an athlete answers *yes*, why is this significant?**
    a. so this athlete can be disqualified before participation
    b. so a more extensive evaluation can be done for a possible inherited medical condition
    c. so the athlete is told to play in a noncontact sport
    d. so the athlete is told to play in a noncontact or noncollision sport
    e. so regular medical checkups are arranged

76. **Which strengthening exercise requires a reciprocal contraction?**
    a. isometrics
    b. isotonic eccentric
    c. isotonic concentric
    d. isokinetics
    e. variable resistance

77. **Why are men more able than women to run and jump faster and higher?**
    a. gender and anatomical differences
    b. hormonal differences
    c. Men have a higher center of gravity.
    d. Men have a greater vital capacity.
    e. Men have more muscles.

78. **Which person will have the slowest resting heart rate?**
    a. a male endurance athlete
    b. a female endurance athlete
    c. a male nonathlete with no activity
    d. a female nonathlete with no activity
    e. a postmenopausal athlete with no activity

79. **Lateral epicondylitis in a tennis player can be prevented by**
    a. hitting a two-handed forehand
    b. using a larger handled racquet
    c. using a racquet with a smaller sweet spot
    d. using the leading elbow technique in backhands
    e. using a lighter racquet

80. **To prevent neck injuries in wrestling, rules have been put into place. These are**
    a. wrestling mats must be a minimum of 2 in. thick
    b. disqualification for slamming an opponent
    c. disqualification for not wearing head gear
    d. disqualification for a previous neck injury
    e. disqualification for not wearing a mouth guard

81. **What is the proper position of the neck when an athlete is about to make a tackle?**
    a. hyperflexed
    b. hyperextended
    c. bulled
    d. flexion
    e. flexion with some lateral rotation

82. **To prevent knee injuries from lateral blows, teach an athlete to**
    a. relax on impact
    b. contract muscles on impact
    c. strengthen leg musculature
    d. wear long-cleated shoes
    e. play on a grass surface

83. **Fatal injuries occur most often to what part of the body?**
    a. chest
    b. head
    c. back
    d. abdominal area
    e. neck

84. **When teaching athletes to fall in a manner that will prevent shoulder injuries, teach them to**
    a. fall onto the outstretched hand
    b. fall onto the tip of the shoulder
    c. fall flat on side of the shoulder
    d. fall so athletes can roll over the shoulder
    e. fall so athletes avoid the shoulder by falling onto the thorax

85. **Cutting the sleeves of a football jersey**
    a. can help decrease heat injuries
    b. can help range of motion of shoulder pads
    c. should be done for quarterbacks and receivers
    d. may predispose the athlete to abrasions
    e. may predispose the athlete to shoulder injury

86. **Which category of sports has the highest risk of fatalities, catastrophic neck injuries, and severe musculoskeletal injuries?**
    a. noncontact
    b. contact
    c. collision
    d. There is no significant difference.
    e. The category isn't important, it's the sport that matters.

87. **Mouth guards provide a reduction in the number of injuries to**
    a. ear
    b. throat

c. hyoid bone

d. palate

e. brain

88. **To prevent litigation as a result of head and neck injuries, the following items should be incorporated** *except*

a. teaching techniques of lowering the head just before impact

b. proper conditioning prior to competition

c. proper fitting of athletes for helmets

d. telling athletes of the risk involved in sports

e. teaching safety to your athletes

89. **An athlete with exercise-induced asthma should use medication**

a. only in cold, dry weather

b. only in cold, humid weather

c. once an asthmatic attack occurs

d. 30 min before exercise

e. as many times daily as desired

90. **How long does it take for an athlete to be acclimatized to a warm environment?**

a. 1 to 2 days

b. 3 to 5 days

c. 5 to 10 days

d. 8 to 12 days

e. about two weeks

91. **Which is the best way to prevent dehydration during athletic activity?**

a. Rehydrate during activity.

b. Wait to rehydrate until after the activity.

c. Hyperhydrate before activity.

d. Hyperhydrate and do not urinate until after activity.

e. No method is better than the other.

92. **You have a swimmer with a previous history of swimmer's shoulder from the freestyle (front crawl). As a preventative measure, how should the swimmer's stroke be modified?**

a. Lengthen arm stroke cadence.

b. Limit abduction and internal rotation.

c. Limit the breathing pattern to one side.

d. Lessen the body roll.

e. Enter the water head down.

93. **An athlete is competing during a hot day. Thirst will replace how much of the fluid lost?**

a. 100%

b. 80%

   c. 60%

   d. 50%

   e. 20%

94. **The AMA statement on alcohol is:**

   a. Drink in moderation.

   b. One drink a day is good for the cardiovascular system.

   c. Alcohol is a poison.

   d. Drink as much as you like.

   e. Drink, but not so much that you vomit.

95. **When should an athlete be within 3 lb of ideal weight for the season?**

   a. 1 week before the season starts

   b. 2 weeks before the season starts

   c. 3 weeks before the season starts

   d. 1 month before the season starts

   e. the day season starts

96. **Rubberized sweat suits contribute to**

   a. chilblains

   b. diabetes

   c. asthma

   d. staleness

   e. heat illnesses

97. **To protect the bladder from injury, the athlete should**

   a. wear a protective supporter

   b. drink plenty of fluids during competition

   c. reduce fluid intake

   d. play with a full bladder

   e. empty the bladder

98. **What is the purpose of the physical examination before activity?**

   a. to eliminate athletes who are out of shape

   b. to determine who is going out for the team

   c. to make money for the medical community

   d. to meet the athletes

   e. to determine if the athlete has any illnesses

99. **The best way to manage athletic injuries is to**

   a. rehabilitate

   b. educate

   c. prevent

   d. evaluate

   e. treat

100. **What energy system supplies the immediate energy for muscular contraction?**

    a. ATP–CP system
    b. oxygen system
    c. nervous system
    d. free-fatty-acid system
    e. lactic-acid system

101. **Which energy system is set up for endurance activities?**

    a. ATP–CP system
    b. oxygen system
    c. nervous system
    d. free-fatty-acid system
    e. lactic-acid system

102. **Active loosening exercises should be a part of**

    a. warm-up and cooldown after activity
    b. the physiological effects of activity
    c. at-home rehabilitation
    d. active daily living skills
    e. long drives or sitting

103. **How long does the ATP–CP energy system function until it switches to the lactic-acid system?**

    a. 10 s maximum
    b. 2 min maximum
    c. 5 min maximum
    d. 30 min maximum
    e. for several hours

104. **Athletes who are sensitive to insect bites should be reminded to avoid**

    a. eating sugary substances when outdoors
    b. standing near garbage cans while outdoors
    c. wearing flowery-scented soaps
    d. running away from insects
    e. swinging at insects

■ Recognition and Evaluation

Directions—Each of the questions or incomplete statements here is followed by five suggested answers or completions. Select the *best* answer in each case.

105. **When using skin-fold calipers to assess body fat, how do you ensure that you are measuring fat and not muscle?**

a. Have the athlete relax.
b. Have the athlete slouch.
c. Have the athlete inhale.
d. Have the athlete exhale.
e. Have the athlete contract the muscle in the area.

106. **Which portion of the clavicle is most frequently fractured?**

a. at the acromioclavicular portion
b. at the sternoclavicular portion
c. in the lateral third
d. at the point where the middle and lateral thirds join
e. at the point where the middle and medial thirds join

107. **What bony portion of the skull is particularly vulnerable to focal impacts?**

a. temporal bone
b. parietal bone
c. occipital bone
d. lacrimal bone
e. zygomatic arch

108. **A Bennett's lesion is associated with**

a. anterior glenohumeral dislocation
b. tears of glenoid labrum and posterior capsule
c. fracture of the humeral head
d. impingement of the supraspinatus muscle
e. repetitive anterior glenohumeral subluxation

109. **An athlete comes to you after a fall. He has a posterior dislocated shoulder. In what position will you expect him to be carrying his arm?**

a. internally rotated
b. externally rotated
c. a neutral position
d. internally rotated and adducted
e. externally rotated and abducted

110. **Synovial fluid containing fibrinolysin**

a. speeds the healing process
b. slows the healing process
c. creates more swelling
d. causes the growth of abnormal tissue
e. increases the size of callus in a healing fracture

111. **Injury to the ulnar nerve causes numbness**
    a. in the palm of the hand
    b. along the palmar aspect of the thumb
    c. in the little finger and lateral aspect of the ring finger
    d. in the index and middle fingers
    e. along the dorsal surface of the hand

112. **A mallet finger is caused by what mechanism?**
    a. radial deviation
    b. flexion
    c. ulnar deviation
    d. extension against active contraction of extensor
    e. flexion against active contraction of extensor

113. **On a banked track, knee pain will result in**
    a. uphill leg with medial soreness and downhill leg with lateral soreness
    b. uphill and downhill legs with medial soreness
    c. uphill and downhill legs with lateral soreness
    d. uphill leg with lateral soreness and downhill leg with medial soreness
    e. uphill leg patellar tendon soreness and downhill leg lateral soreness

114. **Osgood–Schlatter disease occurs in the area of the**
    a. patella
    b. patellar tendon
    c. quadriceps
    d. tibial tubercle
    e. femoral condyle

115. **What separates the lateral meniscus from the lateral collateral ligament?**
    a. popliteus
    b. iliotibial
    c. biceps femoris
    d. plantaris
    e. pes anserinus

116. **Fluid drawn from a swollen knee joint found to have blood and fat droplets is an indication of?**
    a. torn ligaments
    b. gout
    c. arthritis
    d. infection
    e. a fracture

117. **Which portion of the eye is responsible for focusing images on the retina?**
    a. conjunction
    b. sclera
    c. cornea
    d. lens
    e. retina

118. **Itching of the eye generally indicates**
    a. a foreign body in the eye
    b. serious eye disease
    c. swelling of the cornea
    d. mucus floating in the eye
    e. an allergy

119. **You have an African-American athlete with sickle cell anemia. What should you look for to recognize symptoms early in a crisis?**
    a. unconsciousness and decreased blood pressure
    b. bounding pulse rate and decreased blood pressure
    c. vomiting, lightheadedness, and increased blood pressure
    d. rapid, weak pulse, sweating, and decreased blood pressure
    e. pain in lower left ribs, weakness, nausea, hematuria

120. **An athlete who cannot recall events that occurred before a concussion has**
    a. retrograde amnesia
    b. posttraumatic amnesia
    c. tinnitus
    d. disorientation
    e. Romberg's sign

121. **What type of joint has the thumb?**
    a. hinge
    b. ball and socket
    c. ellipsoidal
    d. saddle
    e. gliding

122. **A rib fracture can be distinguished from a rib contusion by**
    a. painful compression of the anterior-posterior rib cage
    b. pain with both inspiration and exhalation
    c. severe pain with inspiration, point tenderness over the fracture
    d. application of a tuning fork to area is painful
    e. partial breathing is extremely painful

123. **The most frequent injury occurring in the thigh is**
    a. myositis ossificans
    b. quadricep contusion

    c. quadricep strain

    d. hamstring strain

    e. adductor group strains

124. **When evaluating the hip and pelvis it is also important to evaluate what other area?**

    a. the spine

    b. the lower extremities

    c. the abdomen

    d. the low back

    e. the reproductive organs

125. **An athlete who is prone to lower leg stress fractures should be evaluated for**

    a. tight Achilles tendon

    b. weak anterior tibialis musculature

    c. tight plantar fascia

    d. pronated foot

    e. leg-length discrepancy

126. **A positive anterior drawer of the ankle will indicate a tear of the**

    a. calcaneofibular ligament

    b. deltoid ligament

    c. anterior talofibular ligament

    d. Achilles tendon

    e. posterior tibialis muscle

127. **The acromioclavicular joint is injured by**

    a. hyperextension and internal rotation

    b. abduction and external rotation

    c. adduction and external rotation

    d. direct impact to the joint

    e. a fall on the tip of the shoulder

128. **A bruise is caused by what type of force?**

    a. tensile

    b. abrasive

    c. shearing

    d. compressive

    e. stretching

129. **Pericoronitis is usually found in conjunction with**

    a. pulpitis

    b. an avulsed tooth

    c. an impacted wisdom tooth

    d. herpes simplex

    e. an aphthous ulcer

130. **A fabella is a(n)**
    a. skin disorder with small lesions
    b. abnormal bone growth
    c. large infection in a joint
    d. loose body in the knee joint
    e. sesamoid bone in the head of the gastrocnemius muscle

131. **In an athlete with a head injury and in shock, remember the**
    a. blood pressure will decrease
    b. need to apply an antishock device
    c. need to look for other injuries contributing to shock
    d. head must be elevated
    e. need for oxygen will decrease

132. **An athlete who coughs up bright-red blood has an injury to the**
    a. spleen
    b. lungs
    c. heart
    d. stomach
    e. throat

133. **Nerve endings are located in the**
    a. epidermis
    b. germinal layer of the skin
    c. dermis
    d. fat cells
    e. pigment layer

134. **Capillary refill testing of the nail beds is invalid if the color**
    a. that returns is blue
    b. returns instantaneously
    c. does not return
    d. is delayed in return
    e. is red

135. **A pulse absent in one extremity but present in *all* other extremities indicates a(an)**
    a. weak heartbeat
    b. neurological injury
    c. alcohol overdose
    d. blockage in the artery to that extremity
    e. blockage in the vein to that extremity

136. **The primary survey includes**
    a. level of consciousness and checking medical identification
    b. checking vital signs
    c. pulse and breathing rate

d. blood pressure, pulse, and breathing rate

e. airway, breathing, and circulation

137. The diaphragm has three openings in it. What are they for?

a. thoracic spine, esophagus, and bronchi

b. thoracic spine, trachea, and esophagus

c. lumbar spine, neurovascular bundles, and esophagus

d. esophagus, aorta, and superior vena cava

e. esophagus, aorta, and inferior vena cava

138. The body's breathing rate is controlled by the amount of

a. oxygen in the venous blood

b. oxygen in the arterial blood

c. oxygen in the brain tissue

d. carbon dioxide in venous blood

e. carbon dioxide in arterial blood

139. What drug is involved in an athlete with bilateral dilated pupils?

a. a stimulant

b. a narcotic

c. an inhalant

d. a depressant

e. a steroid

140. The classic symptom of Sever's disease is

a. pain in the anterior heel

b. swelling on the lateral aspect of the ankle

c. swelling in the posterior aspect of the ankle

d. pain in the posterior heel

e. crepitus of the Achilles tendon

141. When evaluating low back pain, it is discovered that an athlete has bilateral pronation of the feet. What compensations will occur in the low back as a result?

a. anterior pelvic tilt and increased lordosis

b. lateral flaring of the iliac crests

c. medial flaring of the iliac crests

d. posterior pelvic tilt on nondominant leg side and anterior pelvic tilt on dominant leg side

e. leg-length discrepancy in the pelvis, yielding scoliosis

142. A classic symptom of iliotibial tract friction is pain in the

a. foot-strike phase

b. take-off phase

c. foot-descent phase

d. forward-swing phase

e. mid-support phase

143. When valgus-stress testing the knee, it is necessary to

a. take the knee into hyperextension
b. flex the hip
c. make sure quadriceps musculature is relaxed
d. make sure hamstring musculature is relaxed
e. have the athlete lie prone

144. A knee hyperextension can injure

a. anterior and posterior cruciate ligaments
b. meniscus
c. patellar tendon
d. patella
e. medial and lateral collateral ligaments

145. The motor function of the ulnar nerve is best tested by

a. abduction of the little finger or index finger against resistance
b. abduction of the thumb against resistance
c. extension of all fingers against resistance
d. flexion of all fingers against resistance
e. flexion of the wrist against resistance

146. A boxer's fracture occurs in what bone?

a. the nasal bones
b. the zygomatic arch
c. the orbit
d. the fifth metacarpal
e. the third metacarpal

147. When attempting to determine the presence of a stress fracture in the shin,

a. have the athlete walk on it and determine the painful area
b. have the athlete shake the leg and determine if this causes pain
c. tape the skin and see if skin pain is resolved
d. put arches in shoes and see if skin pain is resolved
e. percuss over and away from the painful area

148. Posterior glenohumeral subluxations are characterized by pain in what anatomical position?

a. abduction and external rotation
b. adduction, forward flexion, and some external rotation
c. internal rotation and adduction
d. forward flexion with direct impact
e. internal rotation and hyperextension

149. Lymphadenitis is evident by

a. a discharge from the nose
b. phlegm in the throat

   c. difficulty swallowing and swollen glands

   d. pain, swelling, and inflammation of tissue

   e. high fever and red streaks from lymph glands toward the heart

150. **The mechanism of injury for an anterior shoulder dislocation is**

   a. external rotation and abduction

   b. direct impact

   c. circumduction

   d. internal rotation and adduction

   e. torsion

151. **The mechanism of injury of a brachial plexus "burner" is**

   a. rotation

   b. depression of shoulder at lateral flexion, away from the depression

   c. depression of shoulder of lateral flexion, toward the depression

   d. direct impact

   e. hyperextension

152. **If swelling of the knee occurs gradually over 24 hours, you should suspect what problem?**

   a. Osgood–Schlatter disease and osteochondritis dissecans

   b. bursitis and chondromalacia patellae

   c. osteochondral fracture

   d. synovial irritation or a small meniscus tear

   e. fracture of the patella

153. **A permanently locked knee is an indication of what injury?**

   a. a meniscus fragment

   b. patellar tendinitis

   c. a loose body in the knee

   d. synovial membrane impingement

   e. a large bucket-handle meniscus tear

154. **A tailor's bunion is located on the**

   a. tip of the index finger

   b. metacarpal joint of the thumb

   c. second metatarsal head on the plantar surface

   d. first metatarsal head

   e. fifth metatarsal head

155. **The normal plantar flexion of the ankle is**

   a. 20 degrees

   b. 30 degrees

   c. 50 degrees

   d. 60 degrees

   e. 90 degrees

156. **Ranges of motion in extremities can be compared to the opposite extremity to determine decreases or losses in range. What is the spine compared to?**

    a. range-of-motion charts
    b. other individuals of the same age and body type
    c. individuals of the same sex and body type
    d. other individuals of the same sex, age, and body type
    e. other individuals with a similar injury

157. **Ankylosis is**

    a. incorrect body alignment
    b. a congenital deformity of a bone increasing range of motion
    c. total loss of motion in a joint
    d. hyperflexability
    e. hypermobility

158. **When measuring the range of motion in the forearm, specifically pronation and supination, where is 0 degrees, or neutral?**

    a. palm side up (supination)
    b. palm side down (pronation)
    c. a thumbs-up position
    d. little-finger-up position
    e. palm side up (supination) with slight ulnar deviation

159. **Cellulitis lesions first appear**

    a. in the adipose tissue
    b. in lymph node
    c. in hair follicles
    d. in the distal aspect of a limb
    e. in the proximal aspect of a limb

160. **If sinusitis is not treated and it progressively gets worse, what secondary problem may occur?**

    a. migraine headaches
    b. brain infection
    c. ear infection
    d. pharyngitis
    e. bronchitis

161. **Periostitis most commonly occurs from what injury?**

    a. a contusion
    b. a laceration
    c. an amputation
    d. a fracture
    e. an infection

162. **Verrucae plantaris are most likely to be found on the**
    a. dorsum of the foot
    b. plantar surface of small toes
    c. lateral malleolus
    d. ball of the foot
    e. longitudinal arch of the foot

163. **A carbuncle is most often found on the back of the neck. What characteristic distinguishes it from a furunculosis?**
    a. A carbuncle is from staphylococci.
    b. A carbuncle discharges greenish-white pus.
    c. A carbuncle is treated by squeezing fluid out.
    d. A carbuncle discharges pus from many sites.
    e. A carbuncle is not contagious.

164. **The Thompson test is used to determine**
    a. Achilles tendon ruptures
    b. contraction of the hip
    c. tibial torsion
    d. thoracic outlet syndrome
    e. thrombophlebitis

165. **Which disease is characterized by a thick, yellow discharge from the urethra, especially in males?**
    a. gonorrhea
    b. urethritis
    c. herpes
    d. AIDS
    e. syphilis

166. **Pale skin color is an indication of what?**
    a. jaundice
    b. lack of oxygen
    c. poisoning
    d. heat stroke
    e. lack of circulation

167. **In what plane does extension of the spine occur?**
    a. coronal
    b. transverse
    c. sagittal
    d. longitudinal
    e. midsagittal

168. **What nerve innervates the biceps femoris?**
    a. inferior gluteal nerve
    b. sciatic nerve

c. peroneal nerve

d. obturator nerve

e. femoral nerve

169. **How is the extensor pollicis brevis examined and differentiated from other muscles that move the thumb?**

a. Have the athlete flex the metacarpophalangeal joint against resistance.

b. Have the athlete flex the interphalangeal joint against resistance.

c. Have the athlete adduct the metacarpal bone.

d. Have the athlete extend the metacarpophalangeal joint against resistance.

e. Have the athlete extend the interphalangeal joint against resistance.

170. **When testing the extensor digitorum communis, stabilize the**

a. distal interphalangeal joint

b. proximal interphalangeal joint

c. metacarpal interphalangeal joint

d. forearm

e. wrist

171. **The action of the quadratus lumborum is to**

a. hip extension

b. back extension

c. back flexion

d. hip abduction and external rotation

e. lateral flexion of lumbar vertebrae

172. **An athlete has fallen on the back of her head, causing flexion of the neck. The athlete complains of dizziness, headaches, and tingling in her feet. You should suspect**

a. neck injury

b. brachial plexus injury

c. migraine

d. sciatica

e. piriformis syndrome

173. **What is the most common mechanism for nerve root injuries of the neck?**

a. hyperflexion

b. hyperextension

c. rotation

d. lateral flexion

e. circumduction

174. **What joint(s) make up the shoulder?**
    a. glenohumeral and acromioclavicular
    b. glenohumeral, acromioclavicular, scapulothoracic, and sternoclavicular
    c. glenohumeral, acromioclavicular, scapulothoracic
    d. glenohumeral and sternoclavicular
    e. glenohumeral

175. **Periorbital ecchymosis can be caused by a**
    a. basilar artery rupture
    b. parietal skull fracture
    c. lacrimal fracture
    d. zygomatic arch fracture
    e. frontalis fracture

176. **What vascular changes occur as the result of histamine release after an acute injury?**
    a. erythema
    b. increased capillary permeability
    c. hematoma
    d. myositis ossificans
    e. red blood cell numbers increase

177. **An athlete has mild headaches regularly and takes aspirin to relieve them. A blood test will show**
    a. increased white blood cell count
    b. mild anemia
    c. low potassium level
    d. low calcium level
    e. decreased HDL

178. **Cervical spinal injuries in ice hockey occur most often by axial loading of the head in contact with**
    a. another player
    b. the puck
    c. the boards
    d. the goalposts
    e. hockey sticks

179. **What heat-related illness is most likely to occur in nonacclimatized athletes?**
    a. salt-depletion heat exhaustion
    b. exertion heat stroke
    c. water-depletion heat exhaustion
    d. anhidrotic heat exhaustion
    e. heat cramps

180. **What age group does not benefit from the Tanner age classification?**
    a. age 12
    b. age 13
    c. age 14
    d. age 15
    e. under age 12

181. **Females have greater _____ than males.**
    a. muscle strength
    b. power
    c. maximum VO$_2$ levels
    d. circulatory capacity
    e. flexibility

182. **If the hyaline cartilage of the knee joint is chronically compressed, what injury results?**
    a. bursitis
    b. Osgood–Schlatter disease
    c. osteochondrosis
    d. dislocation
    e. synovitis

183. **If pain in a joint increases during the day, the cause is**
    a. tendinitis
    b. synovitis
    c. bursitis
    d. edema
    e. fracture

184. **The largest tarsal bone in the body is the**
    a. calcaneus
    b. talus
    c. navicular
    d. cuboid
    e. lateral cuneiform

185. **The shoes of athletes who spend a lot of time on their toes will wear out under the**
    a. medial aspect of the great toe
    b. great toe and second toe
    c. lateral heel only
    d. metatarsal arch area
    e. metatarsal arch area and lateral heel

186. **What artery supplies blood to the meniscus of the knee?**
    a. the peroneal artery
    b. the femoral artery

c. the anterior tibial artery
d. the popliteal tibial artery
e. the middle genicular artery

187. **With femoral anteversion, what degree of hip internal rotation is involved?**

a. 5 degrees
b. 15 degrees
c. greater than 35 degrees
d. greater than 45 degrees
e. greater than 60 degrees

188. **Tissue that binds a fracture site together is referred to as a**

a. calcium deposit
b. myositis
c. callus
d. osteochondritis
e. myositis ossificans

189. **The supportive structure of bones is the**

a. lacuna
b. haversian canal
c. trabecula
d. epiphyseal growth plate
e. metaphysis

190. **Why is decreased flexibility common in young athletes?**

a. Bones grow faster than musculature.
b. Condyles are larger during youth.
c. Young athletes fail to stretch regularly.
d. Young athletes fail to stretch properly.
e. Young athletes lack fitness role models.

191. **The most common cause of anemia in females is**

a. strenuous exercise
b. menstrual blood loss
c. high rates of injury
d. high usage of aspirin
e. amenorrhea

192. **Females are prone to stress fractures as a result of**

a. osteoporosis
b. lack of calcium intake
c. amenorrhea
d. anemia
e. inflexibility

193. **An athlete who has exercise-induced bronchospasm is most likely to show signs of the illness at what point during exercise?**
    a. only when strenuous exercise occurs
    b. as soon as exercise begins
    c. within the first eight minutes
    d. when maximum VO_2 levels are reached
    e. when the oxygen debt begins

194. **A characteristic of slow-twitch muscle fibers is**
    a. more I bands
    b. high amounts of mitochondria
    c. low concentration of enzymes
    d. high amounts of ATP
    e. fewer Z bands

195. **Oxygen being transported through the blood is attached to**
    a. platelets
    b. leukocytes
    c. plasma
    d. hemoglobin
    e. erythrocytes

196. **Menstruation will result in the loss of what mineral?**
    a. iron
    b. calcium
    c. sulfur
    d. sodium
    e. chromium

197. **The resting pH level of the blood is**
    a. 10
    b. 8.3
    c. 7.4
    d. 7.0
    e. 5.4

198. **Which of these alter blood pH?**
    a. maximal effort exercise, diarrhea, and rich food intake
    b. maximal effort exercise, diarrhea, and acidic food intake
    c. hepatitis, hyperventilation, and ulcers
    d. diabetes, lactic-acid buildup, and vomiting
    e. fractures, diarrhea, and vomiting

199. **Where does the majority of digestion take place?**
    a. in the cecum and jejunum
    b. in the duodenum and jejunum
    c. in the ileum and ascending colon

d. in the ascending colon and transverse colon

e. in the cecum and appendix

200. What is the major secretion in the large intestine?

a. bacteria for fermentation

b. enzymes for digestion

c. hydrochloric acid for digestion

d. urea, a by-product

e. mucus to hold fecal material together

201. A functional leg-length discrepancy results from

a. one leg being shorter than the other

b. anterior tilting of the pelvis

c. lateral tilting of the pelvis

d. bilateral contractions of the quadriceps

e. bilateral contractions of the hamstrings

202. Hyperpnea is also called

a. hyperventilation

b. cluster breathing

c. Cheyne–Stokes respiration

d. apnea

e. Biot's breathing

203. The normal adult pulse rate is

a. 50 to 80 beats per min

b. 60 to 90 beats per min

c. 120 beats per min

d. 12 to 20 beats per min

e. 12 beats per min

204. An athlete indicates she felt crepitus over the area of injury. What do you suspect as the injury?

a. sprain of the joint

b. bone fracture

c. hematoma

d. apnea

e. complete musculature rupture

205. What somatotype is more prone to heat-related illnesses?

a. an extreme mesomorph

b. a mesomorphic ectomorph

c. an extreme endomorph

d. an ectomorphic mesomorph

e. an endomorphic ectomorph

206. The ponderal index is used to determine

a. height
b. weight
c. predisposition to injury
d. laxity of the anterior cruciate
e. somatotype

207. What type of bone is the scapula?

a. a long bone
b. an irregular bone
c. a sesamoid bone
d. a short bone
e. a flat bone

208. Crutch paralysis specifically affects what nerve?

a. brachial plexus
b. musculocutaneous nerve
c. radial nerve
d. median nerve
e. ulnar nerve

209. Which of the following is a diarthrosis joint?

a. pubic synthesis
b. costal chondral
c. shoulder
d. suture of cranium
e. tibiofibular articulation

210. Hinge joints are capable of what motions?

a. flexion and extension
b. retraction and protraction
c. pronation and supination
d. abduction and adduction
e. gliding and rotation

211. The portion of the muscle that remains stationary during a contraction is called the

a. insertion
b. belly
c. origin
d. gaster
e. skeletal

212. Cellular death resulting from trauma is called

a. necrosis
b. inflammation
c. hypoxia

    d. gangrene

    e. aseptic

213. **Signs of inflammation are:**

    a. pain, crepitus, and necrosis

    b. redness, swelling, and heat

    c. discoloration and hypoxia

    d. loss of function and loss of sensation

    e. pain and leakage from an open wound

214. **Scar formation occurs in the**

    a. collagen phase

    b. wound healing phase

    c. fibroplasia phase

    d. maturation phase

    e. adhesion phase

215. **Which layer of skin is responsible for new cell formation?**

    a. stratum germinativum

    b. stratum spinosum

    c. stratum granulosum

    d. stratum lucidum

    e. stratum corneum

216. **A laceration is identified by**

    a. bleeding and oozing

    b. smooth edges and bleeding freely

    c. a flap of skin that bleeds freely

    d. jagged edges and bleeding freely

    e. a hole that seals itself

217. **A skin lesion that is characterized by a skin elevation with sero fluid is called a**

    a. papule

    b. crust

    c. fissure

    d. nodule

    e. vesicle

218. **An accumulation of blood at the site of an injury is called**

    a. a hematoma

    b. ecchymosis

    c. edema

    d. a contusion

    e. a myositis ossificans

219. A sprain is an injury to

   a. muscle
   b. tendon
   c. ligamentous structures
   d. periosteum
   e. synovium

220. Stress fractures are not seen on plain radiographs until _____ week(s), postinjury.

   a. 1
   b. 1 to 2
   c. 5
   d. 2 to 3
   e. 4 to 6

221. The weakest part of a long bone in children is the

   a. articular surface
   b. diaphysis
   c. periosteum
   d. endosteum
   e. epiphysial plate

222. What nerve is involved in the winged-scapula injury?

   a. axillary nerve
   b. suprascapular nerve
   c. long thoracic nerve
   d. spinal accessory nerve
   e. median nerve

223. A Bennett's fracture occurs in the

   a. hamate bone
   b. ulna
   c. navicular
   d. metacarpal of the thumb
   e. styloid process of the radius

224. A mallet finger occurs because of flexion or hyperflexion, causing

   a. rupture of the collateral ligament structure
   b. an injury to the volar plate
   c. a tear of the extension tendon slip, yielding a flexion contracture
   d. avulsion of the extension mechanism
   e. avulsion of the flexor mechanism

■ *Management, Treatment, and Disposition*

Directions—Each of the questions or incomplete statements here is followed by five suggested answers or completions. Select the *best* answer in each case.

225. **Which items are important to have readily available at an athletic event?**
    a. an ambulance and athletes' parents
    b. athletes' insurance policy numbers and permission for care
    c. money for the pay telephone and a map to the local hospital
    d. spine board and insect-bite lotion
    e. neck collar and waiver-of-injury forms

226. **To make sure all training kits have the proper supplies, it is best to**
    a. stock them yourself
    b. have a student athletic trainer stock them
    c. take two training kits
    d. have a checklist of supplies needed
    e. stock all kits to overflowing without regard for need

227. **An athlete's medical record should be**
    a. long and detailed
    b. filled with personal comments
    c. done in a weekly format even if no progress or changes were made
    d. done in pencil to erase any mistakes later
    e. in SOAP format

228. **Individual report forms are helpful because**
    a. they are not legally binding
    b. they can be given to scouts without the need for athletes' permission
    c. the athletic trainer does not have to go to the athlete's file as often
    d. they are usually available to coaches and other athletes
    e. they do not have to be placed in the athlete's injury record

229. **An injury report to a parent is more helpful than a telephone call because**
    a. it avoids confrontations with parents
    b. they will surely get their mail, but may not get the telephone message
    c. you can put it off for a while
    d. it avoids confusion and misunderstandings
    e. it is less time consuming than a telephone call

230. **A physician's referral form is an indication that**

   a. the athletic trainer does not know what is wrong
   b. the athletic trainer has no interest in what is wrong
   c. the athletic trainer is too busy to care for the athlete
   d. the athletic trainer does not like the athlete
   e. the athletic trainer is concerned for the athlete

231. **A physician referral form is helpful because**

   a. information can be transferred more effectively
   b. you will not have to call
   c. referrals do not have to be placed in the athlete's record, so they are less time consuming
   d. they are not legally binding
   e. they show that you are not concerned about the welfare of the athlete

232. **An EMS dispatcher can give helpful information before the ambulance arrives. What information may save an athlete's life?**

   a. your location
   b. cardiopulmonary resuscitation instructions
   c. the time the ambulance will arrive
   d. the number of emergency personnel on the ambulance
   e. the level of training of the ambulance personnel

233. **What information must be given to the EMS dispatcher concerning an injury?**

   a. location and sex of athlete
   b. hospital the athlete desires and insurance information
   c. number of people injured and care being given
   d. allergies, height, and weight of the athlete
   e. telephone number you are calling from and athlete's age and race

234. **An athlete is in cardiac arrest. Which type of EMS unit will be dispatched if all units are equally close?**

   a. a simple transfer unit
   b. a first responder unit
   c. a basic life-support unit
   d. an advanced life-support unit
   e. medevac helicopter

235. **Which physician specializes in fractured noses and deviated septa?**

   a. otolaryngologist
   b. neurosurgeon
   c. dentist
   d. urologist
   e. orthopedist

236. **The easiest way to maintain effective communication to all members of the athletic training team regarding an injury is to**
    a. hold weekly meetings
    b. use forms that are in triplicate
    c. make telephone calls on a regular basis
    d. review athletes' files monthly
    e. send letters to all members weekly

237. **An athlete with itchy, watery eyes and sneezing needs a referral to which specialist?**
    a. a dermatologist
    b. an optometrist
    c. an allergist
    d. an orthopedist
    e. a general surgeon

238. **What is the team physician's role?**
    a. injury prevention
    b. conditioning of athletes
    c. increasing the workload
    d. supervision of the athletic training program
    e. ordering supplies

239. **A player with a possible anterior cruciate tear leaves the playing field and goes to the sideline by**
    a. walking
    b. being carried in a stretcher
    c. an arm-supported three-point gait
    d. being carried in a seated position
    e. hopping off

240. **When should an accident report be written?**
    a. only if the athlete requires services of a physician
    b. only if litigation will be involved
    c. immediately following the incident
    d. if you have been subpoenaed as a result of an incident
    e. once you receive an unpaid medical bill

241. **What role should a nurse play on the athletic training team?**
    a. coverage of athletic contests
    b. diagnosis of athletic injuries
    c. evaluation of skin disorders
    d. disqualification of athletes because of medical concerns
    e. a liaison between the athletic trainer and coaching staff

242. **A runner who complains of patellar tendinitis should avoid running on**
   a. soft surfaces
   b. hard surfaces
   c. uphill terrain
   d. downhill terrain
   e. curves of any surfaces

243. **When can an underage athlete give consent for treatment of an injury?**
   a. in an emergency situation
   b. anytime when injured
   c. when a parent cannot be reached
   d. at age 16
   e. never

244. **A medical diagnosis can be made only by a**
   a. physician
   b. athletic trainer
   c. nurse
   d. coach
   e. athlete

245. **You have the entire athletic training team together evaluating an injury. Whose role is it to contact the parent of a high school athlete who has suffered a serious injury?**
   a. the team physician
   b. the athletic trainer
   c. the athlete
   d. the school nurse
   e. the student athletic trainer

246. **Who is responsible for calling an ambulance in an emergency?**
   a. the person designated by procedure policy
   b. the team physician
   c. the athletic trainer
   d. the coach
   e. the student athletic trainer

247. **SOAP, with regard to clinical note taking, means:**
   a. short term goals, objective, assessment, and plan
   b. short term goals, objective, assessment, and progress
   c. seriousness of injury, outcome, assistance, and progress
   d. subjective, objective, assessment, and plan
   e. subjective, objective, assessment, and progress

248. **Which of the following is important for record keeping in an acute injury?**
    a. witnesses to injury
    b. names of bystanders who assisted in care
    c. athlete's date of birth
    d. time of injury
    e. mechanism of injury

249. **Which of the following athletes *cannot* give consent for treatment?**
    a. a married athlete
    b. an unconscious athlete
    c. a mentally incompetent athlete
    d. an emancipated minor
    e. a 16-year-old athlete

250. **When beta-blocking drugs are used, what is the heart response under stressful situations?**
    a. increased cardiac output
    b. decreased ventricular output
    c. decreased atrial output
    d. increase in heart rate
    e. decrease in heart rate

251. **What drug is banned by the International Olympic Committee?**
    a. theophylline
    b. salbutamol
    c. any antihistamine
    d. dextromethorphan
    e. codeine

252. **The best treatment for athlete's foot fungus is**
    a. the application of moist heat
    b. oral medications
    c. over-the-counter creams
    d. surgical removal of the diseased area
    e. prevention

253. **Why do fractures of the proximal scaphoid (navicular) take extended periods of time to heal?**
    a. because of continual impact with the styloid process
    b. because they are usually displaced
    c. because of nerve entrapment
    d. because of inadequate blood supply
    e. because of local edema

254. **A thumb metacarpophalangeal joint dislocation should be reduced by**

a. pulling the thumb longitudinally

b. adducting thumb while pulling longitudinally

c. adducting thumb while pushing it dorsally

d. abducting thumb while pushing it dorsally

e. a physician

255. **How long should a small-chip fracture of the proximal interphalangeal joint be splinted?**

a. 6 to 8 weeks

b. 2 to 4 weeks

c. 3 weeks

d. 1 week

e. 1 to 2 days

256. **A volar plate injury requires splinting for**

a. 2 to 4 weeks

b. 5 weeks, minimum

c. 3 weeks

d. 1 to 2 weeks

e. only as long as decreased range of motion is apparent

257. **A fracture of the first rib is treated by**

a. placing the athlete in a clavicular harness

b. placing the athlete in a sling

c. placing the athlete in a sling with a cross-chest strap

d. placing an elastic bandage across the athlete's chest

e. doing nothing

258. **After an eye injury, an athlete should be referred to an opthamologist if he has**

a. double vision and eye fatigue

b. stabbing pain and tearing

c. tearing and loss of some visual field

d. loss of some visual field or blurred vision

e. blurred vision and eye fatigue

259. **An athlete loses a filling. What material is used as a temporary filling?**

a. dycal

b. cavit

c. oil of clove

d. a mixture of eugenol and zinc oxide

e. calcium hydroxide

260. **A brain injury may lead to long-term difficulties, such as**
    a. aniscoria and vertigo
    b. epilepsy and dementia
    c. hyphema
    d. vertigo
    e. hearing loss

261. **The acuscope is used to assist in the treatment of**
    a. myositis ossificans
    b. edema
    c. sympathetic reflex dystrophy
    d. nonunion fractures
    e. fungal infections

262. **Low-voltage electrical stimulators are used to assist in the treatment of**
    a. nonunion fractures and sympathetic reflex dystrophy
    b. pain and muscle spasms and to enhance venous returns
    c. myositis ossificans, nonunion fractures, and pain
    d. osteoporosis, osteoarthritis, and enhanced venous return
    e. osteochondritis dissecans, pain, and muscle spasms

263. **The use of massage in the intermediate stage of an injury can facilitate**
    a. an increase of muscle spasm
    b. a decreased vasodialation
    c. removal of waste products
    d. an increase of swelling
    e. hardening of muscle tissue

264. **Following an injury, heat therapy begins**
    a. when the patient has some pain-free range of motion
    b. once histamine is released
    c. when edema is stabilized
    d. when the discoloration is subsiding
    e. as soon as the injury occurs

265. **If tape is applied to the skin after hot or cold treatments, what will likely result?**
    a. The tape adhesive will be less effective.
    b. More tincture of benzoin will be needed.
    c. The skin may be damaged when tape is removed.
    d. The tape will help retain the cold or heat therapy longer.
    e. The support from the tape will be less effective.

266. **For taping to be effective,**
    a. tape tension is greater over the injured part
    b. the trainer must know what motions must be limited

    c. skin oils should be removed or covered

    d. tape should be applied at 10 °F lower than room temperature

    e. it must be comfortable so have the athlete move around during taping

267. **Control of pain can be accomplished by self-control. What would the technique be?**

    a. denial and isolation of injury

    b. affective negative imagery

    c. biofeedback

    d. exercise

    e. sleeping

268. **The treatment for osteitis pubis is:**

    a. ice, muscle stimulation, and crutches

    b. ice and the Trendelenburg position

    c. ice, neoprene compression, and rest

    d. hydroculator pack and anti-inflammatory medication

    e. TENS, ice, and ultrasound

269. **When dealing with a furunculosis, which of the following is correct?**

    a. Squeeze the pus out.

    b. Apply hot packs.

    c. Apply drawing salves.

    d. Apply an astringent.

    e. Refer to a physician for antibiotics.

270. **A sty is best treated by**

    a. application of a hot cloth

    b. application of a drawing salve

    c. being left alone

    d. covering the eye for 2 days

    e. applying yellow oxide

271. **Hydrocortisone can be used as a drying agent for what skin disorder?**

    a. herpes

    b. ringworm

    c. impetigo

    d. warts

    e. tinea versicolor

272. **The treatment for scabies and pediculosis pubis is**

    a. benzoyl peroxide

    b. topical antibiotics

    c. gamma benzene hexachloride

d. an antimicrobial agent

e. an antifungal agent

273. **Treatment for a black eye is**

a. a cold steak

b. a warm tea bag

c. ice

d. ice and compression

e. ice, compression, and elevation

274. **Elastic bandages should be moistened prior to compressing an acute injury to**

a. help absorb any leaking water

b. keep skin supple

c. keep the body part cold

d. prevent frostbite

e. make the bandage more snug

275. **When applying a pressure bandage to an acutely sprained ankle, apply the bandage**

a. loosely

b. from distal to proximal

c. from proximal to distal

d. tightly at the proximal aspect

e. tightly over the injury and loose at each end

276. **Why is it important for a compression bandage to be tighter distally?**

a. It aids arterial flow.

b. It aids venous return.

c. It raises blood pressure in the area.

d. It decreases blood pressure in the area.

e. It decreases blood flow in the area.

277. **In what position is a shoulder taped in if it is being taped for return to competition after a dislocation?**

a. internal rotation and adduction

b. internal rotation and abduction

c. external rotation and abduction

d. external rotation and adduction

e. in a position of comfort

278. **An athlete who is high on a hallucinogenic drug and is exhibiting paranoid behavior refuses to go to the hospital. What needs to be done?**

a. Call for an ambulance and leave the athlete alone.

b. Take charge and get angry, as this will cause athlete to become submissive.

    c. Protect yourself from aggressive behavior and call for an ambulance.

    d. Put the athlete in a cold shower and give black coffee.

    e. Restrain the athlete and call for an ambulance.

279. An athlete is obviously dead, but other people are concerned because you have not started resuscitation efforts. You should

    a. start resuscitation efforts

    b. cover the athlete with a sheet

    c. pronounce the athlete dead and console the other people

    d. tell the people ambulance personnel will deal with the athlete

    e. explain to the people why you should not start resuscitation efforts and cover the athlete's body

280. In what situations would you refer an athlete to a physician after a throat injury?

    a. loss of voice, or hoarseness

    b. sinus drainage

    c. cold

    d. laceration less than 0.5 in. in length

    e. coughing up phlegm

281. To break a testicular spasm, the athlete

    a. is lifted at the waist while lying supine

    b. breathes deeply through his nose and out through his mouth

    c. brings both knees to his chest

    d. applies ice for 20 min

    e. does a couple of bent-knee sit-ups

282. When moving an athlete off the field on a stretcher, move the athlete

    a. feet first

    b. head first

    c. sideways

    d. whichever way is convenient

    e. so feet are higher than the heart

283. When moving an athlete down a stairway on a stretcher, move the athlete

    a. feet first

    b. head first

    c. sideways

    d. whichever way is convenient

    e. so feet are higher than the heart

284. **Irreversible brain damage occurs after** _____ **of oxygen deprivation**
    a. one min
    b. 2 to 3 min
    c. 4 to 6 min
    d. 1 hr
    e. 10 min

285. **Mouth-to-nose ventilation is given when**
    a. there are severe mouth injuries
    b. there is vomitus in the mouth
    c. there is an airway obstruction
    d. there is a stoma
    e. there is gastric distention

286. **When treating a total airway obstruction in a conscious patient, use**
    a. a finger sweep
    b. Heimlich maneuvers or abdominal thrusts
    c. mouth-to-mouth breathing
    d. five back blows
    e. encouragement of coughing

287. **You can stop giving cardiopulmonary resuscitation for** _____ **to move a patient.**
    a. 4 min
    b. 1 min
    c. 45 s
    d. 15 s
    e. 10 s

288. **A fracture of the second toe is taped in what way?**
    a. There is no need to tape it.
    b. Tape it to the third toe.
    c. Tape it to the second toe.
    d. Tape it to the first and third toes.
    e. Basket weave the second toe only.

289. **An athlete has been bitten during a wrestling match. To treat this injury,**
    a. wash the wound with soap and water and keep it clean
    b. cover the wound with a dressing and bandage
    c. apply ice for the first 2 days, then apply heat
    d. find the athlete who bit and swab that athlete's mouth for infection
    e. wash the wound with soap and water, bandage, and refer to a physician for antibiotics

290. **To treat a felon of the finger,**
    a. drill a hole through fingernail and apply pressure
    b. soak the finger in hot water for 3 days
    c. clip ends of the fingernail in a U-shape
    d. refer to a physician for surgical drainage
    e. bandage and soak the finger in hot water daily

291. **A complication of an inappropriately treated felon is**
    a. osteochondritis
    b. myositis
    c. osteomyelitis
    d. Kienböck's disease
    e. osteitis

292. **After a proximal interphalangeal joint dislocation is reduced, how should this finger be taped for athletic participation?**
    a. Flex the finger beyond 90 degrees and tape to the next finger.
    b. Buddy tape the finger with some flexion and basket weave the affected joint.
    c. Basket weave the affected joint.
    d. Buddy tape the joint into full extension.
    e. Buddy tape the joint into 20-degree flexion.

293. **Treatment of an acute sternal contusion is**
    a. ice and a protective pad over area
    b. heat and a protective pad over area
    c. circumferential elastic taping
    d. massage
    e. ice and compression by an elastic bandage

294. **A contusion of the spinous process is treated by**
    a. massage over area
    b. ice; application of a pad for participation
    c. pain-killing medication
    d. heat
    e. William's flexion exercises

295. **An athlete has a wrist splint in place for a contusion. The athlete has pain with pronation and supination while immobilized. What should be done?**
    a. Place the athlete in a sling and swathe.
    b. Immobilize the athlete above the elbow.
    c. Tell an athlete to avoid pronation and supination.
    d. Ice and tell the athlete to avoid pronation and supination.
    e. Sling and tell the athlete to avoid pronation and supination.

296. **An athlete has a proximal finger nail avulsion with the fat pad protruding. What is your treatment?**
   a. Apply a pressure bandage and ice.
   b. Apply a pressure bandage and allow the nail to go into place on its own.
   c. Apply a bandage and refer to a physician.
   d. Push the fat pad under the nail and then apply a pressure bandage.
   e. Cut the proximal nail off and apply a pressure bandage to the fat pad.

297. **Lymphadenitis is treated by**
   a. squeezing the gland
   b. application of ointment to the area
   c. massage of the area
   d. immobilization
   e. antibiotics

298. **An athlete who was unconscious for a couple minutes**
   a. can return to competition once appearance returns to normal
   b. can return to competition once conscious
   c. can return to competition if all head injury assessments are normal
   d. cannot return and is out for the rest of the season
   e. should not return to activity until evaluation by a physician

299. **A fracture of the clavicle is held in place by**
   a. a sling
   b. a yoke
   c. a sling and swathe
   d. a splint
   e. a splint and sling

300. **An athlete is sitting in a chair on the sideline and is complaining of swelling and cervical spine pain. The athlete had fallen hard to the floor 10 min before. What should you do?**
   a. Give the athlete an ice pack and call for an ambulance.
   b. Indicate the athlete was fine 10 min ago and give ice.
   c. Use a long spine board and backboard the athlete.
   d. Use a short spine board and transfer the athlete to a long backboard.
   e. Have athlete move the head around to see if this increases pain.

301. **In what position should the elbow be placed if there is a complete rupture of the biceps brachii?**
   a. flexion
   b. hyperflexion
   c. adduction and internal rotation

d. extension

e. hyperextension

302. **Which of the following is the most effective way to control bleeding from an open wound?**

a. a tourniquet

b. a pressure bandage

c. a pressure point

d. elevation

e. direct pressure

303. **You have controlled bleeding from an external wound. What should be done with the soiled dressings on the wound?**

a. Take dressings off and apply sterile ones.

b. Take dressings off and apply sterile bandage over wound.

c. Bandage over the top of the soiled dressings.

d. Apply pressure point pressure, remove dressing, and apply bandage.

e. Apply tourniquet, remove dressing, and apply bandage.

304. **You have evaluated an athlete with a painful, swollen tibia. You are unsure if it is strained or fractured. What is your treatment?**

a. Have the athlete walk and jump on it to test it.

b. Apply ice and give the athlete crutches.

c. Varus- and valgus-stress test the tibia.

d. Recommend ice and apply a compression wrap.

e. Splint the lower leg and refer to a physician.

305. **An athlete has sustained a penetrating injury of the cheek that goes from outside to inside of the mouth. To stop the bleeding,**

a. apply pressure to the carotid artery

b. apply a pressure point to the jugular vein

c. apply direct pressure over the wound on the outside of the mouth

d. apply direct pressure over the wound, both on the outside and inside of the mouth

e. apply direct pressure over the wound inside the mouth

306. **To treat a traumatic pneumothorax,**

a. cover the wound and give oxygen

b. elevate the head

c. elevate the feet

d. backboard the athlete

e. use antibiotics and oxygen therapy

307. **To treat hyperventilation,**

a. have the athlete breathe into a paper bag

b. have the athlete breathe into a plastic bag

    c. give oxygen at 10 L/min

    d. have the athlete sit in a semireclining position

    e. give humidified oxygen at 10 L/min

308. To treat a third-degree critical burn,

    a. apply cool water for at least 5 min

    b. apply sterile saline for at least 5 min

    c. cover the burn with a dry, sterile dressing

    d. cover the burn with sterile dressing and apply sterile water

    e. break any blister and apply sterile dressing and water

309. An avulsed piece of tissue is initially treated by

    a. trimming the piece off and cleaning the wound

    b. debriding the wound with a brush and trimming off the piece

    c. debriding the wound with a brush

    d. cleaning the wound and sending the athlete to a physician for care

    e. cleaning the wound, dressing it daily, and watching it for infection

310. A scalp wound is referred to a physician if

    a. it is dirty

    b. the wound is more than 0.5 in. in length

    c. it bleeds a lot

    d. it is a laceration

    e. it is an abrasion

311. Examples of stimulant drugs are:

    a. nicotine, alcohol, and beta blockers

    b. caffeine, cocaine, and amphetamines

    c. alcohol, THC, and caffeine

    d. ephedrine, THC, and heroin

    e. PCP, morphine, and cocaine

312. Side effects caused by the use of anabolic steroids include

    a. stunting of growth in children, acne, and aggression

    b. breast enlargement in males and decreased aggression

    c. shrinkage of testicles, high blood pressure, and increased body fat

    d. decreased sperm production and increased height in children

    e. premature atherosclerosis and increasing lean-body muscle mass

313. How is a laceration cleaned?

    a. with a circular motion

    b. with alcohol

    c. only by a physician

    d. in a lengthwise direction

    e. in a sideways direction

314. **With an unconscious athlete, ammonia fumes should**
   a. never be used
   b. be used if the athlete has a suspected head injury
   c. be used if the athlete has been unconscious for more than 2 min
   d. be used if the athlete has dilated pupils
   e. be used if the athlete has a syncope episode

315. **When treating an orbital hematoma, instruct the athlete to avoid**
   a. blowing the nose
   b. blinking the eye
   c. crying
   d. touching the eye
   e. icing

316. **A volar plate injury of proximal interphalangeal joint is splinted in what position?**
   a. 20 to 30 degrees of flexion
   b. 0 degrees of extension
   c. into hyperextension
   d. the distal interphalangeal joint into flexion and the proximal interphalangeal joint into extension
   e. the distal interphalangeal joint into extension and proximal interphalangeal joint into flexion

317. **Which of the following athletes would be triaged as a high priority?**
   a. a multiple fracture
   b. a dislocation with absence of a pulse
   c. a back injury without spinal cord involvement
   d. an athlete who was decapitated
   e. a minor bleeding head wound

318. **When should an athlete be placed on crutches?**
   a. whenever there is swelling in the lower extremity
   b. whenever there is an injury to the lower extremity
   c. whenever the athlete cannot walk normally
   d. whenever there is pain in the lower extremity
   e. whenever the athlete is in a cast of the lower extremity

319. **When treating a thigh contusion in the acute stage, what should be used?**
   a. massage and anti-inflammatory medication
   b. cryotherapy and compression
   c. active stretching of the area
   d. ultrasound and passive stretching of the area
   e. cortisone injection

320. **A wound should be referred for suturing**
    a. when it is on the face
    b. when it bleeds a lot
    c. when it is at a joint
    d. when athlete plays contact sports
    e. when it has a gap

321. **In what type of sling should a third-degree shoulder separation be treated?**
    a. a Kenny Howard sling
    b. a triangular bandage
    c. a figure-eight bandage
    d. a sling and swathe
    e. a shoulder harness

322. **When taping a joint, one principle that the athletic trainer needs to know is**
    a. how to clean the area
    b. allergy to tape adherent
    c. overlapping of tape
    d. that the joint needs movement so activity can occur
    e. the common mechanism of injury of the joint

323. **At what point after a contusion of the thigh would it be best to get an X ray and check for the presence of myositis ossificans?**
    a. the same day as the injury occurs
    b. only if normal range of motion does not occur in 1 month
    c. 2 to 4 weeks postinjury
    d. 3 months
    e. There is no need to get an X ray, because you can palpate the myositis ossificans.

324. **What injury to the hand or finger is splinted in hyperextension?**
    a. avulsion of the collateral ligament at the distal phalange
    b. mallet finger or volar dislocations of phalange
    c. metacarpal fractures
    d. boutonniere deformity or mallet finger
    e. dorsal dislocation of distal phalangeal joint

325. **The treatment for an athlete with a sore throat is**
    a. taking cough medication
    b. gargling with warm salt water
    c. using an antihistamine medication
    d. gargling with mouthwash
    e. using throat lozenges

326. **For acute cervical spinal cord contusion,**
    a. have the athlete move the arms and legs
    b. check the grip strength
    c. backboard the athlete
    d. ice and keep the athlete out of the game
    e. place the athlete in a soft collar and remove from the game

327. **An athlete with an inguinal hernia who wishes to continue to participate should be instructed to**
    a. wear a truss
    b. seek the advice of a physician
    c. eat a high-fiber diet
    d. avoid a high-fiber diet
    e. weight lift and build up abdominal musculature before returning

328. **An athlete with a blow to the solar plexus is treated by**
    a. lifting the lumbar spine up
    b. giving 6 to 8 L of oxygen
    c. having the athlete breathe in short inspirations and exhale long expirations
    d. having the athlete hold her breath
    e. having the athlete breathe into a paper bag

329. **Proper cane fitting is done by**
    a. measuring from the armpit to tip of finger
    b. measuring from greater trochanter to the floor with shoes on
    c. measuring from greater trochanter to the floor without shoes
    d. measuring from the full extension of the elbow to the floor
    e. measuring from the full extension of the hand to the floor

330. **You have an athlete who is unconscious. What is your first step in care?**
    a. Stabilize the head and neck.
    b. Check the pupils.
    c. Check the athlete for breathing and circulation.
    d. Call the emergency medical service.
    e. Do a head-to-toe evaluation.

331. **An athlete is able to walk off the field, but needs some support. What minimum aid should be given?**
    a. backboard aid
    b. vehicular aid
    c. firemen's carry aid
    d. ambulatory aid
    e. stretcher aid

332. **The most effective way to open the airway when there is a cervical spinal cord injury is to use the**
   a. head tilt
   b. neck lift
   c. jaw thrust without a head tilt
   d. head tilt and chin lift
   e. forehead lift

333. **When an athlete exhibits partial paralysis from a head impact, the athlete trainer should**
   a. have the athlete walk around
   b. immobilize the spine and have the athlete transported to a hospital
   c. have the athlete move the parts that are in paresis
   d. splint the parts that are in paresis
   e. have the athlete rest until paresis is resolved

334. **An intermittent compressive device is being used to decrease edema in an ankle. What physiological effect results?**
   a. decreased blood flow
   b. decreased lymphatic flow
   c. The lymphatic capillaries remove plasma and water.
   d. Increased muscular contraction at bridges occurs.
   e. Gravity causes plasma to flow toward the heart.

335. **You are using galvanic electrical stimulation for a 10-day-old injury and notice that there is a decreased (contraction) response to this treatment. What do you suspect is wrong?**
   a. a degeneration of the nerve
   b. incorrect modality
   c. incorrect frequency
   d. improper pad placement
   e. rupture of the muscle

336. **The initial treatment for a quadriceps contusion is:**
   a. ice, application of knee immobilizer, and crutches
   b. ice, compression with knee straight, and crutches
   c. ice, compression with knee flexed to 90 degrees or more, and crutches
   d. ice, massage with knee flexed to 90 degrees or more, and crutches
   e. heat, massage, and crutches

337. **What is the best splint to be used for a femur fracture?**
   a. a board splint
   b. a vacuum splint
   c. a box splint
   d. an air splint
   e. a traction splint

338. **What type of brace should be applied to an athlete with an acute shoulder separation?**
    a. a triangular bandage
    b. a sling
    c. a yoke
    d. a Kenny Howard sling
    e. a sling and swathe combination

339. **Which of the following cold therapies is in order of the most effective to least effective?**
    a. cold compression machine, gel packs, cold packs, ice, and cold sprays
    b. ice, gel packs, chemical packs, cold compression machines, and cold sprays
    c. cold sprays, cold compression machine, ice, gel packs, and chemical packs
    d. ice, chemical packs, cold compression machine, gel packs, and cold sprays
    e. chemical packs, cold sprays, ice, cold compression machine, and gel packs

340. **How soon after a tooth has been avulsed must it be reimplanted for the highest success rate?**
    a. 24 hr
    b. 12 hr
    c. 8 hr
    d. 4 hr
    e. 2 hr

341. **To care for a luxated tooth,**
    a. wash the tooth with saline and place in the socket
    b. push the tooth into place in the socket and refer the athlete to a dentist
    c. place the tooth in gauze and under the tongue, and refer the athlete to a dentist
    d. place the tooth in milk, and refer the athlete to a dentist
    e. place a mouth guard in the athlete's mouth

342. **When should the face mask of a head-neck injury patient be removed?**
    a. when the athlete is wearing a mouth guard
    b. when athlete is having difficulty breathing
    c. once the athlete is backboarded
    d. when the athlete is face down
    e. when the athlete is groggy

343. **An athlete with a cervical spine injury is lying face down and is to be backboarded. How is the head moved?**
    a. Use the cross-arm technique and roll.
    b. Slightly lift the head and spine board athlete face down.
    c. Sandwich the head and roll the leaders arms in-line.
    d. Straighten the neck and roll the leaders arms in-line and rolled.
    e. Straighten the neck and spine board athlete face down.

344. **How is an airway opened in an athlete wearing a helmet?**
    a. Use the head tilt and chin lift.
    b. Use the head tilt and neck lift.
    c. Use the jaw thrust.
    d. Use the finger crossover.
    e. The airway will be open, because the athlete is wearing a helmet.

■ Rehabilitation

Directions—Each of the questions or incomplete statements here is followed by five suggested answers or completions. Select the *best* answer in each case.

345. **An athlete has a serious knee injury that you know will require surgery and extensive rehabilitation. The athlete has not seen a physician about the injury. You tell the athlete**
    a. that the prognosis is poor
    b. nothing, just ice and immobilize the body part
    c. that the prognosis, and reassure the athlete you'll help with rehabilitation
    d. that there is an injury that needs to be seen by a physician
    e. that everything will be OK

346. **At what point during knee rehabilitation after meniscus surgery is an athlete allowed to walk using two crutches?**
    a. when swelling has decreased
    b. when the athlete can do a single straight-leg raise
    c. when the athlete can do cocontractions
    d. when the athlete can do cocontractions and straight-leg raises
    e. as soon as the athlete stops using pain relievers

347. **When should flexion exercises begin for an interphalangeal joint fracture dislocation of the proximal end?**
    a. 4 to 6 weeks after injury
    b. as soon as full range-of-motion is obtained
    c. 2 to 4 weeks after injury

d. 3 weeks after injury

e. 1 week after injury

348. **Avascular necrosis of the lunate is also known as**

a. carpal tunnel syndrome

b. de Quervain's disease

c. Kienböck's disease

d. lunate disease

e. lunate compaction disorder

349. **A nerve contusion that lingers, causing hyperthesia, is dealt with by**

a. straightening exercises

b. icing

c. contrast therapy

d. surgery

e. stretching

350. **When the knee is in a flexed position, the posterior capsule of the knee is**

a. unstable

b. loose

c. taut

d. overly taut

e. semitaut

351. **A brace for footdrop forces the foot to remain**

a. everted and dorsiflexed

b. inverted and plantarflexed

c. dorsiflexed

d. plantarflexed

e. internally rotated and dorsiflexed

352. **An athlete with an acute anterior shoulder dislocation is able to return to competition**

a. after 6 weeks of immobilization and rehabilitation

b. after 3 weeks of immobilization and rehabilitation

c. after a shoulder harness is fitted

d. immediately, because no rehabilitation will hold this shoulder in place

e. only after this competitive season

353. **For articular cartilage to regenerate,**

a. active movement is necessary

b. non-weight bearing is necessary

c. casting is necessary

d. regular competitive activity is helpful

e. surgical intervention is necessary

354. **What area of the intervertebral disc produces most disc protrusions?**

    a. the anterior longitudinal nucleus pulposus
    b. the hyaline plate
    c. the posterolateral corner of annulus
    d. the anterior aspect of annulus
    e. the posterior aspect of nucleus pulposus

355. **What muscles are in the rotator cuff?**

    a. supraspinatus, infraspinatus, teres minor and subscapularis
    b. supraspinatus, infraspinatus, teres major, and subscapularis
    c. deltoid, scalenus, pectoralis major and minor
    d. deltoid, pectoralis major and minor, and teres minor
    e. supraspinatus, infraspinatus, and subscapularis

356. **Wrist drop results from injury to the**

    a. vascular structures
    b. distal radius
    c. median nerve
    d. radial nerve
    e. ulnar nerve

357. **Inversion of the subtalar joint of the ankle yields how many degrees of motion?**

    a. 45 degrees
    b. 30 degrees
    c. 15 degrees
    d. 5 degrees
    e. 0 degrees

358. **Normal hyperextension of the distal interphalangeal joint is**

    a. 20 degrees
    b. 15 degrees
    c. 10 degrees
    d. 5 degrees
    e. 0 degrees

359. **The normal alignment of the anterior portion of the lower extremity is**

    a. medial malleolus, patella, and greater trochanter
    b. lateral malleolus, patella, and greater trochanter
    c. talus, tibia, and femur
    d. fifth toe and greater trochanter
    e. between first and second toes, patella, and anterior superior iliac crest

360. **The normal abduction range of motion of the glenohumeral joint, without scapular motion, is**

a. 30 degrees
b. 45 degrees
c. 60 degrees
d. 20 degrees
e. 180 degrees

361. **The usual limited range of motion of hip flexion after an injury is**

a. 0 to 120 degrees
b. 0 to 90 degrees and 110 to 130 degrees
c. 0 to 30 degrees and 60 to 90 degrees
d. 0 to 60 degrees and 90 to 120 degrees
e. 0 to 30 degrees and 90 to 120 degrees

362. **The usual limited range of motion of knee flexion after an injury is**

a. 0 to 30 and 100 to 130 degrees
b. 0 to 30 degrees and 90 to 135 degrees
c. 0 to 10 degrees and 90 to 135 degrees
d. 0 to 15 degrees and 130 to 160 degrees
e. 0 to 15 degrees and 90 to 110 degrees

363. **What form of energy is produced with a paraffin bath?**

a. high frequency mechanical oscillation
b. shortwave infrared rays
c. ultraviolet rays
d. molecular motion
e. high-frequency electrical oscillations

364. **The application of heat to an injured area causes**

a. sweating that becomes acidic
b. decreased blood volume
c. increased circulatory rate
d. increased blood pressure
e. decreased elimination by the kidneys

365. **What is the heart rate of an athlete receiving a full-body warm whirlpool?**

a. 10 beats per min faster for each degree Fahrenheit above 98.6 °F
b. the same as without the whirlpool
c. 10 beats per min slower for each degree Fahrenheit above 98.6 °F
d. 5% to 15% slower than normal
e. It will decrease at the same rate as respiration, as relaxation occurs.

366. **What effect does low voltage galvanic stimulation produce?**
    a. a chemical effect
    b. a kinetic effect
    c. an electrokinetic effect
    d. a thermal effect
    e. a cryothermal effect

367. **The closing (starting) of a direct current is called**
    a. a make
    b. a break
    c. a contraction
    d. the cathode
    e. a broken circuit

368. **A running back with a recently injured ankle is ready to return to practice. What functional assessment is appropriate for this athlete?**
    a. With taping the athlete can participate in straight-ahead running.
    b. The athlete has full range of motion.
    c. The athlete has 90% muscle strength and is able to do toe raises.
    d. The athlete can participate in running forward, cutting and back pedaling.
    e. The athlete can participate in biking.

369. **During anterior shoulder dislocation, rehabilitation emphasis is placed on strengthening the**
    a. abductors and external rotators
    b. horizontal extensors
    c. adductors and internal rotators
    d. extensor muscles
    e. flexor

370. **Back rehabilitation in Stage 1 (the earliest stage) focuses on**
    a. gaining range of motion by stretching
    b. strengthening the back musculature
    c. strengthening the abdominal musculature
    d. returning to athletic activity
    e. cardiovascular fitness

371. **Criteria for return to play after an acute knee injury includes**
    a. the ability to run figure eights and zigzag while under local anesthetic after cryotherapy
    b. the ability to run figure eights and zigzag
    c. the ability to run backwards and to cut
    d. the absence of abnormalities in all functional tests
    e. the recovery of the full range of motion

372. At what point in an ankle rehabilitation program can an athlete begin heel raises on the injured ankle?
    a. when full range of motion returns in the affected ankle
    b. when full range of motion is present on both heel raises without support
    c. when the affected ankle is pain free
    d. when the affected ankle has no swelling
    e. when the proprioceptive exercises are complete

373. When applying the contract–relax technique of proprioceptive neuromuscular facilitation, the athlete should achieve
    a. a greater range of motion in the body part
    b. greater strength in the body part
    c. greater coordination in the body part
    d. greater endurance in the body part
    e. less endurance in the body part

374. When returning an athlete to competition from a knee injury, what criteria must be met?
    a. The athlete has no swelling.
    b. The athlete has 90% of range of motion.
    c. The athlete experiences no pain from the injury.
    d. The athlete must have 80% strength, compared to unaffected knee.
    e. The athlete must have 80% of knee circumference, compared to unaffected knee.

375. The shoulder wheel is used to provide
    a. proprioception
    b. flexibility and strength
    c. flexibility
    d. strength
    e. agility

376. As intensity of a rehabilitative workout increases, how often should it be done?
    a. 3 days a week
    b. 5 days a week
    c. 7 days a week
    d. 5 days a week, twice a day
    e. 3 days a week, twice a day

377. How much time should be used when lowering a weight, if lifting the weight took 2 to 3 s?
    a. 2 to 3 s
    b. 4 to 6 s
    c. 8 s

d. whatever the athlete decides
e. more than 15 s

378. Which muscle group is worked first during a rehabilitation-exercise program?

a. accessory muscle groups
b. antagonist muscle group
c. the largest muscles
d. the smallest muscles
e. the intricate muscles

379. A double-leg raise for low back rehabilitation is done

a. once a single-leg raise is not taxing
b. right after William's flexion exercises are performed
c. once a regular straight-legged sit-up can be done
d. not at all, as it should not be done in these circumstances
e. once abdominal curls can be done

380. What is the SAID principle?

a. Muscle fibers contract maximally.
b. static antagonistic isometric dynamics
c. static adaptation isometric demands
d. standard adaptation isometric deviation
e. Training and rehabilitation must adapt the athlete to demands during athletic activity.

381. Which of the following exercises is used in the early stage of shoulder rehabilitation?

a. dumbbell circles
b. dumbbell flies
c. latissimus pull downs
d. upright rowing
e. codman pendulum exercises

382. Presurgical rehabilitation is done to

a. build strength to possibly aid in determining the extent of injury
b. increase endurance
c. increase pain-tolerance level
d. educate the athlete on exercises for postsurgery
e. determine the extent of rehabilitation necessary for postsurgery

383. An athlete with an acute knee injury is unable to do cocontractions or straight leg raises due to pain. What is the best alternative for rehabilitation?

a. Use ice, a compression wrap, and crutches until contractions can occur.
b. Rest until contractions can occur.

c. Rehabilitation of the secondary muscle groups, like the hip and ankle.

d. Do side, straight leg raises.

e. Do only hamstring contractions.

384. **An athlete is in a full-leg cast and is unable to perform straight-leg raises due to pain. What should be done to help accomplish straight-leg raises?**

a. Have the athlete rest until pain subsides.

b. Have the athlete try straight-leg raises daily.

c. Passively lift the leg into a straight-leg-raise position and have the athlete contract the musculature.

d. Have the athlete push leg downward against the table until straight-leg raises can occur pain free.

e. Have the athlete stand on crutches and swing leg in flexion and extension.

385. **During rehabilitation after anterior cruciate ligament reconstruction the athlete should do**

a. no slow exercises

b. no negative resistance exercises

c. no positive resistance exercises

d. no jerky movements or forced extension

e. no jerky movements or hip adduction

386. ***Extensor lag* in the quadriceps refers to the**

a. inability to extend the hip actively

b. inability to flex the hip actively

c. inability to extend the knee actively

d. inability to flex the knee actively

e. inability to extend the knee passively

387. **For a muscle to be stimulated with an electrical current, membranes must**

a. become less dense

b. become more dense

c. depolarize

d. hyperpolarize

e. depolarize or hyperpolarize

388. **A denervated muscle requires what frequency of electrical stimulation to elicit a response?**

a. 0.5 to 20 Hz

b. 20 to 50 Hz

c. 50 to 85 Hz

d. 90 to 100 Hz

e. 100 to 500 Hz

389. The skin has an impedance of 200 Ω per cm for electrical stimulation currents. What would increase the impedance?

a. moisture on the skin
b. skin diseases
c. scar tissue
d. dry skin
e. coarser hair

390. An athlete who has a partial denervation in the peripheral nervous system requires an electrical stimulating current that is

a. surging in frequency
b. alternating in frequency
c. lower in frequency to stimulate a response
d. higher in frequency to stimulate a response
e. variable in frequency to stimulate a response

391. To reduce skin impedance when applying electrical stimulation,

a. apply lotion
b. wash the body part with soap and water
c. dry the skin thoroughly
d. increase the intensity
e. use direct current instead of alternating current

392. Which electrode will stimulate more with direct current?

a. a small positive electrode
b. a large negative electrode
c. a small negative electrode
d. The electrodes produce equal stimulation.
e. the dispersive pad

393. A motor point is where

a. the contractile fibers are located
b. the muscle shortens
c. the cross-bridges are located
d. a nerve attaches to a muscle
e. a nerve runs through a muscle

394. Which of the following creates more discomfort with electrical stimulation for the athlete?

a. oily skin
b. soft, hydrated skin
c. application of the stimulation to a motor point
d. coarse hair
e. obesity

395. When using infrared therapy, what skin reaction occurs after 30 min of tissue temperature rise?
   a. increased body temperature
   b. swelling
   c. redness of the skin
   d. charring of the skin
   e. white patches and red blotches

396. An athlete is totally rehabilitated. How can the athlete be helped mentally to return to competition?
   a. by boosting the athlete's self-esteem
   b. by giving the athlete a starting roll
   c. by throwing a congratulatory party
   d. with hypnosis
   e. with bracing or support on the injured part

397. Which of the following is *not* a factor in deciding on a rehabilitation plan?
   a. the severity of injury
   b. the type of injury
   c. age of the athlete
   d. use of protective equipment
   e. the time of season

398. The angle at which a muscle has significant weakness is called the
   a. zero angle
   b. sticking point
   c. atrophy point
   d. point of concentration
   e. reconditioning angle

399. During knee rehabilitation, the application of weights to the foot
   a. may stretch ligamentous structures
   b. is the best way to strengthen the extensor mechanism
   c. should be avoided until 90 degrees of flexion is achieved
   d. should progress at 2-lb increments
   e. should begin once muscular contraction is felt

400. When returning an athlete to athletic competition after knee rehabilitation, thigh circumference 3 in. above the patella should be within what percent of the unaffected knee?
   a. 100%
   b. 90%
   c. 80%

d. 75%

e. 70%

401. An athlete with an acute thigh contusion is prone to myositis ossificans if

a. the athlete's calcium intake is high

b. the athlete has had previous blows to the thigh

c. the blood supply to the area is decreased

d. the athlete is returned to activity too soon

e. the muscle tissue is injured

402. Proprioception for a lower leg can be accomplished by using

a. strengthening exercises

b. stationary bike riding

c. zigzag running

d. stretching exercises

e. carioca running

403. Athletes who overwork during rehabilitation show

a. pain away from the injury site

b. increased girth measurements

c. pain lasting more than 3 hr after exercise

d. loss of feeling in the affected body part

e. depression stemming from the need to do rehabilitation

404. What is the main goal of the early-exercise phase of rehabilitation?

a. to achieve full range of motion

b. to decrease swelling

c. to return the athlete to competition

d. to increase proprioception

e. to rebuild muscular contractions to a painful level

405. What is the main goal of the advanced exercise phase of rehabilitation?

a. to rebuild strength and range of motion to within 90% of normal

b. to make sure the athlete is psychologically ready

c. to build agility, proprioception, and an absence of pain

d. to have the athlete complete sport-specific rehabilitation

e. to improve kinesthetic ability and psychological readiness

406. The chemical substance that is responsible for producing pain in the area of an injury is

a. histamine

b. prothrombin

c. thromboplastin

d. thrombin

e. bradykinin

407. Scar tissue formation takes up to _____ in the remodeling phase.
   a. a year
   b. 6 months
   c. 3 months
   d. 4 to 6 months
   e. 2 weeks

408. Hard callus formation to repair a bone fracture takes _____ to be completed.
   a. 6 months
   b. 2 months
   c. 1 month
   d. 4 to 6 weeks
   e. 2 weeks

409. Arthritis is the body's response after an injury resulting from
   a. muscular atrophy
   b. inadequate circulation
   c. a lack of iodine
   d. an overdose of calcium
   e. the athlete's being returned to activity too soon

410. A muscular cramp that is characterized by a constant contraction is termed
   a. tightness
   b. inflexibility
   c. spasm
   d. clionic cramp
   e. tonic cramp

411. An ultrasound machine is frequently used at an operating frequency of 1 MHz. If the unit is used at 4 MHz, what will the penetration be compared to 1 MHz?
   a. One MHz will penetrate 75% deeper.
   b. Four MHz will penetrate 50% deeper.
   c. Four MHz will penetrate 25% deeper.
   d. Four MHz will penetrate to the same depth as 1 MHz.
   e. Four MHz will penetrate less than 1 MHz.

412. The beam nonuniformity ratio (BNR) of ultrasound is
   a. the intensity indicated by the power meter
   b. the average intensity indicated by the power meter
   c. the highest intensity found in the beam compared to the average intensity indicated by the power meter
   d. the lowest intensity found in the beam compared to the average intensity indicated by the power meter
   e. uneven intensity caused by some areas of the body, especially bony areas

413. **What decreases the effects of ultrasound?**
    a. too much coupling medium
    b. covering too small a surface area at one time
    c. moving the sound head too slowly
    d. moving the sound head too fast
    e. increasing intensity

414. **Ligamentous strength after an 8-week immobilization is**
    a. unchanged
    b. increased
    c. decreased
    d. nearly normal
    e. not measurable

415. **In the coronal plane, what postural points should line up in the ideal alignment?**
    a. lateral malleolus and transverse process of the cervical spine
    b. calcaneous, greater trochanter, and the spine of the scapula
    c. half-way between both calcaneous, the body of the sacrum, and the atlas of the cervical spine
    d. second metatarsal, anterior superior iliac spine, and maxilla
    e. lateral malleolus, bodies of the lumbar spine, shoulder joint, and external auditory meatus

416. **Continuous anterior postural deviation causes the posterior muscles of the lower leg and trunk to**
    a. become weak
    b. become stretched
    c. become malaligned
    d. be in a continuous state of contraction
    e. be in a continuous state of relaxation

417. **Criteria for returning an athlete to competition are:**
    a. reabsorption of acute swelling, 80% or more strength, pain-free range of motion, no instability, and physician permission
    b. 80% range of motion, 80% strength, and 80% pain free
    c. normal endurance of body part, strong desire by the athlete to return, full range of motion, and beginning a cardiovascular program
    d. normal-size muscle mass, normal cardiovascular endurance, and instabilities supported by tape
    e. control of the instability, 75% strength, no swelling, and full range of motion

418. **What is the cause of an athletes's inability to lift 50 lb with the quadriceps (something normally done daily) after suffering a mild medial collateral ligament tear?**
    a. immobilization
    b. pain from the injury, causing reflex inhibition

c. instability of the ligament
d. possible referred pain to the quadriceps
e. a poor psychological state of mind

419. **What are the criteria for progressing from the initial to the intermediate stage of rehabilitation?**
    a. edema stabilized, almost full range of motion, range is pain free, progress with ice has plateaued, and no hyperemia
    b. edema stabilized, progress increasing with ice, and decreasing hyperemia
    c. ischemia decreasing, range of motion can be noted, and pain free through the range
    d. initial contractions can be felt, no ischemia, decreasing edema, and full range of motion
    e. athlete is motivated, full range of motion, pain-free range, and decreasing edema

420. **What are contraindications to intervertebral joint mobilization?**
    a. ligament sprain
    b. defects of facets
    c. hypermobility of joints
    d. sciatica
    e. acute pain

421. **Which nerve-fiber type transmits motor information the fastest?**
    a. A-alpha
    b. A-beta
    c. A-delta
    d. A-gamma
    e. B fibers

422. **Which nerve-fiber types are controlled using electrical stimulation when it is necessary to control pain?**
    a. A-delta and B fibers
    b. A-beta and C fibers
    c. A-gamma and C fibers
    d. C fibers and B fibers
    e. A-alpha and B fibers

423. **Capacitance is**
    a. a current spread over a large area
    b. the ability to store energy as a result of separation of charge
    c. a shift from positive to negative charge
    d. a phase configuration
    e. amonophasic unidirectional flow of current

424. Point stimulators are used to

a. reduce pain
b. reeducate muscle tissue
c. reduce edema
d. reduce spasm
e. improve circulation

425. When is the use of heat indicated?

a. to help with wound healing
b. with circulatory problems
c. with hyposensitivity to heat
d. with hypersensitivity to heat
e. with decreased sensation of the injured area

426. Healing time in an acute injury is directly related to

a. atrophy, edema, and fibrous tissue
b. the amount of fibrin released and the amount of fibrotic tissue formed
c. the number of phagocytes released and macrophages in the area
d. pain, edema, and the amount of fibrin released
e. the number of fibroblasts, pain, and edema

427. The final results of treatment (healing, regaining full range of motion) are achieved how long after an injury?

a. 2 to 4 weeks
b. 4 to 6 weeks
c. 2 to 8 months
d. 1 year
e. 1 to 2 years

428. An athlete who is just out of a cast needs rehabilitation. The athlete has high blood pressure. What type of exercise is contraindicated?

a. isometric
b. isodynamic
c. isotonic
d. concentric
e. eccentric

429. Why is it important that a coupling agent be used during ultrasound?

a. to prevent damage to the crystal
b. to help absorb superficial skin moisture
c. to avoid superficial tissue destruction
d. to apply moisture to dry skin
e. to make it easier to move the ultrasound head

430. Which stroke in massage employs long stroking toward the heart and has a soothing effect?

a. petrissage
b. percussion, or tapotement
c. friction
d. effleurage
e. vibration

431. Low frequency (1 to 5 Hz), high intensity stimulation of the body causes excitement of β-endorphins. β-endorphins yield which of the following?

a. an anti-inflammatory effect
b. an opening of the gate control
c. an increase in pain level
d. an analgesic effect
e. an increase in nociceptors

432. What mechanism of heat transfer occurs with the warm whirlpool?

a. conduction
b. convection
c. conversion
d. radiation
e. conduction and convection

433. Hunting reaction occurs

a. to increase blood pressure
b. to decrease blood pressure
c. to prevent local tissue injury resulting from cold
d. due to muscle spasms
e. because of pain

434. For what body type does the application of cold require a shorter icing treatment time?

a. mesomorphic
b. endomorphic
c. ectomorphic
d. neuromorphic
e. none, because treatments times are the same for all body types

435. What is the physiological basis for the stinging, burning, or aching and numbness sensations caused by the application of cold?

a. increased metabolism
b. temporary cessation of nerve-ending function
c. vasodilation of vessels
d. vasoconstriction of vessels
e. decreased metabolism

436. Adding salt to ice creates a slushy mixture. Why is using a slushy mixture important when treating an injury?

a. Melting ice is colder.
b. Salt prevents frostbite.
c. Melting ice is warmer.
d. Treatment time is reduced.
e. Melting helps hold ice in place.

437. Cold whirlpool temperature for treatment of a body part should be

a. 33 to 40 °F
b. 40 to 50 °F
c. 50 to 60 °F
d. 60 to 70 °F
e. 65 to 80 °F

438. Why are cold sprays successful in reducing pain?

a. because they frost the body part
b. because they cause vasoconstriction of the capillaries
c. because muscle-spindle response is activated
d. because A-fibers are stimulated to reduce painful arc
e. because the athlete believes they work

439. You have an obese athlete with myositis ossificans in the quadriceps muscle group. What modality should be used to treat this condition, given the athlete's obesity?

a. diathermy
b. cold whirlpool and active range of motion
c. ultrasound
d. warm whirlpool
e. heat packs

440. A pes anserinus transfer is done to control what?

a. anterior femoral translation
b. posterior femoral translation
c. lateral collateral instability
d. rotatory instabilities
e. posterior cruciate instability

441. A freestyle swimmer needs balanced exercise to counteract one-sided repetitive stress. What swim stroke would you suggest?

a. the breaststroke
b. the side stroke
c. the butterfly
d. the backstroke
e. the overarm side stroke

442. **For the best results in restoring full muscle function,**
   a. always ice before exercise
   b. use maximum amounts with low repetitions
   c. make sure the muscles are contracted throughout the entire range of motion
   d. work the range of motion that is pain free
   e. fatigue the muscle group

443. **The three commonly used modes with isokinetics are:**
   a. gravity, antigravity, and pendulum
   b. strength, power, and endurance
   c. active, passive, and active resistive
   d. concentric, eccentric, and progressive resistive
   e. motor performance, endurance, and aerobic conditioning

444. **In what instance would use of a continuous, passive motion modality be contraindicated?**
   a. joint contracture
   b. total joint replacement
   c. intraarticular surgery
   d. noncompliant patients
   e. synovectomy

445. **To limit hypoxia as a result of an acute injury, the most important effect when applying cold is to decrease**
   a. circulation
   b. muscle spasm
   c. pain
   d. metabolism
   e. stiffness

446. **Which of the following does *not* need to equal or exceed preinjury levels as part of a completed rehabilitation program?**
   a. muscular endurance
   b. power
   c. muscle tension
   d. skill patterns
   e. agility

447. **The swelling that occurs immediately after an injury is due to what?**
   a. edema
   b. hemorrhaging
   c. hypoxia
   d. breakdown of tissue by macrophages
   e. negative hydrostatic pressure of capillaries

448. **What indicates that an athlete has regained full strength after an Achilles tendon rupture?**
   a. The athlete has greater dorsiflexion and less plantar flexion on the injured side than on the noninjured side.
   b. The athlete can use a wobble board in planes of motion.
   c. The athlete can bear weight in a toe-walking position.
   d. The athlete can bear weight in a heel-walking position.
   e. The athlete can tolerate manual resistive exercises three times per day.

■ Organization and Administration

Directions—Each of the questions or incomplete statements here is followed by five suggested answers or completions. Select the *best* answer in each case.

449. **An athletic trainer who compiles statistical information about injuries and their causes is using the**
   a. epidemiological method
   b. statistical method
   c. catastrophic method
   d. injury occurrence method
   e. detail method

450. **An athlete is considered legally blind, but still desires to participate in contact athletic activities. You should**
   a. provide protective eye guards for all athletes
   b. buy extra insurance
   c. get a waiver from the coach
   d. assign a person to assist this athlete
   e. get parental permission and athlete permission waiver

451. **Participating in a nationwide computer injury registry is helpful because**
   a. you can meet new people
   b. you can find new jobs
   c. it's great for networking
   d. your school can be compared with others
   e. you can brag about how good a job you are doing, because fewer athletes were injured

452. **Electrical outlets in the hydrotherapy area of the training room should**
   a. be 2 to 3 ft above the floor
   b. be 220 V
   c. be grounded

    d. have cords near pipes

    e. have long cords

453. **At the finish line of a race, how many medical personnel should be available to care for injured runners?**

    a. one medical person per runner

    b. one medical person per every two runners

    c. one medical person per every three runners

    d. one medical person per every 10 runners

    e. a minimum of nine medical personnel per 1,000 runners

454. **When compiling an annual report on the function of the training room, what items should be included?**

    a. the types of injuries the training room would like to service

    b. an analysis of the entire athletic program

    c. the number of athletes not served

    d. an evaluation of administration and custodial services

    e. recommendations for improvements

455. **An injury data collection system should consider**

    a. extrinsic factors

    b. intrinsic factors

    c. extrinsic and intrinsic factors

    d. position, age, and environment

    e. level of play, time of day, and previous injuries

456. **What is the minimum cases of tape necessary for a high school that has 1,000 students and 20 athletic teams in a year?**

    a. 10 cases or more

    b. 20 cases or more

    c. 35 cases or more

    d. 50 cases or more

    e. 75 cases or more

457. **What is the minimum number of paper cups to be used as ice cups for a high school that has 1,000 students and 20 athletic teams in a year?**

    a. 1,000

    b. 2,000

    c. 3,000

    d. 4,000

    e. 5,000

458. **You are a new athletic trainer and will be responsible for the budget. How can you determine what to order?**

    a. Just order what you want.

    b. Always try to stockpile supplies, so order more.

    c. Take an inventory.

    d. Look at past purchase orders and reorder them.

    e. First inventory, evaluate a few years of purchase orders, and then do your budget.

459. **The standard procedure policy is a written statement that**

    a. can be changed as needed

    b. is needed when it is necessary to fire someone

    c. the athletic training staff uses only in an emergency

    d. establishes all procedures from budgeting to rehabilitation

    e. is established by the athletic director

460. **Putting injury records on the computer helps to**

    a. keep you organized

    b. conserve space used by records

    c. review your role

    d. provide a resource for statistics

    e. keep track of injury trends

461. **What agency is responsible for computerized monitoring of emergency room reports of athletic injuries?**

    a. the National Electronic Injury Surveillance System

    b. the Head and Neck Registry

    c. the National Athletic Injury Reporting System

    d. the National High School Injury Registry

    e. the National Operating Committee for Standards in Athletic Equipment

462. **Which of the following is the role and responsibility of the athletic trainer as a member of the athletic training team?**

    a. nutrition

    b. rest

    c. organization

    d. hiring/firing

    e. record keeping

463. **An athlete with Marfan's syndrome has personal physician approval to play basketball. What should you do (if anything) to decrease the school's risk of liability in the event of the athlete's death?**

    a. Do nothing.

    b. Make sure the family has medical insurance.

    c. Explain to the family that the athlete is at increased risk and record the conversation.

    d. Require the athlete and a parent to sign a release form that explains the increased risk of participation.

    e. Disqualify the athlete from competition.

464. **To ensure successful record keeping,**
    a. hire a secretary to record your work
    b. carry a minicassette and record every evaluation
    c. take the time to write daily
    d. update records weekly
    e. have a student athletic trainer update your records

465. **When setting up staffing of the training room, consider**
    a. marital and family status of each athletic trainer
    b. events needing coverage
    c. financial requirements of each athletic trainer
    d. athletes' needs
    e. athletes' convenience

466. **Having a parent's and athlete's signature on a sports participation form acknowledging they understand the risk of play is not enough to prevent a lawsuit. Therefore, the athletic trainer should**
    a. assume parents and athletes know the risk of play
    b. provide continual reinforcement of the risk
    c. use a school nurse at athletic competitions
    d. carry liability insurance
    e. carry malpractice insurance

467. **To assist in reducing liability,**
    a. keep the training room open long hours to take care of all injuries
    b. give athletes your home phone number
    c. buy malpractice insurance
    d. post warning signs about the risks of sport and improper equipment use
    e. preventively tape all athletes

468. **Accident insurance is used to cover**
    a. accidents on school grounds
    b. accidents that may lead to lifetime disability
    c. errors and omissions by employees
    d. negligence
    e. hospitalization and general medical services

469. **To deter theft, it is best to**
    a. keep all expensive modalities up high, out of the way
    b. give coaches keys to the athletic training facility
    c. keep a sign-out sheet for equipment loaned out
    d. leave cabinets and doors unlocked
    e. allow outside visitors

470. **The least expensive way to prevent ankle injuries is to**
    a. stretch the Achilles tendon and strengthen the key musculature
    b. tape all ankles
    c. put lace-up braces on all ankles
    d. ankle wrap all ankles
    e. apply elastic ankle braces

471. **When purchasing a high grade of adhesive tape, the most important item to consider is the**
    a. type of adhesive
    b. tension as it comes off the roll
    c. weight
    d. number of fibers
    e. grade of linen

472. **When storing tape, remember to**
    a. store it in a high place
    b. store it in a warm place
    c. store it where there is good ventilation
    d. store it in a humid place
    e. keep it cool and flat

473. **To avoid legal problems resulting from equipment use, the athletic trainer should**
    a. buy equipment based on lowest price
    b. use equipment even if unsure of its proper use
    c. customize equipment to meet your needs
    d. follow the manufacturer's instructions for use
    e. maintain the equipment based on the ability to have it checked

474. **Which of the following is part of an emergency plan?**
    a. designating a person to call the emergency medical system
    b. taking vital signs
    c. giving cardiopulmonary resuscitation
    d. raising consciousness about emergency preparedness
    e. prevention

475. **What is more important in prevention of injuries in a football stadium?**
    a. the watering system
    b. a good playing surface
    c. padding of goal posts
    d. seating placement
    e. height of the grass

476. **Which of the following is *not* a hazard on a playing surface?**
    a. fences next to the end zone
    b. a chain gang holding onto the rods

    c. players standing near the sideline
    d. benches near the sideline
    e. end-zone markers that are not staked

477. **An athletic program that provides an easy warm-up game before the regular schedule creates what hazard?**
    a. an easy win
    b. self-confidence
    c. overconfidence
    d. unbalanced competition and increased injuries
    e. lack of discipline

478. **To ensure athletic trainers on staff are kept current on the latest techniques, they should**
    a. practice their basic level skills
    b. keep all certifications updated (NATA, first aid, CPR)
    c. have the staff experiment on athletes
    d. have the staff discuss their feelings about education
    e. have the staff watch an "emergency" television show

479. **The school is responsible to provide what services to its athletes?**
    a. prevention, treatment, rehabilitation, evaluation of injuries, and first aid
    b. a safe environment, proper record keeping, and funding
    c. athletic equipment, winning seasons, and effective coaching
    d. a uniform, good facilities, and a large spectator crowd for events
    e. no services

480. **As a part of the emergency plan, the local emergency medical service should yearly**
    a. design your plan
    b. tour your various athletic facilities
    c. review the route to the school
    d. give you 911 stickers for the telephone
    e. know your football schedule

481. **When informing an athlete about an injury, the physician should present**
    a. the next scheduled appointment for evaluation
    b. alternatives in treatment and potential hazards of this injury
    c. a note indicating everything that was discussed about the injury
    d. a note to be given to the coach
    e. only positive aspect and goals regarding the injury

482. **To prevent confusion in your emergency plan,**
    a. do not tell people about it
    b. write the plan down, but put it away

c. it should not have any details

d. practice it

e. just do what comes naturally when an emergency occurs

483. **The key in any emergency plan is**

a. the number of injuries

b. the first aid being given

c. the first aid equipment needed

d. the initial evaluation

e. distance of the ambulance

484. **The training room provides many services. Which one(s) should be closest to the entrance?**

a. whirlpools

b. athletic trainer's desk with sign-in sheet

c. modalities

d. taping table and the ice machine

e. wheelchair and stretcher

485. **When a young man becomes a quadriplegic as a result of an injury, he and his family sue. What is the most likely defense whereby the athletic trainer, team physician, and institution would win the case?**

a. assumption of risk

b. foreseeability

c. negligence

d. standard of care

e. informed consent

486. **Which of the following athletes has the priority in triage?**

a. an athlete near death

b. an athlete with chest wounds

c. an athlete in shock

d. an athlete with a fracture

e. an athlete with a sprain

487. **You are using a modality. What is the safest assurance that your patient won't be electrocuted?**

a. Use an internal fuse.

b. Use a ground fault circuit breaker.

c. Use a three-pronged electrical plug.

d. Use the on-off switch on the modality.

e. Use an insulated electrical unit.

488. **How often should ground fault circuit breakers be checked?**

a. every time the unit is used

b. weekly

    c. monthly

    d. biannually

    e. yearly

489. **A fatality could result from use of a modality that applies current to the body At what current can this occur?**

    a. 1 to 15 mA

    b. 20 mA

    c. 15 to 100 mA

    d. 100 to 200 mA

    e. more than 200 mA

490. **Calibration of electrical modalities should be done**

    a. weekly

    b. monthly

    c. every 3 months

    d. biannually

    e. yearly

491. **Which of the following athletes has the highest priority in triage?**

    a. an athlete with uncomplicated burns

    b. an athlete in cardiac arrest

    c. an athlete with an eye injury

    d. an athlete with multiple fractures

    e. an athlete with lacerations and abrasions

492. **The strength of tape is based on**

    a. the number of threads per inch

    b. the type of adhesive used

    c. the type of material used

    d. how the tape is applied

    e. the body part to which the tape is applied

493. **Which of the following athletes have delayed priority in triage?**

    a. athletes who are dead

    b. athletes with head injuries

    c. athletes with severe burns

    d. athletes with an ankle sprain

    e. athletes in shock

494. **The Good Samaritan Law protects the athletic trainer's**

    a. wanton misconduct

    b. errors or omissions

    c. negligence

    d. abandonment

    e. gross negligence

495. In athletic training, boric acid is used for
   a. treatment of itching
   b. skin protection from sunlight
   c. control of odor
   d. an analgesic effect
   e. a seductive effect

496. If athletes desire the information from their physicals to be given to their coach, the athletic trainer should
   a. obtain athletes' verbal permission
   b. obtain parents' verbal permission
   c. have parents send a note
   d. just tell the coach, as there are no legal difficulties
   e. have a signed release of information form on file

497. To avoid litigation when releasing information to a college scout concerning a player's health, the athletic trainer should
   a. tell the scout the entire medical history
   b. tell the scout only insignificant medical history
   c. tell the scout only surgeries
   d. get a written release from the athlete and parents
   e. get a written release from the athletic director

498. The size of the doorway in an athletic training facility should be
   a. wide enough to carry a person via a seat carry
   b. wide enough for a wheelchair or stretcher
   c. wide enough to get supplies in
   d. wide enough to carry a person via a fireman's carry
   e. as wide as a normal door (32 in.)

499. The optimum number of entrances to an athletic training facility is
   a. one
   b. two
   c. three
   d. four
   e. five

500. Outdoor lighting for right-handed athletic trainers needs to enter the athletic training facility from
   a. the east
   b. the north
   c. above
   d. the left
   e. the right

501. The level of lighting for an athletic training facility is
   a. 30 foot-candles
   b. 50 foot-candles

    c. 80 foot-candles

    d. 100 foot-candles

    e. 120 foot-candles

502. **How much of the athletic training facility should be set aside as an electrotherapy area?**

    a. 10%

    b. 20%

    c. 25%

    d. 35%

    e. 50%

503. **How much of the athletic training facility should be set aside as a hydrotherapy area?**

    a. 15%

    b. 20%

    c. 25%

    d. 35%

    e. 50%

504. **Electrical outlets in the hydrotherapy area need to be placed how high off the floor?**

    a. 1 ft

    b. 2 to 3 ft

    c. 4 to 5 ft

    d. 6 to 8 ft

    e. 8 to 10 ft

505. **An athletic training facility should have a minimum of two whirlpools, one of which must care for**

    a. the upper extremities

    b. burns

    c. the feet

    d. the full body

    e. the immobile athlete, so it must be mobile

506. **Who can legally dispense a prescription drug to an athlete?**

    a. a chiropractor

    b. an athletic trainer

    c. a physical therapist

    d. anyone authorized by state law

    e. a nurse

507. **When filling out an accident report form, why is it important to do so promptly?**

    a. to keep track of injury statistics

    b. so details will not be forgotten

    c. so changes can be made to reduce future injuries

    d. to avoid legal action

    e. to process insurance forms promptly

508. To avoid lawsuits, the athletic trainer should

    a. refer all injuries to the team physician

    b. let others on staff treat injured athletes

    c. stay within their medical training

    d. use their own car to transport injured athletes

    e. request the administration to drop high-risk sports

509. Once an athlete has completed the testing, what is the next step for those giving the preparticipation fitness examination?

    a. Assess conditions and deficits.

    b. Have the physician sign the participation form.

    c. Review the family medical history.

    d. Check the athlete's height and weight.

    e. Check the athlete's blood pressure.

510. When designing a medical history form, the athletic trainer should remember to

    a. make the form brief and short

    b. use lay terms when possible

    c. limit questions on family history

    d. use medical terminology

    e. keep the form complex

511. To help avoid lawsuits as a result of giving preparticipation fitness examinations, athletes

    a. must bring their parents with them

    b. must have a signed consent form

    c. must have a physical examination after the preparticipation fitness exam

    d. must have the same physician perform all aspects of the preparticipation fitness examination

    e. must have the same physician perform the preparticipation fitness examination and physical examination

512. An athlete who has only one testicle and still chooses to participate in football must have

    a. an insurance rider beyond school insurance

    b. an informed consent form on file

    c. a physician's approval to participate

    d. informed an athletic trainer

    e. an emergency card on file

513. Most commonly, injuries from using electrical modalities (i.e., whirlpools, electrical stimulators, ultrasound devices) are caused by
    a. overly prolonged treatment time
    b. improper use of the device
    c. inappropriate use for the injury involved
    d. too frequent use
    e. damage, breakdown, or short circuit of the power cord

514. When assuming your role as athletic trainer, you should check your facility and make sure safety precautions have been taken with the electrical system. To ensure this,
    a. assume all three-pronged outlets are grounded
    b. check all electrical modalities every 5 years against National Electrical Code standards
    c. use electrical extension cords, as this will decrease intensity
    d. pull on the electrical cord when unplugging the device to keep your distance
    e. check all modalities yearly and be sure they are properly grounded

515. You need to use a whirlpool with a three-prong plug, but you do not have a three-prong outlet, so you will use a three-wire-to-two-wire converter. How do you ensure everyone's safety while using this whirlpool?
    a. Have the athlete turn on the whirlpool before getting in.
    b. Attach the pigtail of the converter to the screw on the outlet box.
    c. Try out the whirlpool yourself.
    d. Have only one athlete in the whirlpool at a time.
    e. Make sure the floor is dry.

516. You need to use a whirlpool with a three-prong plug, but you do not have a three-prong outlet. What is the safest course?
    a. Use a three-wire-to-two-wire converter.
    b. Pull the ground blade off the plug.
    c. Use a long extension cord to get to a three-way plug.
    d. Have an electrician replace the old outlet with a grounded plug.
    e. Use a short extension cord with a three-way plug.

517. When should whirlpools be checked and cultures taken to check for bacteria?
    a. once a day
    b. once a week
    c. biweekly
    d. monthly
    e. bimonthly

518. **Candidates for the position of team physician should specialize in what field of medicine?**
    a. pediatrics
    b. internal medicine
    c. emergency medicine
    d. orthopedics
    e. general surgery

519. **The training room should be next to**
    a. all practice fields
    b. the gymnasium
    c. the swimming pool
    d. the football stadium
    e. the men's and women's locker rooms

520. **To be assured supplies for your training room will arrive in time for fall sports, equipment and supplies must be ordered by**
    a. June 1
    b. July 1
    c. April 1
    d. May 1
    e. August 1

521. **To be assured you get the quality supplies you need at the cheapest price,**
    a. have athletes purchase their own supplies
    b. discourage athletes' use of supplies
    c. buy a cheaper grade
    d. buy lower quality goods
    e. use the bid system

522. **The NOCSAE (National Operating Committee on Standards for Athletic Equipment) seal on football helmets indicates that**
    a. the helmet is comfortable
    b. the helmet is completely safe
    c. the athlete is safe when wearing the helmet
    d. the helmet meets NOCSAE safety standards
    e. the helmet meets a legal standard

523. **How long should records of an athlete's injury be kept?**
    a. for as long as the athlete is in your "program"
    b. for seven years
    c. for two years after the athlete leaves your program
    d. for two years longer than your state's statue of limitations
    e. for the athlete's lifetime

524. **A permission-for-treatment form is**
    a. not necessary after age 18
    b. only necessary if athlete is unconscious
    c. necessary under the age of 18
    d. only necessary when there are objections to treatment
    e. only necessary if athlete is an emancipated minor

■ Education and Counseling

Directions—Each of the questions or incomplete statements here is followed by five suggested answers or completions. Select the *best* answer in each case.

525. **An athlete reports to you that an injury is the result of being hit by a parent with a coat hanger. You should**
    a. treat the injury and ignore the mechanism
    b. treat the injury and wait until you see proof of child abuse before reporting it
    c. treat the injury and report this to authorities as a child abuse case
    d. call the parent and let them know you are concerned
    e. tell the coaching staff and athletic director so everyone can watch for any further signs of abuse

526. **An athlete reports to you that he was stabbed by a knife while running from the scene of a robbery. You should**
    a. treat the wound and report the incident to police
    b. report the incident to the school public relations personnel, so they can avoid bad publicity
    c. treat the wound and say nothing
    d. treat the wound and tell all staff members what happened
    e. give the athlete medical supplies for self-treatment and excuse the athlete from practice

527. **Combining two drugs may result in**
    a. a potentiation effect
    b. habitual addiction
    c. tolerance
    d. idiosyncrasy
    e. a counterirritant effect

528. **What are the six classes of nutrients?**
    a. salt, water, fats, proteins, carbohydrates, and vitamins
    b. carbohydrates, water, fats, minerals, proteins, and vitamins
    c. calcium, niacin, iodine, fiber, water, free-fatty acids

d. amino acids, fiber, free-fatty acids, vitamins, water, and salt

e. saline, amino acids, fiber, free-fatty acids, vitamins, and water

529. **Use of water bottles can contribute to spread of which communicable disease?**

a. hepatitis A, hepatitis B, and viral meningitis

b. bacterial meningitis and AIDS

c. viral meningitis and syphilis

d. pneumonia, mononucleosis, and measles

e. tuberculosis, mononucleosis, and AIDS

530. **Certain athletes are more prone to trochanteric bursitis due to certain anatomical features. These are**

a. a small hemipelvis and a long second toe

b. a tight piriformis and an externally rotated femur

c. lordosis and a small hemipelvis

d. lordosis and a wide pelvis

e. a wide pelvis and leg-length discrepancy

531. **A complication from using corticosteroids for long periods of time is**

a. fluid retention

b. gastric upset

c. increased muscular size

d. disorientation

e. facial acne

532. **What are the signs that an athlete is becoming stale?**

a. illness, irritability, and poor performance

b. increased desire to go to practice and stay there

c. increased injuries and increased enjoyment at practice

d. The athlete is easily distracted and experiences a decrease in injuries.

e. irritability

533. **When bent-knee sit-ups and push-ups are done regularly and in great repetition, what postural deformity can occur?**

a. anterior pelvic tilt

b. kyphosis

c. lordosis

d. flat back

e. forward head

534. **What are the psychological reactions to injury?**

a. denial, anger, bargaining, depression, and acceptance

b. denial, anger, and acceptance

c. withdrawal from peers and teammates

d. blaming others for the injury

e. self-defeating behaviors

535. **How can the athlete trainer assist an athlete into accepting an injury?**

   a. Be evasive about the seriousness of the injury and pad the athlete with hope.
   b. Be honest, give the athlete accurate information, and give the athlete hope.
   c. Refer the athlete to a counselor.
   d. Hurry the athlete through treatment and rehabilitation.
   e. Have other athletes give their encouragement.

536. **What happens to an athlete's rate of metabolism as body temperature rises?**

   a. Nothing will happen if the air temperature is cool.
   b. It will rise 13% for each degree Fahrenheit.
   c. It will remain constant.
   d. It will rise.
   e. It will decrease.

537. **How can an athlete deal with a dry mouth?**

   a. Take deep breaths.
   b. Chew gum.
   c. Eat salty food.
   d. Drink an electrolyte drink.
   e. Eat sugary food.

538. **An athlete is depressed about having just sustained a career-ending injury. What should the athletic trainer do?**

   a. Show pity.
   b. Be curt and tell the athlete to accept reality.
   c. Tell the athlete this is acting foolishly.
   d. Have the athlete talk about feelings.
   e. Tell the athlete a joke.

539. **An athlete is angry and upset before entering a contest, and so is likely to**

   a. injure an opponent
   b. play better
   c. play worse
   d. regain emotional control as competition continues
   e. become injured

540. **Weight loss should not be greater than _____ lb per week.**

   a. 1 to 3 lb
   b. 2 lb
   c. 2 to 5 lb
   d. 7 lb
   e. 10 lb

541. Pain tends to be worse

a. at night
b. when an athlete talks about it
c. in the morning
d. during cryotherapy treatments
e. when an athlete's team is competing

542. How long are tetanus boosters good for?

a. 1 year
b. 2 years
c. 10 years
d. 30 years
e. for life

543. In an anorexic, basal metabolic rate

a. increases initially, then decreases
b. decreases initially, then increases
c. decreases
d. increases
e. equalizes, based on activity

544. When are nutritional problems usually found?

a. when an athlete begins to feel poorly
b. during a routine physical examination
c. after an injury
d. when dieting
e. after an illness

545. Under which circumstances is a male athlete most likely to inherit a predisposition to obesity?

a. when both parents are slim
b. when only one parent is slim
c. when both parents are obese
d. when the father is obese
e. when the mother is obese

546. Which of the following would you recommend for an athlete who is overweight and would like to lose weight?

a. a liquid diet
b. Overeaters Anonymous
c. eating smaller amounts of food more often
d. liposuction
e. wearing a rubberized suit and using saunas

547. White adolescent females are the population most likely to become anorexic, and they are usually perfectionists and

overachievers. **What characteristics do white adolescent anorexic males exhibit?**

a. Type A personalities
b. depression
c. underachievement
d. popularity
e. excellence in athletics

548. **An athlete comes to you about a problem the athlete believes is abnormal. What is the best way to move into a problem-solving mode rather than focus on "abnormal thoughts"?**

a. Tell the athlete everything will be OK.
b. Tell the athlete it's not so bad.
c. Indicate that "other people feel the same way."
d. Tell the athlete a pretend story about your similar experience.
e. Tell the athlete one of your own problems to give reassurance.

549. **An athlete injures a forearm. The coach indicates this athlete is injury prone and "really plays it up." Evaluation reveals nothing noteworthy, but the athlete is in gross pain. What should be done?**

a. Splint the injury as if it were a fracture.
b. Assume the injury is a bruise and ice.
c. Tell the athlete to stop wasting your time.
d. Say that the athlete will be OK.
e. Tell the athlete to see a psychiatrist.

550. **An athlete who seeks a third opinion regarding a serious injury may be**

a. in denial of an injury
b. angry about the injury
c. in a depressed state about the injury
d. accepting the injury
e. logical about the injury

551. **The two most common psychological factors an athletic trainer has to deal with in an athlete who is rehabilitating are**

a. anger and denial
b. acceptance and impatience
c. bargaining and denial
d. anger and bargaining
e. depression and impatience

552. **Which of the following is *not* transmitted by sexual intercourse?**

a. gonorrhea
b. syphilis
c. AIDS

d. herpes zoster

e. herpes simplex type 2

553. **If an athlete were to touch his or her mouth to the team water bottle, what infectious disease might be transmitted?**

a. gonorrhea

b. measles

c. typhoid fever

d. AIDS

e. hay fever

554. **When talking with a parent about a child's injury, it is important to**

a. communicate at the parent's level

b. use medical terminology

c. impress the parent with your knowledge

d. talk a lot

e. do not say anything specific about the injury

555. **Which of the following best describes an athlete who is a malingerer?**

a. The athlete gets injured when physically exhausted.

b. The athlete takes chances during activity.

c. The athlete has a decreased performance level.

d. The athlete is overly aggressive during activity.

e. The athlete lies about an injury to take a day off.

556. **Athletes who use foul language may do so to**

a. show how grown up they are

b. cover for their lack of ability

c. motivate teammates

d. show team leadership

e. attract others' attention

557. **An athlete who is overly aggressive despite collision sport involvement should be**

a. referred to counseling

b. cut from the team

c. put on the bench and allowed to cool off

d. put in a position of the most impact

e. given a pat on the back

558. **An athlete who is frustrated before and during an athletic event is**

a. likely to play more aggressively

b. likely to be unable to play

c. more prone to injury

d. in need of therapeutic counseling

e. in no great need of concern

559. Relaxation techniques are used to

a. increase stress
b. decrease the ability to work
c. assist in weight loss
d. relieve stress and tension
e. help one escape

560. What is a positive development resulting from stress?

a. burnout
b. an acute awareness of surroundings
c. a state of readiness
d. a state of greater aggressiveness
e. mental growth and development

561. Which of the following athletes have the least tolerance for pain?

a. immature athletes
b. aggressive athletes
c. relaxed athletes
d. passive-aggressive athletes
e. unemotional athletes

562. An athlete who was injured while sliding is having difficulty attempting the skill again. What should be done?

a. Send the athlete to a counselor.
b. Drop the athlete from the team.
c. Have the athlete take muscle relaxants.
d. Teach the athlete relaxation techniques.
e. Have the athlete perform in front of the team so they can give encouragement.

563. Desensitization of an athlete following a surgically repaired injury includes

a. negative images of the injury
b. a cold whirlpool
c. a breakdown of defense mechanisms
d. a full-body warm whirlpool
e. positive images of successful surgery

564. One sign that an athlete is a substance abuser is

a. a change in friends and increased eating
b. the smell of drugs, uncharacteristic behavior, and drug paraphernalia
c. reads material about drugs and is well versed about them
d. denial of drug use and improvement in work habits
e. is more alert and has disregard for others

565. **An athlete with a painful back needs instructions for lifting. Tell the athlete to**
   a. bend at the waist and keep the head up
   b. tighten the gluteals and abdominals and bend at knees
   c. flatten the back and lift with the arms
   d. stretch before lifting and twist as the object is lifted
   e. keep the knees under the hips and lift with the arms

566. **An athlete is confused as a result of an injury. The athletic trainer needs to**
   a. write everything down for the athlete
   b. restrain the athlete
   c. speak slowly and precisely
   d. ignore the confusion and assess the injury
   e. have two athletic trainers talk to the athlete about the injury

567. **The team physician has declared an athlete dead. In consoling the friends, you should**
   a. try to hide any morally wrong things
   b. let friends see the body even if they don't want to, because they will get over the loss faster
   c. answer questions with only information you know to be true
   d. be reassuring and tell friends everything will be OK
   e. cry along with the athlete's friends

568. **An athlete is certain to die, based on signs you have seen. What should be done with family and friends who are standing around?**
   a. Separate family and friends from the athlete, allowing the athlete to die in peace.
   b. Cover the athlete with a sheet so no one has to see the death.
   c. After the athlete dies, gather family and friends in another room and tell them.
   d. Allow friends and family to share the final moments with the athlete.
   e. Allow friends and family in the room, but ask them to remain quiet.

569. **An athlete is attempting suicide. You, as athletic trainer, should**
   a. tell the athlete you understand what they are going through
   b. tell the athlete things aren't that bad
   c. stay with the athlete and have someone call EMS
   d. dare the athlete to do it, because you know the athlete is not serious
   e. tell the athlete you would be sad if the suicide were successful

570. **When designing a course in athletic training, what is the first thing to establish?**
   a. the topics to be taught
   b. the resources available

c. class size

d. course objectives

e. the textbook

571. **What are the six domains defined by the Role Delineation Study, set forth by the NATA?**

    a. first aid and cardiopulmonary resuscitation; evaluation; prevention; budgeting; counseling; and rehabilitation

    b. prevention and padding; predisposing factors; first aid; communication; therapeutic modalities; and taping

    c. principals of rehabilitation; taping and wrapping; prevention; evaluation; counseling; and administration

    d. referral procedures; instructional techniques; public relations; psychological counseling; taping; and rehabilitation

    e. prevention; recognition and devaluation; management, treatment, and disposition; rehabilitation; organization; and administration

572. **Which teaching technique allows immediate feedback from students?**

    a. the objective technique

    b. the subjective technique

    c. the library assignment technique

    d. the informal technique

    e. the formal technique

573. **The main function of continuing education after certification is to**

    a. make more money for the NATA

    b. keep the economy going

    c. keep athlete trainers current and up to date

    d. weed out poor candidates who "just got by" the certification process

    e. discourage those who are not serious about athletic training as a profession

574. **A psychological stress response before athletic competition is indicated by**

    a. increased speed of talking and increased control of voice

    b. increased ability to concentrate and increased breathing rate

    c. increased heart rate and increased decision-making ability

    d. increased sweating and increased focus on feelings

    e. increased saliva production and increased sweating

575. **Effective learning of material before a lecture can be accomplished through**

    a. answering questions after the lecture

    b. reading assignments

c. relaxation

d. physical exercise

e. visualization

576. **To evaluate a teacher's effectiveness, which tests are most helpful?**

a. objective tests, either written or essay

b. informal tests

c. subjective essay tests

d. cognitive multiple-choice tests

e. formal tests

577. **To keep track of a student's practical-experience progress, it is best**

a. to have several staff members remember it

b. to write it down and keep it

c. to have the student write it down and keep it

d. to have the head student athletic trainer keep track of it

e. that you and the student remember it

578. **Student feedback of an instructor and athletic training program provides information on**

a. who likes the program

b. who dislikes the program

c. strengths and weaknesses of the program

d. changes that need to be made

e. objectives of the program

579. **A good clinical experience provides the student with**

a. selected injuries or situations that an athletic trainer is most likely to see

b. hands-on experience with infrequently seen, but traumatic, situations

c. involvement in as many injuries and situations as possible

d. experience in as many injuries and situations as possible

e. exposure to as many injuries and situations as possible

580. **A periodic evaluation is most helpful if it**

a. notes strengths

b. notes weaknesses

c. is negative and subjective

d. is objective and positive

e. is constructive and positive

581. **An athletic trainer who finds it difficult to communicate with the team physician and others needs to**

a. find a new job

b. find a new team physician

c. take a public relations class

d. take an assertiveness training course

e. tell the others to communicate more

582. **An athlete who thinks irrationally about an injury**

a. shows greater improvement faster

b. shows no difficulty with other aspects of life

c. rarely exaggerates the significance of the injury

d. rarely oversimplifies the significance of the injury

e. takes longer to get through the rehabilitation process

583. **To assure successful communication with an injured athlete, it is important to**

a. build the athlete's self-confidence

b. build the athlete's self-esteem

c. have knowledge of the athlete's injury

d. take an interest in the athlete as a person

e. have knowledge of the athlete's acceptance of the injury

584. **The NATA Code of Ethics for athletic trainers states that athletic trainers should**

a. follow only state regulation concerning care

b. discriminate based on the disease an athlete has

c. provide services for which they are qualified

d. advocate higher salaries

e. be unsportsmanlike

585. **When carbohydrate loading, how can an athlete know without a needle muscle biopsy whether glycogen stores are increasing?**

a. by weight gain while loading

b. by not eating anything but carbohydrates

c. by abdominal bloating

d. by an increased energy level

e. by an increase in alertness

586. **The use of refined sugar in the diet contributes to many health problems, but not to**

a. diabetes

b. cavities

c. hyperactivity

d. allergic reactions

e. premenstrual syndrome

587. **In what phase of the menstrual cycle is a female most likely to have heat-related problems?**

a. the luteal phase

b. none, as there is no difference associated with any phase

c. the menstrual phase

d. the ovulatory phase

e. the endometrial phase

588. How many calories are there in 1 g of fat?

a. 1 cal

b. 5 cal

c. 9 cal

d. 15 cal

e. 32 cal

589. An athlete desires to loose fat in the hips. How would you recommend this be done?

a. Have the athlete do hundreds of straight-leg raises.

b. Have the athlete lift quadricep and hamstring weights.

c. Have the athlete lift hip flexor and gluteal weights.

d. Have the athlete go on a reduced-calorie diet.

e. Have the athlete wear a rubberized sweat suit when working out.

590. What is the most effective weight-loss program?

a. increasing exercise time

b. reducing calories

c. using laxatives and diuretics

d. using diet pills

e. reducing calories and increasing exercise

591. An athlete on the wrestling team has refused to admit a bulimic disorder, even with overwhelming evidence. What should the athletic trainer do?

a. Continue to check with the athlete from time to time.

b. Consult a person with expertise in eating disorders.

c. Give the athlete the benefit and believe him.

d. Ask the athlete's friends about the disorder.

e. Assume the athlete will eat correctly once given a diet.

592. One g of carbohydrate equals how many calories?

a. 4 cal

b. 10 cal

c. 15 cal

d. 9 cal

e. 7 cal

593. When asking an athlete about substance abuse, the questions should be

a. straightforward

b. asked indirectly

c. nonjudgemental

d. intimidating

e. accusational

594. **When counseling an athlete about an injury, it is most important to**
   a. be sure to make a referral to the team physician
   b. document the conversation
   c. consider the athlete's long-term health
   d. tell others on staff about the counseling session
   e. protect yourself from litigation

595. **When counseling an athlete about a condition that disqualifies that person from a sport, it is also helpful to**
   a. tell the athlete's friends about the situation
   b. tell the athlete's parents about the situation
   c. offer the athlete a position as a student athletic trainer
   d. refer the athlete to a sport psychologist
   e. remind the athlete that things could be worse

596. **An athlete who indicates a family history of alcohol abuse**
   a. is usually an enabler
   b. is in need of a twelve-step program
   c. should be referred to Alcoholics Anonymous
   d. is at higher risk of alcohol abuse themselves
   e. needs to have a urine drug test

597. **If an athlete desires weight loss and cuts back food intake by 1,000 cal per day, how many pounds will this athlete lose per week?**
   a. 2 lb
   b. 3 lb
   c. 5 lb
   d. 7 lb
   e. 10 lb

598. **What role do proteins play in the body?**
   a. They regulate body temperature, and are a source of energy and growth.
   b. They support cellular structure, regulate nerve activity, and support the energy system.
   c. They move the body, transport oxygen, and regulate metabolism.
   d. They assist growth and development and formation of enzymes, and they are a source of energy.
   e. They regulate body composition, growth and development, and body temperature.

599. **A wrestler who has lost body weight primarily from muscle mass will show a decreased performance because of**
   a. lack of development
   b. lack of iron
   c. lack of energy stores

    d. anemia

    e. increased waste products

600. Which vitamins are antioxidants?

    a. A, D, E, and K

    b. B_1, B_{12}, and niacin

    c. B_6, C, D, and E

    d. niacin, biotin, and A

    e. A, E, and C

7

CHAPTER

Study Questions for the Oral/Practical Test

The following questions simulate the oral/practical test. During this portion of the certification examination you will have an opportunity to explain and demonstrate your skills. These situations are typical of those which a certified athletic trainer must face daily. The examiner's evaluation is based only on your explanations and demonstrations in response to the question asked. In the examination you will demonstrate your skills, using a model, a person who does not answer your questions but does only what you direct. Materials will be available for your use, but if some item you normally use is not available, tell the examiners.

In this chapter your goal is to obtain as many positive responses as you can. Questions in this area range from acute injuries, equipment fitting, taping and wrapping, rehabilitation, and management of life-threatening injuries.

You will need another person to assist you in this chapter by reading the questions and checking yes or no for correct and incorrect responses. You will also need a volunteer to be the model. You can follow along in this study guide as your selected examiner reads the questions from Appendix B. The selected examiner can tell you if you have passed a certain oral/practical question, as I have listed a 70% passing point range at the end of each question in Appendix B.

■ Oral/Practical Questions

1. This situation allows you to explain and demonstrate the application of a hydroculator pack. First explain the effects, advantages and

disadvantages, indications, precautions, and contraindications of hydroculator pack use. Second, explain and demonstrate preapplication and application procedures for use of a hydroculator pack. You have 8 min to complete this task. Supplies—several towels, hydroculator, and a steam pack

2. Demonstrate the taping of a longitudinal arch. You have 5 min to complete this task. Supplies—tape adherent, white tape, 2-in. elastic tape, elastic bandage, under wrap, and scissors

3. This situation will give you an opportunity to tape an athlete who has previously sustained a hyperextension of the knee. Please demonstrate taping to prevent knee hyperextension. You have 8 min to complete this task. Supplies—3-in. elastic tape, elastic bandage, white tape, under wrap, white petroleum jelly on pads, and tape adherent

4. The following question will give you an opportunity to demonstrate your ability to evaluate an injury to the ankle. Explain and demonstrate your initial evaluation of an ankle. You have 10 min to complete this task. Supplies—goniometer

5. The following question will give you an opportunity to demonstrate your ability to fit a set of football shoulder pads. Explain and demonstrate the fitting of these pads. You have 8 min to complete this task. Supplies—a set of shoulder pads, measuring tape, and calipers

6. The following question will give you an opportunity to demonstrate your ability to inspect a padded style football helmet for possible damage and for an athlete's use. Explain and demonstrate the inspection of a football helmet. You have 8 min to complete this task. Supplies—a padded football helmet with a distorted face mask

7. The following question will give you an opportunity to demonstrate your ability to initially evaluate a conscious athlete with an acute head injury. *The athlete does not have a neck injury.* The athlete is lying in the supine position. Explain and demonstrate the evaluation of a head injury. You have 10 min to complete this task. Supplies—penlight, ruler, paper clip, note pad, pen, blood pressure cuff, stethoscope, and tongue depressor

8. This situation gives you an opportunity to explain and demonstrate caliper testing for body fat percentage. You have 8 min to complete this task. Supplies—measuring tape and skin-fold calipers

9. The following question will give you an opportunity to explain and demonstrate your ability to educate an athlete with low-back problems in correct back care. Teach the athlete the proper sleeping, sitting, standing, and lifting procedures to protect the low back. You have 10 min to complete this task. Supplies—empty box, pillow, soft chair, and a high-backed chair

10. The following situation will give you an opportunity to explain and demonstrate your ability to evaluate an abdominal injury. *This athlete does not have a spinal cord injury.* You have 10 min to complete this task. The model is on the table, lying on the side with knees drawn up to the chest. Supplies—blood pressure cuff and stethoscope

11. In this situation you are to demonstrate the treatment of an unconscious athlete with a total airway obstruction. You have 5 min to complete this task. Supplies—a mannequin positioned supine with an object in the throat

12. The following question will give you an opportunity to demonstrate your ability to rehabilitate an athlete who has a cervical spine injury. Explain and demonstrate the initial, intermediate, and advanced rehabilitation of this athlete as well as the criteria for returning this athlete to participation. You have 10 min to complete this task. Supplies—surgical tubing and two ankle weights (equal in weight)

13. The following question will give you an opportunity to demonstrate your ability to rehabilitate an athlete with an acute anterior glenohumeral subluxation injury who is currently in a sling. Explain and demonstrate the initial, intermediate, and advanced rehabilitation of this athlete as well as the criteria for returning to participation. You have 10 min to complete this task. Supplies—two ankle weights (equal in weight), goniometer, and surgical tubing

14. The following question will give you an opportunity to demonstrate your ability to tape an athlete to prevent Achilles tendon injury. You have 5 min to complete this task. Supplies—tape adherent, elastic bandage, white tape, 2-in. elastic tape, and under wrap

15. The following question will give you an opportunity to demonstrate your ability to treat an athlete who is having a seizure caused by epilepsy. Explain and demonstrate treatment of this illness. (The model is demonstrating an active seizure near a chair; the seizure will resolve in 30 s.) You have 5 min to complete this task.

16. The following question will give you an opportunity to demonstrate your ability to rehabilitate an athlete who has had an anterior cruciate ligament reconstruction. Explain and demonstrate the initial, intermediate, and advanced rehabilitation of this athlete as well as the criteria for returning this athlete to participation. The athlete is currently in an adjustable-range-of-motion knee immobilizer. You have 10 min to complete this task. Supplies—adjustable knee brace and an ankle weight

17. The following question will give you an opportunity to demonstrate your ability to evaluate an acutely injured knee. Explain and demonstrate the evaluation of an injured knee. You have 10 min to complete this task. Supplies—paper clip, goniometer, and measuring tape

18. The following question will give you an opportunity to demonstrate your ability to evaluate an acutely injured low back. Explain and demonstrate the evaluation of an injured low back. You may assume there is no cervical spine injury. You have 10 min to complete this task. Supplies—plumb line, measuring tape, paper clip, and goniometer

19. The following question will give you an opportunity to demonstrate your ability to evaluate an acutely injured wrist/hand. Explain and demonstrate the evaluation of an injured wrist and hand. You have 10 min to complete this task. Supplies—goniometer, measuring tape, and paper clip

20. This situation will give you an opportunity to tape an athlete with a recently hyperextended elbow. Please demonstrate what you would do to tape a hyperextended elbow. You will have 5 min to complete this task. Supplies—tape adherent, under wrap, 2-in. elastic tape, 4-in. elastic bandage, and a roll of 2-in. white tape.

21. This situation will give you an opportunity to use ultrasound on a thigh. Please give the following explanations and demonstrations; first explain how ultrasound works and its effects on tissues, then explain indications and contraindications for use of ultrasound. Then, explain and demonstrate the use of ultrasound on a thigh. You have 10 min to complete this task. Supplies—ultrasound machine and ultrasound gel

22. This situation will give you an opportunity to control bleeding from a laceration of the hand. Please explain while you demonstrate your treatment of a hand laceration, while at the same time also protecting yourself from blood-borne pathogens. You have 8 min to complete this task. Supplies—several sterile gauze pads, a pair of latex gloves, tape, and a garbage can with a plastic liner labeled Biohazardous. (*Note.* Examiner is to indicate no need for a tourniquet if applicant attempts to apply one.)

23. This situation will give you an opportunity to splint a fracture of the forearm. Please explain and demonstrate what you would do to splint a radial fracture. You have 10 min to complete this task. The model is sitting with the arm bent ninety degrees at the elbow. Supplies—two padded aluminum splints, several rolls of gauze, a sling, and a roll of tape

24. This situation will give you an opportunity to give a massage. This athlete has general soreness in his back. Please explain and demonstrate the massage techniques you would use to aid in reducing an athlete's general soreness. You have 10 min to complete this task. Supplies—massage oil, towels, massage table, sheets, and a bolster

8
CHAPTER

Study Questions for the Written Simulation

The written simulation in this textbook is designed to be similar to what you will encounter in the certification examination. In the written simulation examination you will be tested on your decision-making skills in situations a certified athletic trainer faces daily. The actual certification examination uses two booklets, a problem guide and an answer guide in which you make your responses with a highlighter pen. In this study guide, highlights are in parentheses in Appendix C. You will need a partner to assist you with this portion of the study guide. As you select an answer your partner should read the (bracketed) "highlight." Based on the information you know from the opening and what you find through answering the questions, select only those answers that are necessary then. You are to read the problem and carefully decide all of the options in each section you would choose for your athlete. Some sections will have more than one appropriate response, so choose all that apply. If you choose an incorrect response, you will receive a penalty. Also, a penalty will be given if you fail to choose all correct responses. As you highlight, answer-specific instructions are given, and you must follow this information to solve the problem correctly.

■ Problem 1

Opening Scene: A 14-year-old soccer player ran into the goalpost during a game. Your evaluation has been completed, and you suspect a first-degree concussion. You can assume no cervical injury, and there is no visual deformity.

Go to Section A.

A.   Immediately after your evaluation you will do which of the following? (Choose only those actions that you believe are essential to resolving the problem at this time.)

1. Apply ice to the head.
2. Return the athlete to competition.
3. Write a note to excuse her from school tomorrow.
4. Return the athlete to competition, but using a soccer helmet.
5. Rest the athlete and periodically recheck blood pressure and level of consciousness.

Go to Section B.

B. The soccer game is now over, and the athlete is in the training room. She is having difficulty recalling the event and does not recognize those around her. Indicate your response at this time. (Choose only those actions that you believe are essential to resolving the problem at this time.)

6. Call an ambulance.
7. Continue to ice the area.
8. Monitor the athlete's airway, breathing, and circulation.
9. Note the athlete's skin color.
10. Monitor blood pressure.
11. Elevate the athlete's feet.
12. Cover the athlete with a blanket.
13. Take the athlete's temperature.
14. Check the athlete's pupils.
15. Elevate the athlete's head.
16. Turn the athlete on her side.
17. Give the athlete aspirin.

Go to Section C.

C. The athlete's parents arrive, insist that she is fine, and wish to drive her to the hospital. An ambulance will arrive in 15 min. What should you do at this time? (Choose only those actions that you believe are essential to resolving the problem at this time.)

18. Try to convince the athlete and her parents to wait for an ambulance.
19. Take a long time to reassess the athlete.
20. Ignore the parents.
21. Have the parents sign a waiver.
22. Keep assessing the athlete's vital signs.
23. Release the athlete into the parents' care.
24. Have a witness to the situation.
25. Write an accident report.

End of Problem 1

■ Problem 2

Opening Scene: A volleyball player has injured her right knee during practice. Your evaluation has been completed and you suspect a possible lateral meniscus tear.

Go to Section A.

A. After your evaluation you will do which of the following? (Choose only those actions that you believe are essential to resolving the problem at this time.)

1. Tape the knee and return the athlete to practice.
2. Have the athlete walk around on the knee.
3. Have the athlete do a deep knee bend.
4. Apply ice to the right knee.
5. Apply a wet compression wrap to the right knee.
6. Have the athlete cold whirlpool the knee.
7. Have the athlete hop on one leg.
8. Have the athlete lift weights.

Go to Section B.

B. The athlete cannot bear weight and has swelling over the lateral aspect of the joint. Indicate your actions at this time. (Choose only those actions that you believe are essential to resolving the problem at this time.)

9. Take a girth measurement of the thigh.
10. Apply a dry compression wrap.
11. Apply a knee immobilizer.
12. Call an ambulance.
13. Write a note excusing the athlete from physical education class tomorrow.
14. Secure, measure, and instruct the athlete in the use of crutches.
15. Instruct the athlete to continue use of ice.
16. Instruct the athlete to keep knee elevated.
17. Instruct the athlete to massage the injured leg.

Go to Section C.

C. The athlete is seen by the team physician, who diagnoses the injury as a subluxation of the patella. She instructs the athlete to use crutches and avoid weight bearing as long as this is painful. She refers the athlete back to you for acute treatment. What action will you take next? (Choose only those actions that you believe are essential to resolving the problem at this time.)

18. Instruct the athlete to use ice treatments.
19. Instruct the athlete to use a warm whirlpool.
20. Instruct the athlete to use an analgesic balm.
21. Instruct the athlete in straight-leg raises.
22. Instruct the athlete in cocontractions of thigh musculature.
23. Call the physician and tell her she has made the wrong diagnosis.

End of Problem 2

■ Problem 3

Opening Scene: You have been requested by the soccer coach to design a year-round training program for the soccer team.

Go to Section A.

A. Please indicate which of the following is important for the off-season portion of the training program. (Choose only those actions that you believe are essential to resolving the problem at this time.)

　1. stretching before and after activity
　2. weight training to improve power
　3. rest—no workout or activity
　4. Build up long-distance running.
　5. weight training to improve strength
　6. soccer practice
　7. interval training
　8. limited ball-handling drills
　9. Begin the athlete on anabolic steroids.
　10. Determine the target heart rate.
　11. recreational soccer or other activity
　12. flexibility program

Go to Section B.

B. The soccer team is in need of a preseason training program. Please select only those answers that are involved in the preseason portion of the program. (Choose only those actions that you believe are essential to the resolving the problem at this time.)

　13. intense development of skills
　14. scrimmages of soccer
　15. upper and lower body weight training 3 days per week
　16. regular games
　17. stretching before and after activity
　18. weight training to improve power
　19. increasing dietary intake
　20. Determine the target heart rate.
　21. Begin heat acclimatization.
　22. a maintenance program
　23. rest—no workouts
　24. a flexibility program

Go to Section C.

C. Finally the season has arrived. Which of the following is (are) a part of the in-season soccer training program? (Choose only those actions that you believe are essential to resolving the problem at this time.)

　25. running intensity at high level twice per week
　26. regular games

27. weight training to improve power, 3 days per week
28. weight training to improve strength, 3 days per week
29. maintenance program
30. intense skill drills
31. flexibility program
32. Begin amphetamine usage.

End of Problem 3

■ Problem 4

Opening Scene: A 17-year-old female athlete who is overweight asks your advice to lose 30 lb.

Go to Section A.

A. What types of recommendations and procedures would you use to assist this athlete? (Choose only those actions that you believe are essential to resolving the problem at this time.)

1. Give the athlete a high-protein diet to follow.
2. Determine the athlete's activity level.
3. Recommend the use of massage to reduce weight.
4. Restrict water intake to two glasses daily.
5. Determine percent body fat.
6. Recommend liposuction.
7. Send the athlete to a physician for a physical.
8. Recommend the athlete eat slowly.
9. Determine the athlete's dietary intake.
10. Recommend the athlete avoid situations where food is involved.
11. Check athlete's height and weight.
12. Recommend multiple vitamins.

Go to Section B.

B. You have determined the athlete is 30 lb overweight. What recommendations and procedures would you use to assist this athlete? (Choose only those actions that you believe are essential to resolving the problem at this time.)

13. Recommend fasting 1 day per week.
14. Have the athlete decrease caloric intake by 500 cal per day.
15. Have the athlete increase energy output by 500 cal per day.
16. Recommend diet pills.
17. Send the athlete to a physician for stomach stapling.
18. Recommend a liquid diet.
19. Recommend only bland foods.
20. Encourage the athlete to lose 5 lb per week.
21. Encourage the athlete to avoid television.
22. Recommend the use of saunas to reduce weight.

23. Recommend the use of rubberized clothing to reduce weight.
24. Recommend the athlete increase caffeine intake.
25. Have the athlete reduce calorie intake by 2,000 cal per day.
26. Give the athlete a list of high-nutrient, dense foods.
27. Recommend a single-food diet plan.
28. Recommend an alternative activity to eating.
29. Give the athlete a well-balanced diet plan to follow.

Go to Section C.

C. The athlete has lost 45 lb and reports that she believes she is still out of shape. Six months has elapsed and her percent body fat is now 19%. She is asking you for a recommendation for a more stringent weight loss program. (Choose only those actions that you believe are essential to resolving the problem at this time.)

30. Determine current body weight.
31. Determine activity level.
32. Determine the athlete's dietary intake.
33. Ask about the athlete's menstrual period.
34. Ask about the athlete's use of laxatives or vomiting.
35. Recommend a well-balanced diet plan.
36. Recommend an increased activity plan.
37. Recommend a particular laxative.
38. Refer the athlete to a physician.
39. Speak to the athlete's friends about her eating habits.
40. Recommend a particular brand of diuretic.
41. Ask the athlete about her perception of her body.
42. Recommend a liquid diet.
43. Refer the athlete to a psychiatrist.
44. Recommend a high-calorie diet.
45. Inquire about the athlete's having constipation or diarrhea.
46. Tell the athlete she is bulimic.
47. Ask about the athlete's dental problems.
48. Assess the athlete's hair and skin.
49. Indicate to the athlete that she is at appropriate body weight.
50. Evaluate the athlete for swollen glands about the neck.
51. Give the athlete a high-fat, high-carbohydrate diet.
52. Recommend a diet that is high in grains, fiber, and protein.
53. Say that you believe the athlete is a diabetic.
54. Say that the athlete is anorexic.
55. Ask if the athlete has food binges.
56. Ask the athlete about fluctuations in weight.
57. Assess the athlete's mood.
58. Check the athlete's blood pressure.
59. Check the athlete's heart rate.
60. Inquire about the athlete's heart rate.

61. Have the athlete take calcium supplements.

Go to Section D.

D. Based on your findings, what is your impression of this athlete? Choose only one answer.

62. anorexic
63. bulimic
64. diabetic
65. a patient with an ulcer
66. a patient with appropriate weight loss
67. a substance abuser
68. hypoglycemic

End of Problem 4

■ Problem 5

Opening Scene: You have been called to the scene of a field hockey game where a 15-year-old player has been pushed into the goalpost.

Go to Section A.

A. What is your initial assessment of this athlete? (Choose only those actions that you believe are essential to resolving the problem at this time.)

1. Do a primary survey.
2. Remove the athlete from the field.
3. Check the athlete for bleeding.
4. Tell the coaches to check that all players are wearing mouth guards.
5. Determine the athlete's level of consciousness.
6. Determine if a goal was scored on the play.
7. Ask the athlete what happened.
8. Ask the athlete if there is pain.
9. Determine the score of the game.
10. Note the athlete's position as you approach.
11. Ask the athlete if she felt or heard a snap.
12. Determine who pushed the athlete into the goalpost.
13. Get rib protectors.
14. Determine if there was a penalty assessed on the play.
15. Have a stretcher brought onto the field.
16. Do a secondary survey of the athlete bilaterally.
17. Have a student athletic trainer call for an ambulance.
18. Have the athlete touch toes.
19. Ask the athlete if breathing is painful on inhalation.
20. Ask the athlete if breathing is painful on exhalation.
21. Auscultate the chest for breath sounds.

22. Ask the athlete to lay down.
23. Apply ice bags.
24. Determine the athlete's blood pressure.
25. Determine the athlete's breathing rate.
26. Have the athlete do a couple sit-ups.

Go to Section B.

B.   The athlete is able to walk off the field and goes to the sideline. Once at the sideline, the athlete's parents arrive and ask for an ambulance to be called. With this request, what actions would you take at this time? (Choose only those actions that you believe are essential to resolving the problem at this time.)

27. Actively test range of motion in all directions.
28. Monitor breathing.
29. Call an ambulance.
30. Apply ice to the injured area.
31. Have the parents get away from the athlete.
32. Indicate that the athlete will require long-term immobilization.
33. Strap the athlete's arm across the chest.
34. Record the athlete's vital signs for ambulance personnel.
35. Apply compression to the athlete's ribs.
36. Apply a sling to the athlete's left arm.
37. Ask the athlete's parents what insurance they have.
38. Tell the coach that the athlete is out for a couple games.
39. Apply rib protectors and allow the athlete to return to the game.

Go to Section C.

C.   The athlete returns from the hospital emergency room. She has a fracture of the eight rib (which requires no treatment) and a shoulder separation. The physician recommends complete immobilization of the shoulder for 2 weeks. (Choose only those actions that you believe are essential to resolving the problem at this time.)

40. Measure the circumference of the athlete's chest with full inflation.
41. Indicate the goals for the athlete's full recovery.
42. Begin the athlete on a stationary-bike exercise program.
43. Have the athlete continue to use ice.
44. Have the athlete lift lower-body weights.
45. Begin Codman pendulum exercises.
46. Begin isometrics.
47. Fit the athlete for rib protectors.
48. Have the athlete begin a forearm exercise program.
49. Begin a flexibility program for the left shoulder.
50. Begin proprioceptive neuromuscular facilitation.
51. Recommend heat therapy.

Go to Section D.

D. Two weeks pass and the athlete is highly motivated to return to field hockey. The team physician has given you permission to get the athlete into the initial phase of rehabilitation. (Choose only those actions that you believe are essential to resolving the problem at this time.)

52. Check the athlete for brachial plexus response.
53. Continue ice treatments after therapy.
54. Check the athlete's instability.
55. Have the athlete do Codman's pendulum exercises.
56. Have the athlete begin a running program.
57. Allow the athlete to begin ball-handling drills.
58. Tell the field hockey coach when the athlete can return to play.
59. Apply ultrasound for pain.
60. Have the athlete begin a progressive resistive-exercise program.
61. Have the athlete begin an upper-body exercise program.
62. Keep the athlete in a sling.
63. Fit the athlete in a shoulder harness.
64. Begin proprioceptive neuromuscular facilitation techniques.

End of Problem 5

■ Problem 6

Opening Scene: An athlete comes to you with dirt in his eye after having slid headfirst into a base. The eye is watering.

Go to Section A.

A. What actions would you take to resolve this situation? (Choose only those actions that you believe are essential to resolving the problem at this time.)

1. Cover the injured eye and refer the athlete to a physician.
2. Have the athlete rub the eye.
3. Flush the eye with water.
4. Use a handkerchief to wipe the dirt out.
5. Use a toothpick to get the dirt out.
6. Test the eye with a fluorescein sodium stain.
7. Apply antibiotic ointment to the eye.
8. Have the athlete blink.
9. Check pupillary reflex with a penlight.
10. Fold the eyelid back.
11. Apply eye drops.
12. Apply a topical anesthetic.
13. Check the eye with funduscope.
14. Ask the athlete what happened.
15. Apply ice to the eye.

Go to Section B.

B. You receive a telephone call from the athlete's parent, who is concerned that the incident will reoccur. The physician indicated no damage to the eye. What will you recommend now? (Choose only those actions that you believe are essential to resolving the problem at this time.)

16. Reassure the parent that eye injuries are rare.
17. Recommend that the athlete wear a batting helmet with a face mask.
18. Have the athlete wear polycarbonate 39 goggles.
19. Ask the athlete to close his eyes when sliding.
20. Say nothing to the athlete.
21. Put a restriction on headfirst sliding.
22. Have the athlete wear sunglasses.
23. Have the athlete wear a baseball hat.

End of Problem 6

■ Problem 7

Opening Scene: A high school wrestler reports to you that he has a red, blotchy rash all over his body.

Go to Section A.

A. What is your initial evaluation of this rash? (Choose only those actions that you believe are essential to resolving the problem at this time.)

1. Put on goggles and a face mask.
2. Ask how long the athlete has had the rash.
3. Touch the rash.
4. Put on rubber gloves.
5. Ask if athlete knows where he got it.
6. Contact the coach and determine how often mats are cleaned.
7. Take athlete's temperature.
8. Wash your hands.
9. Disinfect the area where you evaluated the athlete.
10. Determine the athlete's age.

   Go to Section B.

B. Given that this athlete has a rash, what treatment would you provide? (Choose only those actions that you believe are essential to resolving the problem at this time.)

11. Cover the rash.
12. Return the athlete to practice.
13. Refer the athlete to a physician.

14. Send the athlete home.
15. Disinfect the entire training room.

Go to Section C.

C. Because this rash may be communicable, what treatment and actions should be taken, given everything that is known at this time? (Choose only those actions that you believe are essential to resolving the problem at this time.)

16. No further action is necessary.
17. Have someone disinfect the athlete's locker.
18. Determine all meets the athlete attended.
19. Determine all wrestlers the athlete competed against.
20. Send all wrestlers home.
21. Have the mats disinfected with bleach.
22. Check all athletes' immunization records.
23. Report the case to the county health department's communicable disease office.
24. Give the school 10 days off.
25. Contact all schools the wrestling team competed against.
26. Contact the school's medical staff.
27. Issue an educational sheet on measles.
28. Send home only those students who show similar signs.
29. Send home and exclude from school all unimmunized students.
30. Have the entire school disinfected.
31. Contact the local newspaper.
32. Remind all students to cover their mouths.
33. Set up an immunization clinic.
34. Make sure athletes use cups rather than water bottles.

Go to Section D.

D. The wrestler with the rash calls to say he is improving and asks when he can return. (Choose only those actions that you believe are essential to resolving the problem at this time.)

35. Say he can return when the school nurse gives him the OK.
36. Say he can return when he is immunized.
37. Say he can return as soon as the coach needs him.
38. Say he can return when a physician gives approval.

End of Problem 7

■ Problem 8

Opening Scene: A defensive back is lying on the field during a game that you are covering.

Go to Section A.

A. This athlete is not moving. What is your initial assessment of this situation? (Choose only those actions that you believe are essential to resolving the problem at this time.)

1. Call the athletes' parents.
2. Remove the athlete's helmet.
3. Determine if the athlete is conscious.
4. Ask if anyone knows what happened.
5. Carry the athlete off the field.
6. Determine if the athlete is breathing.
7. Roll the athlete supine while controlling the head and neck.
8. Determine if the athlete has a heartbeat.
9. Auscultate the athlete's chest.
10. Check blood pressure.

Go to Section B.

B. Given the information you have at this time, what would you do next to resolve this issue? (Choose only those actions that you believe are essential to resolving the problem at this time.)

11. Send a student athletic trainer to direct the ambulance.
12. Have the procedure videotaped.
13. Open the athlete's airway with a head tilt.
14. Have a student athletic trainer call the ambulance.
15. Remove the athlete's face mask.
16. Begin CPR.
17. Remove the athlete's well-fitted helmet.
18. Backboard the athlete.
19. Begin mouth-to-mouth breathing.
20. Cover the athlete with a blanket.
21. Remove the athlete's mouth guard.
22. Remove the athlete's shoulder pads and neck roll.
23. Open the athlete's airway with a jaw thrust.

Go to Section C.

C. A second athletic trainer has done a secondary survey, with no other injuries noted. The ambulance arrives, along with athlete's parents, who are rather alarmed. What would you do at this time? (Choose only those actions that you believe are essential to resolving the problem at this time.)

24. Stop CPR long enough to get the athlete on a backboard.
25. Ask a school administrator to speak with the parents.
26. Have the announcer make a statement about the athlete's condition.
27. Ask that the game be forfeited.
28. Determine the athlete's insurance coverage.
29. Determine the hospital to be used.

30. Call the hospital about the athlete.
31. Allow paramedics to assume CPR.
32. Determine the other athlete involved.
33. Have the athlete's parents driven to the hospital.
34. Have the lights turned off so spectators do not get upset.
35. Have coaches try to motivate the other athletes to play.
36. Make sure you have all athletes' liability waivers.
37. Tell the other athletes the defensive back will be fine.

Go to Section D.

D. What will need to be done to prepare for the possible death of this athlete? (Choose only those actions that you believe are essential to resolving the problem at this time.)

38. Get a drink of alcohol to calm you down.
39. Indicate the proper tackling technique to other athletes.
40. Check the school's liability insurance.
41. Call the coordinator of the grief support team.
42. Debrief the athletic training staff about their feelings.
43. Purchase additional malpractice insurance.
44. Write a detailed report about the incident.
45. Have all staff present write detailed reports about the incident.
46. Review films of the athlete's injury.
47. In event of death of an athlete, go over the guidelines with athletic training staff.
48. Go to the hospital.

Go to Section E.

E. What should you do now to deal with the death of this athlete? (Choose only those actions that you believe are essential to resolving the problem at this time.)

49. Call the coordinator of the grief support team.
50. Call the school's public relations office.
51. Disconnect your telephone.
52. Send a sympathy card and flowers to the athlete's family.
53. Provide counselors for the other athletes.
54. Call the football team together and inform them of the death.
55. Assist the athlete's family with transportation and lodging.
56. Have the registrar's office contact all students with same last name.
57. Collect the athlete's belongings from the locker room.
58. Hide your own feelings.
59. Address players' concerns about continuing to play.
60. Contact the school's attorney about liability.
61. Try to isolate yourself to avoid the football players.
62. Obtain the athlete's equipment from the hospital.

63. Close the training room for the day.
64. Pretend nothing happened.
65. Answer media questions.
66. Glamorize the athlete's death.
67. Contact the opposing team.

End of Problem 8

■ Problem 9

Opening Scene: A rugby player is carried into the training room by three of his teammates.

Go to Section A.

A. What is your initial assessment of this situation? (Choose only those actions that you believe are essential to resolving the problem at this time.)

1. Ask teammates what happened.
2. Apply ice.
3. Call an ambulance.
4. Ask the athlete what happened.
5. Ask about a previous injury.
6. Determine if the athlete is conscious.
7. Palpate low back for point tenderness.
8. Ask the athlete about crepitus, or popping.
9. Have the athlete try and walk.
10. Ask if the athlete has pain anywhere else other than where already noted.
11. Massage the athlete's thigh.
12. Apply an analgesic balm.
13. Ask the athlete about previous abdominal injury.
14. Apply direct pressure over the wound.

Go to Section B.

B. You have completed your primary examination. What is your evaluation of this athlete's injury? (Choose only those actions that you believe are essential to resolving the problem at this time.)

15. Determine active range of motion in both of the athlete's lower extremities.
16. Palpate the anterior superior iliac spines bilaterally.
17. Check pupillary reflex with a penlight.
18. Place a hydroculator pack on the injury.
19. Check the athlete's strength in both lower extremities.
20. Palpate the athlete's abdomen.
21. Palpate both thighs for point tenderness and spasm.
22. Check the athlete's dorsal pedal pulses.

23. Check the athlete's carotid pulse.
24. Give mouth-to-mouth breathing.
25. Visually check both thighs for swelling or deformity.
26. Remove the athlete's mouth guard.
27. Perform bilateral femoral grinding tests.
28. Test patellar reflex bilaterally.
29. Ask the athlete about nausea.
30. Ask the athlete to perform a leg squat.
31. Ask the athlete to run.
32. Ask the athlete to perform a sit-up.

Go to Section C.

C. What specific tests would be performed to assess the severity of this injury? (Choose only those actions that you believe are essential to resolving the problem at this time.)

33. Perform Lachman's drawer test bilaterally.
34. Perform active hip flexion of the athlete's right leg.
35. Perform McMurray test bilaterally.
36. Continue mouth-to-mouth resuscitation.
37. Check the athlete's pulse every four cycles.
38. Test both knees for hyperextension.
39. Perform an apprehension test on the athlete's right knee.
40. Stress test both knees for varus and valgus.
41. Stress test both knees for varus and valgus at 20 degrees of flexion.
42. Check the athlete for Kehr's sign.
43. Perform Yergason test bilaterally.

Go to Section D.

D. Based on your evaluation, what is your impression of this injury? Select only one answer.

44. anterior cruciate tear
45. posterior cruciate tear
46. abdominal injury
47. lateral collateral injury
48. femur fracture
49. thigh contusion
50. patellar subluxation
51. medial meniscus injury
52. respiratory arrest

Go to Section E.

E. What is your immediate treatment of this injury? (Choose only those actions that you believe are essential to resolving the problem at this time.)

53. Use a neoprene brace.
54. Place the athlete's knee in a locked, hinged knee immobilizer bent at 60 degrees.
55. Instruct the athlete on crutches use.
56. Use a hydroculator pack.
57. Refer the athlete to a physician.
58. Call an ambulance.
59. Take the athlete's blood pressure.
60. No treatment is necessary.
61. Compression wrap the injury.

Go to Section F.

F. The athlete returns to the training room the next day. The physician recommends that you develop a treatment plan for the first week for this athlete's acute thigh contusion and myositis ossificans (from a previous injury). (Choose only those actions that you believe are essential to resolving the problem at this time.)

62. Measure the athlete's thigh circumference.
63. Check the athlete's active range of motion.
64. Apply ice several times a day.
65. Use cocontraction of the thigh.
66. Have the athlete start an upper-body lifting program.
67. Have the athlete do straight-leg raises of the injured thigh while immobilized.
68. Have the athlete start a lifting program for uninjured leg.
69. Massage the injured thigh.
70. Have the athlete do deep knee bends.
71. Ultrasound the injured thigh.
72. Recommend that the athlete use crutches.
73. Apply electrical stimulation to the injury.
74. Apply heat to the injury for the first few days.

Go to Section G.

G. The athlete is a week postinjury and is pain free. What treatment program is appropriate? (Choose only those actions that you believe are essential to resolving the problem at this time.)

75. straight-leg raising—no weights
76. ultrasound
77. deep knee bends
78. light jogging
79. leg press
80. electrical stimulation
81. massage of the injured thigh
82. active range-of-motion exercises
83. application of analgesic balm
84. cocontraction of the thigh

Go to Section H.

H. The athlete is three weeks postinjury. He has full range of motion. The myositis ossificans is nearing resolution. What is the appropriate treatment at this time? (Choose only those actions that you believe are essential to resolving the problem at this time.)

85. biking
86. doing leg presses
87. duck walking
88. sport-specific exercises
89. massage
90. using hydroculator packs
91. jogging
92. progressive resistive-quadriceps exercises
93. isokinetics

Go to Section I.

I. What is the criteria to return this athlete to competition? (Choose only those actions that you believe are essential to resolving the problem at this time.)

94. ability to duck walk
95. physician permission
96. The injured leg is at 90% of strength, compared to noninjured leg.
97. The athlete is pain free.
98. maintenance of the athlete's weight program
99. The athlete has full range of motion.
100. special padding
101. The coach needs the athlete.
102. The athlete is mentally prepared.
103. The athlete uses an elastic compression bandage over the area.
104. The athlete is able to perform sport-specific activities.

End of Problem 9

■ Problem 10

Opening Scene: You are covering a hockey game when a hockey player who got checked is rolling around on the ice across from you. The official stops play and calls you to care for the athlete.

Go to Section A.

A. With the information you have, which of the following will you do? (Choose only those actions that you believe are essential to resolving the case at this time.)

1. Ask the athlete what happened.
2. Determine the athlete's level of consciousness.

    3. Put on skates to get across the ice.
    4. Check the athlete for bleeding.
    5. Have other skaters drag the athlete over to you.
    6. Determine who hit the athlete.
    7. Ask the athlete to skate off the ice.
    8. Ask the athlete where the pain is.
    9. Determine if the check was legal.
   10. Determine if the athlete is breathing.
   11. Determine if the athlete has heartbeat.
   12. Determine the athlete's blood pressure.
   13. Determine the athlete's skin color.
   14. Check the athlete's body temperature.
   15. Visually examine the head and neck.
   16. Remove the athlete's mouth guard.

Go to Section B.

B. Given the information you have available, which of the following will you do? (Choose only those actions that you believe are essential to resolving the problem at this time.)

   17. Give the athlete ice.
   18. Have the athlete skate off the ice.
   19. Check the athlete's pupil size and reflex.
   20. Remove the athlete's helmet.
   21. Open the athlete's airway with a chin lift or jaw thrust.
   22. Call for an ambulance.
   23. Insert an oral airway.
   24. Put a soft neck collar on the athlete.
   25. Give the athlete's asthma medication.
   26. Keep the athlete calm and encourage slow breathing.
   27. Determine the athlete's breathing rate.
   28. Position the athlete supine.
   29. Position the athlete on the side.
   30. Stabilize the athlete's head and neck.

Go to Section C.

C. An ambulance has arrived to take the athlete to the hospital. What do you think was wrong with this athlete? Select only one choice.

   31. a fracture of the larynx
   32. a head injury
   33. cardiac arrest
   34. a seizure
   35. epiglottitis
   36. hyperventilation
   37. croup
   38. an asthma attack

End of Problem 10

■ Problem 11

Opening Scene: Two soccer players collide. Play is stopped and an official waves you onto the field.

Go to Section A.

A. With the information you have, which of the following will you do? (Choose only those actions that you believe are essential to resolving the problem at this time.)

1. Note the position of Player A's body.
2. Ask Player B to get up and walk.
3. Ask Player B if she injured her shoulder before.
4. Determine if Player A is conscious.
5. Send a student athletic trainer for ice.
6. Ask Player B if there is pain anywhere.
7. Determine if Player B is conscious.
8. Ask Player A what happened.
9. Note the position of Player B's body.
10. Ask Player A to get up and walk.
11. Ask Player B what happened.
12. Call an ambulance.
13. Ask Player A if there is pain anywhere.
14. Apply ice to the injured areas.
15. Position both athletes in a supine position.
16. Apply a sling to the shoulder of Player B.

Go to Section B.

B. Given the information you have, what actions would you perform at this time? (Choose only those actions that you believe are essential to resolving the problem at this time.)

17. Visually examine Player A's lower extremities (no problems).
18. Ask Player A if she heard a snap or pop.
19. Check dorsal pedal pulse and sensation in both of Player A's feet.
20. Palpate Player A's ankle.
21. Ask Player A if she injured the ankle before.
22. Tell Player A to be more careful next time.
23. Palpate Player B's leg.
24. Tell Player B to wear thicker shin guards next time.
25. Ask Player B if she heard a snap or pop.
26. Ask other players if they are tired.
27. Check dorsal pedal pulse and sensation in both of Player B's feet.
28. Visually examine Player B's lower extremities for swelling, deformity, and bleeding.

29. Have Player B move her lower leg.
30. Have Player A move her ankle.
31. Externally rotate and abduct Player B's shoulder.
32. Check range of motion bilaterally of Player B's shoulders.
33. Examine Player B's shoulder for swelling or deformity.
34. Palpate the left acromioclavicular joint of Player B.

Go to Section C.

C. Given the information you have, what actions would you perform for Player B? (Choose only those actions that you believe are essential to resolving the problem at this time.)

35. Give the athlete ice.
36. Carry the athlete off on a stretcher.
37. Visually examine Player B's lower extremities for swelling, deformity, and bleeding.
38. Adjust the crutches and show the athlete how to use them.
39. Have the athlete walk off the field.
40. Splint the athlete's leg.
41. Clap for the athlete as she leaves the field.
42. Place the athlete's arm in a sling.
43. Splint the athlete's humerus.

Go to Section D.

D. Given the information you have, what actions would you perform for Player A? (Choose only those actions that you believe are essential to resolving the problem at this time.)

44. Palpate the ankle for deformity.
45. Bilaterally compare both ankles (left to right).
46. Splint the athlete's ankle.
47. Have the athlete actively move the injured ankle.
48. Have the athlete carried off on a stretcher.
49. Test the athlete's active-resistive range of motion.
50. Clap for the athlete as she leaves the field.
51. Call an ambulance to transport the athlete.
52. Apply an anterior drawer stress test.
53. Manually carry the athlete from the field.
54. Provide ambulatory aid off the field.

Go to Section E.

E. Player B returns the next day in full-leg cast. She has a greenstick fracture of the tibia. What is your initial rehabilitation for this athlete? (Choose only those actions that you believe are essential to resolving the problem at this time.)

55. four-way straight-leg raises
56. upper body workouts

57. a swimming program
58. a running program
59. strengthening for the unaffected leg
60. riding the stationary bike

Go to Section F.

F. After 3 months this athlete's cast is removed. What do you initially evaluate before beginning rehabilitation? (Choose only those actions that you believe are essential to resolving the problem at this time.)

61. goniometer active range of motion measurement of the knee
62. girth measurements
63. goniometer passive range of motion measurement of the knee
64. goniometer active range of motion measurement of the ankle
65. goniometer measurement of ankle passively
66. Ask about pain.
67. Palpate fracture site.
68. Note how hairy the leg is.
69. Note how the leg smells.
70. Check the athlete's gait.
71. Note the general condition of the athlete's skin.

Go to Section G.

G. What will you now have the athlete do for rehabilitation? (Choose only those actions that you believe are essential to resolving the problem at this time.)

72. Stretch the gastroc and soleus.
73. Do ball-handling drills.
74. Stretch the quadriceps and hamstrings.
75. Keep the knee active through normal range of motion.
76. Do four-way straight-leg raises.
77. Use ice or a cold whirlpool after activity.
78. Do hip range-of-motion exercises.
79. Do ankle range-of-motion exercises.
80. Do toe raises with weight.
81. Do patellar mobilization.

Go to Section H.

H. The athlete is now ready for what rehabilitation? (Choose only those actions that you believe are essential to resolving the problem at this time.)

82. active ankle plantarflexion with resistance
83. proprioceptive knee exercises
84. active ankle eversion with resistance
85. active ankle inversion with resistance
86. active knee flexion with resistance

87. toe touches
88. jumping on the previously casted leg
89. analgesic balm application
90. active ankle dorsiflexion with resistance
91. proprioceptive ankle exercises
92. active knee extension with resistance
93. running
94. swimming
95. biking

End of Problem 11

■ Problem 12

Opening Scene: You have an athlete who is semicarried in and limping, indicating he just injured his ankle.

Go to Section A.

A. What is your initial evaluation of this injury? (Choose only those actions that you believe are essential to resolving the problem at this time.)

1. Ask the athlete if he has pain anyplace else.
2. Activate your emergency plan.
3. Ask the athlete if anyone else was injured.
4. Ask the athlete what happened.
5. Put the athlete on crutches.
6. Ask if the athlete has injured the ankle before.
7. Apply ice.
8. Ask what type of shoes the athlete was wearing.
9. Check the athlete's blood pressure.
10. Check the athlete's temperature.
11. Ask if the athlete continued to play after getting hurt.
12. Visually inspect the injured area for swelling, bleeding, or deformity.
13. Send a student athletic trainer to the gymnasium to find a supervisor.
14. Check the athlete's level of consciousness.
15. Check the athlete's skin color.
16. Check the athlete's pupil reflex.
17. Palpate the athlete's right ankle.
18. Ask the athlete to plantarflex and dorsiflex the left ankle.
19. Apply a pressure bandage to the injury.
20. Manipulate the athlete's right ankle.
21. Palpate the athlete's left ankle.
22. Have the athlete hop on the ankle.
23. Ask the athlete to plantarflex and dorsiflex the right ankle.

24. Ask the athlete to invert and evert the right ankle.
25. Ask the athlete to invert and evert left ankle.
26. Manipulate the athlete's left ankle.
27. Use traction on the injured ankle.

Go to Section B.

B. What special test would you perform at this time? (Choose only those actions that you believe are essential to resolving the problem at this time.)

28. Test the right foot for anterior drawer.
29. Give a heel-pound test.
30. Place the athlete in warm whirlpool.
31. Give the heel-pound test on the right foot.
32. Do a Thompson test on the right foot.
33. Massage the injured ankle.
34. Give a heel-pound test on the left ankle.
35. Test the left ankle for anterior drawer.
36. Do a McMurray test bilaterally.
37. Put the athlete in a splint.
38. Do a Thomas test bilaterally.
39. Do a Thomas test of the right foot.
40. Varus test the knees bilaterally.
41. Do a Lachman's test bilaterally.

Go to Section C.

C. What is the initial treatment of this injury? (Choose only those actions that you believe are essential to resolving the problem at this time.)

42. Spray ethyl chloride on the injury.
43. Elevate the lower extremity.
44. Put the athlete on crutches.
45. Have the athlete walk.
46. elastic compression of the ankle
47. ultrasound
48. toe-raise exercise
49. Have the athlete exercise on a stationary bike.
50. Have the athlete use a warm whirlpool.
51. massage
52. ice

Go to Section D.

D. What instructions would you give this athlete when at home? (Choose only those actions that you believe are essential to resolving the problem at this time.)

53. Apply ice several times, but not longer than 20 min.
54. Use over-the-counter pain medication.

55. Increase calcium intake.
56. Apply analgesic balm.
57. Keep the lower extremity elevated.
58. Eat red meat.
59. Apply a heating pad at night.
60. Walk on the ankle as much as possible.
61. See a physician.
62. Use over-the-counter anti-inflammatory medication.

Go to Section E.

E. The acute ankle sprain is edematous. How can the edema be removed in the acute stage? (Choose only those actions that you believe are essential to resolving the problem at this time.)

63. Ice for an hour.
64. Use hydroculator packs.
65. Use an intermittent compression device.
66. Use infrared therapy.
67. Use biofeedback.
68. Use ultrasound.
69. Use a TENS unit.
70. Run on the ankle.

Go to Section F.

F. Set up the device you have chosen to reduce this acute edema. (Choose only those actions that you believe are essential to resolving the problem at this time.)

71. Apply electrodes.
72. Place ankle horizontally to infrared unit.
73. Place ice on the injured body part.
74. Apply a pressure wrap over ice.
75. Place the ice pack in towels.
76. Instruct the athlete on distance and speed of runs.
77. Place the injured ankle in a compression sleeve.
78. Instruct the athlete to contract the injured body part.
79. Set the unit to tentenization.
80. Set unit for W/cm^2.
81. Set the pressure to 65 mmHg.
82. Move the ultrasonic head in an overlapping motion.
83. Place an ice pack on the injury for 15 min.
84. Set on-off sequence.

End of Problem 12

■ Problem 13

Opening Scene: A freestyle swimmer who wants to improve times asks you for a strengthening program.

Go to Section A.

A. Please give your initial assessment of this athlete. (Choose only those actions that you believe are essential to resolving the problem at this time.)

1. Recommend the athlete see the coach for this analysis.
2. Recommend the athlete weight lift.
3. Have a student athletic trainer write a physician referral.
4. Strength test the athlete's shoulder extensor.
5. Strength test the athlete's shoulder flexors.
6. Check the athlete's shoulder range of motion.
7. Strength test the athlete's shoulder rotator cuffs.
8. Strength test the athlete's abdominals.
9. Strength test the athlete's neck musculature.
10. Strength test the athlete's horizontal shoulder flexors.
11. Strength test the athlete's horizontal shoulder extensors.
12. Strength test the athlete's elbow extensors.
13. Strength test the athlete's elbow flexors.
14. Ask if the athlete's coefficient of friction has ever been measured.
15. Strength test the athlete's neck rotators.
16. Strength test the athlete's toe flexors.
17. Strength test the athlete's toe extensors.
18. Have the athlete watch other athletes swim in the pool.
19. Determine the athlete's arm length.
20. Strength test the athlete's hip adduction.
21. Strength test the athlete's hip abduction.
22. Strength test the athlete's knee extension.
23. Strength test the athlete's hip extension.
24. Strength test the athlete's knee flexion.
25. Strength test the athlete's back extensor.
26. Strength test the athlete's hip abductors.
27. Strength test the athlete's foot plantar flexors.
28. Determine the length of the race the athlete will complete in.
29. Strength test foot dorsiflexion.
30. Determine the athlete's stroke count.

Go to Section B.

B. What specific strengthening exercises would you recommend for this athlete, based on need to improve freestyle times and deficiencies of this swimmer? (Choose only those actions that you believe are essential to resolving the problem at this time.)

31. toe raises with shoulder weight
32. shoulder shrugs with weights
33. bench press
34. military press

35. leg press
36. leg squats
37. barbell flies
38. wrist barbell curls
39. four-way neck weights
40. running with leg weights
41. four-way straight leg raises
42. empty can exercises with light weights
43. increasing the stroke count
44. decreasing breathing rate
45. doing more rotation in the stroke
46. using swim fins at practice
47. using a kickboard at practice
48. leg extention with weight
49. arm curls
50. hip sled
51. jumping rope
52. running in waist-deep water
53. practicing race dive form

End of Problem 13

■ Problem 14

Opening Scene: You have been assigned to use high-voltage galvanic stimulation with an athlete who has an acute knee sprain.

Go to Section A.

A. What are the positive polarity characteristics? (Choose only those actions that you believe are essential to resolving the problem at this time.)

1. vasodilates blood vessels
2. hardens tissues
3. the same as negative polarity characteristics
4. creates an alkaline reaction under the pad
5. acts as a pain reliever
6. irritates nerves
7. increases spasms
8. repels hydrogen ions
9. Its most effective use is for acute conditions.
10. Its most effective use is for chronic conditions.

Go to Section B.

B. The athlete then asks about the negative polarity characteristics of high-voltage galvanic stimulation. What are these? (Choose only those actions that you believe are essential to resolving the problem at this time.)

11. absorbs fat
12. absorbs blood clots
13. decreases hemorrhaging
14. softens tissues
15. vasoconstricts blood vessels
16. repels oxygen and acids

Go to Section C.

C. The athlete wants to know if there are any contraindications for using this machine. Indicate these contraindications of high-voltage galvanic stimulation. (Choose only those actions that you believe are essential to resolving the problem at this time.)

17. Do not use with ectomorphs.
18. Do not use over muscle motor points.
19. Do not use over resolved hemorrhaging.
20. Do not use over carotid sinus.
21. Do not use with acute spasms.
22. Do not use over metal implants.
23. Do not use with a pregnant patient.
24. Do not use with muscle atrophy.
25. Do not use with pacemakers.

Go to Section D.

D. The athlete is concerned about being electrocuted by the high-voltage galvanic stimulator. What safety procedures have been taken to ensure the athlete's safety? (Choose only those actions that you believe are essential to resolving the problem at this time.)

26. The equipment is checked yearly for safety.
27. Cords are kept close to pipes.
28. A ground-fault-interrupter plug is used.
29. A three-pronged cord is used.
30. Other people have used this unit without injury.
31. A long cord is used.
32. The athlete can turn off the machine.
33. Many cords come out of the same wall.

Go to Section E.

E. The athlete has stopped the questioning and would like you to set up the equipment. What would you use to set up this athlete on a high-voltage galvanic stimulator? The athlete has an acute knee sprain with edema. (Choose only those actions that you believe are essential to resolving the problem at this time.)

34. an 8-pulse-per-s switch rate
35. treatment three times per day
36. Place the pad at the motor point of the muscle.

37. Use the stimulator in conjunction with a hydroculator pack.
38. 128 pulses per s switch rate
39. a treatment time of 45 min
40. intensity set to patient's tolerance
41. Use the negative lead at treatment site.
42. Use the stimulator in conjunction with ice at the same time.
43. Place a dispersive pad at the injury site.

End of Problem 14

■ Problem 15

Opening Scene: You must design a program for next fall to prevent heat illnesses. It is to be given to all athletes before they leave for summer vacation.

Go to Section A.

A. What is the initial part of this program? (Choose only those actions that you believe are essential to resolving the problem at this time.)

1. Recommend athletes drink plenty of water.
2. Recommend athletes work out in air conditioning.
3. Recommend athletes follow a conditioning program.
4. Have athletes monitor their daily diets.
5. Have athletes monitor their weight daily.
6. Have athletes wear sweats on warm days.
7. Have athletes monitor their body temperature.
8. Have athletes take cold showers.
9. Have athletes take salt tablets.

Go to Section B.

B. Athletes have returned to school. What measures are now appropriate before participation to prevent heat injuries? (Choose only those actions that you believe are essential to resolving the problem at this time.)

10. Set practice times for early mornings.
11. Get a physical examination of each athlete.
12. Have athletes take salt tablets.
13. Test all athletes' physical conditioning.
14. Check all athletes' body temperature.
15. Check all athletes' blood pressure.

Go to Section C.

C. The first day of practice begins. What procedures should be followed to prevent heat illnesses? (Choose only those actions that you believe are essential to resolving the problem at this time.)

16. Withhold water until the end of practice.
17. Have a list of athletes' names and phone numbers.

18. Have athletes use salt tablets before going to practice.
19. Weigh all athletes after practice.
20. Use graduated physical conditioning.
21. Watch overweight athletes.
22. Take sling psychrometer readings before practice.

End of Problem 15

■ Problem 16

Opening Scene: You have been called to care for an athlete who has collapsed on the cross-country course.

Go to Section A.

A.   What are your initial actions? (Choose only those actions that you believe are essential to resolving the problem at this time.)

1. Grab a pair of crutches to take with you.
2. Ask the athlete what happened.
3. Determine if the athlete has been disqualified.
4. Hold the athlete's head and neck still.
5. Determine if the athlete has a pulse.
6. Visually check the athlete's body position.
7. Go get a stethoscope to auscultate the athlete's chest.
8. Ask others what happened.
9. Determine if the athlete is breathing.
10. Determine the athlete's skin color.
11. Ask the athlete about pain.
12. Ask if the athlete is allergic to anything.

Go to Section B.

B.   What is your treatment of this athlete? (Choose only those actions that you believe are essential to resolving the problem at this time.)

13. Call for an ambulance.
14. Put the athlete in a comfortable position.
15. Give the athlete CPR.
16. Monitor the athlete's breathing rate.
17. Encourage the athlete to breathe slowly.
18. Give the athlete oxygen.
19. Give the athlete abdominal thrusts.
20. Give the athlete a tracheotomy.
21. Have the athlete breathe into a paper bag.
22. Give the athlete glucose.
23. Place athlete on the side.
24. Move everything away from the athlete.
25. Monitor the athlete's blood pressure.

Go to Section C.

C. Given previous information, what illness or injury has this athlete suffered? Choose only one answer.
   26. a collapsed lung
   27. an airway obstruction
   28. a bee sting
   29. insulin shock
   30. an asthma attack
   31. hyperventilation
   32. a seizure
   33. a contusion of the larynx
   34. pneumonia
   35. a pulmonary embolism
   36. a heart attack

End of Problem 16

A
APPENDIX

Answers to the Written Examination Study Questions

Written examination study questions are numbered 1 through 600. Each question is answered here, with a reference and a page number for further study. Reference numbers correspond to the numbered bibliography. Thus, Reference 1 indicates *The Athlete's Eye* by the American Academy of Ophthalmology. Following the reference number is the page number in the reference work where additional information can be found.

Appendix A is divided, as are the questions, into five sections—prevention, recognition and evaluation, treatment, rehabilitation administration, and education and counseling. At the end of each section a passing-point total is given: I consider these totals, which equate to 70%, minimum passing scores. If you did not pass or you feel uneasy about a section, refer to the textbooks listed as references in these sections to obtain more information about the subject area. If you do not have the indicated reference, use another textbook to gain similar information.

■ *Prevention Answers*

	Answer	Reference	Page Number		Answer	Reference	Page Number
1.	a	51	315	7.	c	32	170
2.	e	32	277	8.	b	32	171
3.	b	32	277	9.	b	32	132
4.	c	32	178	10.	c	32	136-137
5.	a	32	175	11.	d	32	145
6.	e	32	174, 176	12.	d	32	89

	Answer	Reference	Page Number		Answer	Reference	Page Number
13.	a	32	183	55.	c	28	23
14.	e	32	24	56.	a	28	12
15.	a	14	412	57.	c	28	11
16.	d	52	349	58.	e	7	301
17.	c	7	484	59.	a	19	515-516
18.	c	52	349	60.	b	45	20
19.	a	52	352	61.	b	2	13
20.	d	40	556	62.	c	7	309
21.	d	40	11	63.	a	7	317
22.	d	40	21	64.	a	7	106
23.	d	6	16	65.	b	7	106
24.	e	6	18	66.	d	7	147
25.	b	41	31	67.	c	7	159
26.	a	41	31	68.	d	7	103
27.	e	6	102	69.	a	45	450
28.	e	6	410	70.	b	45	452
29.	a	6	343	71.	e	45	490
30.	d	6	49	72.	e	45	492
31.	e	52	350	73.	b	45	493
32.	c	7	49	74.	e	45	500
33.	a	25	185	75.	b	7	46
34.	d	19	191	76.	d	7	86
35.	c	6	104	77.	a	7	93
36.	d	6	107	78.	a	7	95
37.	e	6	107	79.	e	45	223
38.	c	6	124	80.	b	45	252
39.	e	6	40	81.	c	32	288
40.	a	6	41	82.	c	45	305
41.	b	6	41	83.	a	7	22
42.	c	6	52	84.	d	45	169
43.	d	6	68	85.	e	45	169
44.	e	6	39	86.	c	7	11
45.	e	7	19	87.	e	32	285
46.	c	6	29	88.	a	49	209
47.	d	7	22	89.	d	35	43
48.	e	7	22	90.	e	32	174
49.	a	6	19	91.	a	53	75
50.	b	6	19	92.	b	50	195
51.	d	7	307	93.	d	32	172
52.	d	6	22	94.	c	40	11
53.	c	26	333	95.	a	40	12
54.	b	14	112	96.	e	6	207

	Answer	Reference	Page Number		Answer	Reference	Page Number
97.	e	32	412	101.	b	53	21
98.	e	6	15	102.	a	33	134
99.	c	6	6	103.	a	53	24
100.	a	53	19	104.	c	7	487

Passing-point total: 73

■ Recognition and Evaluation Answers

	Answer	Reference	Page Number		Answer	Reference	Page Number
105.	e	28	36	136.	e	4	45
106.	d	14	476	137.	e	4	71
107.	a	49	29	138.	e	4	72
108.	b	32	318	139.	a	7	251
109.	a	32	333	140.	d	7	553
110.	b	32	358	141.	a	45	427
111.	c	32	364	142.	d	45	432
112.	e	32	398	143.	c	45	309
113.	a	32	443	144.	a	45	321
114.	d	32	460	145.	a	45	232-233
115.	a	32	464-465	146.	d	45	240
116.	e	32	467	147.	e	45	130-131
117.	c	1	19	148.	b	50	174
118.	e	1	23	149.	d	48	984
119.	e	32	56	150.	a	14	486
120.	a	6	420	151.	b	14	487
121.	d	14	50-51	152.	d	14	411
122.	c	6	389	153.	e	14	411
123.	b	6	366	154.	e	14	378
124.	d	6	369	155.	c	5	73
125.	d	6	333	156.	b	5	5
126.	c	6	321	157.	c	5	6
127.	e	6	152	158.	c	5	12
128.	d	6	138	159.	d	45	500
129.	c	16	99-100	160.	b	7	818
130.	e	40	566	161.	a	7	214
131.	c	40	97	162.	d	7	472
132.	b	4	131	163.	d	7	474-475
133.	c	4	151	164.	a	2	311
134.	a	4	41	165.	a	2	482
135.	d	4	43	166.	e	2	39

	Answer	Reference	Page Number		Answer	Reference	Page Number
167.	c	27	28	196.	a	26	121
168.	b	27	36	197.	c	26	32
169.	d	27	67	198.	d	26	35
170.	e	27	79	199.	b	26	44
171.	e	27	227	200.	e	26	49
172.	a	32	291	201.	c	14	295
173.	b	32	293	202.	a	14	222
174.	b	32	301	203.	a	14	225
175.	a	32	270	204.	b	14	204-205
176.	b	32	183	205.	c	14	13
177.	b	32	29	206.	e	14	14
178.	c	49	126	207.	e	14	25
179.	a	52	208	208.	c	47	193
180.	e	28	58	209.	c	14	46
181.	e	28	59	210.	a	14	50
182.	c	7	206	211.	c	14	62
183.	d	7	282	212.	a	14	96
184.	a	7	491	213.	b	14	97
185.	d	7	541	214.	c	14	99
186.	e	7	569	215.	a	14	122
187.	c	7	633	216.	d	14	124
188.	c	33	197	217.	e	14	130
189.	c	7	210	218.	a	14	139
190.	a	28	59	219.	c	14	146
191.	b	28	59	220.	d	14	150
192.	c	28	60	221.	e	14	152
193.	c	28	11	222.	c	50	208-209
194.	b	26	182	223.	d	50	238
195.	d	26	195	224.	d	50	243

Passing-point total: 84

■ Management, Treatment, and Disposition Answers

	Answer	Reference	Page Number		Answer	Reference	Page Number
225.	c	3	32	230.	e	3	81
226.	d	3	33	231.	a	3	81
227.	e	3	76-78	232.	b	4	541
228.	c	3	78	233.	c	4	540
229.	d	3	78-80	234.	d	4	540-541

	Answer	Reference	Page Number		Answer	Reference	Page Number
235.	a	3	17	277.	a	2	53
236.	b	3	17	278.	c	4	450
237.	c	3	17	279.	a	4	453
238.	d	3	19-20	280.	a	14	339
239.	b	45	345	281.	c	14	329-330
240.	c	7	55	282.	a	4	478
241.	c	7	37	283.	a	4	478
242.	d	45	422	284.	e	4	75
243.	a	2	18	285.	a	4	82
244.	a	7	36	286.	b	4	84-85
245.	a	3	18	287.	d	4	105
246.	a	3	30-31	288.	d	40	666
247.	d	3	76-77	289.	e	40	296
248.	e	4	547	290.	d	40	297
249.	e	4	16	291.	c	40	297
250.	e	35	4	292.	b	40	310-311
251.	e	35	45, 47	293.	a	40	346
252.	e	7	482	294.	b	40	385
253.	d	32	380	295.	b	40	258-259
254.	e	32	384	296.	c	40	293
255.	c	32	393	297.	e	40	89
256.	b	32	395	298.	e	40	103
257.	b	32	407	299.	b	40	129
258.	d	1	20-21	300.	d	4	504-505
259.	b	32	286	301.	a	40	62
260.	b	32	267	302.	e	4	125
261.	c	32	207	303.	c	4	125
262.	b	32	208	304.	e	4	188
263.	c	32	190	305.	d	4	252
264.	e	32	189	306.	a	4	260
265.	c	32	181	307.	a	4	333
266.	b	32	180	308.	c	4	415
267.	c	32	156	309.	d	7	468
268.	e	45	287	310.	b	7	470
269.	e	7	474	311.	b	53	83
270.	e	7	478	312.	a	53	104-105
271.	a	2	487	313.	d	7	470
272.	c	2	494-495	314.	a	7	711
273.	c	2	412	315.	a	7	728
274.	c	2	48	316.	a	7	808
275.	b	2	48	317.	b	2	43
276.	b	2	48	318.	c	45	391

	Answer	Reference	Page Number		Answer	Reference	Page Number
319.	b	45	300-301	333.	b	14	290
320.	e	45	148	334.	c	43	210
321.	a	45	176	335.	a	47	159
322.	e	45	56	336.	c	32	429
323.	c	50	111	337.	e	7	266
324.	e	6	480	338.	d	55	142
325.	b	6	493	339.	b	18	30
326.	c	6	413	340.	e	49	636
327.	b	6	384	341.	b	49	636
328.	c	6	385	342.	b	49	229
329.	b	6	238	343.	a	49	229
330.	c	6	195	344.	a	49	230
331.	d	6	198				
332.	c	14	190-191	Passing-point total: 84			

■ Rehabilitation Answers

	Answer	Reference	Page Number		Answer	Reference	Page Number
345.	d	2	113	367.	a	47	144
346.	b	32	483	368.	d	3	154
347.	d	32	393	369.	c	45	196
348.	c	32	378	370.	a	45	283
349.	a	40	90	371.	d	45	346
350.	b	40	477	372.	b	45	395
351.	c	40	428	373.	a	7	403
352.	a	40	189	374.	c	7	397
353.	a	40	85	375.	b	7	765
354.	c	45	268	376.	a	40	679
355.	a	50	174	377.	b	40	679
356.	d	14	550	378.	c	40	679
357.	d	5	75	379.	d	40	683
358.	e	5	88	380.	e	18	53
359.	e	14	362	381.	e	40	684
360.	d	24	23	382.	a	40	689
361.	e	5	59	383.	c	40	690
362.	b	5	69	384.	c	40	690
363.	d	47	13	385.	d	40	692
364.	c	47	14-15	386.	c	40	693
365.	a	47	31	387.	e	21	31
366.	a	47	111	388.	a	21	33

	Answer	Reference	Page Number		Answer	Reference	Page Number
389.	b	21	36	420.	c	32	242
390.	c	21	41	421.	a	32	193
391.	b	21	59	422.	b	32	193
392.	c	21	61	423.	b	32	194
393.	d	21	74	424.	a	32	205
394.	e	21	75	425.	a	32	189
395.	e	21	151	426.	a	32	183
396.	d	36	32	427.	e	32	184
397.	c	36	32	428.	a	32	27
398.	b	36	40	429.	a	43	130
399.	a	6	357	430.	d	43	228
400.	b	6	358	431.	d	43	9
401.	d	6	365	432.	e	7	355
402.	e	6	234	433.	c	43	83
403.	c	6	235	434.	c	43	84
404.	e	6	236	435.	b	43	89
405.	a	6	237	436.	a	43	95
406.	e	6	219	437.	c	43	96
407.	a	6	215	438.	d	43	98
408.	b	6	217	439.	c	43	123-124
409.	e	6	149	440.	d	32	489
410.	e	6	68	441.	d	33	308
411.	e	32	215	442.	c	18	58
412.	c	32	217	443.	b	18	75
413.	d	32	217	444.	d	18	82
414.	c	32	228	445.	d	30	8
415.	e	27	19	446.	c	30	9-10
416.	d	27	279	447.	b	30	20
417.	a	32	229	448.	c	50	82
418.	b	32	231				
419.	a	32	235	Passing-point total: 73			

■ Organization and Administration Answers

	Answer	Reference	Page Number		Answer	Reference	Page Number
449.	a	6	27	454.	e	7	58
450.	e	1	49	455.	c	7	8
451.	d	3	33	456.	c	3	28
452.	c	7	42	457.	e	3	28
453.	e	52	353	458.	e	3	30

	Answer	Reference	Page Number		Answer	Reference	Page Number
459.	d	3	30-31	493.	d	4	484
460.	e	3	33	494.	b	4	18
461.	a	3	11	495.	c	7	432
462.	e	3	20-21	496.	e	28	72
463.	d	3	73	497.	d	45	4
464.	c	3	66	498.	b	7	39
465.	b	3	30	499.	c	7	39
466.	b	6	11	500.	d	7	41
467.	d	6	12	501.	a	7	41
468.	a	6	14	502.	b	7	41
469.	c	3	30	503.	a	7	41
470.	a	6	313	504.	c	7	42
471.	d	6	263	505.	d	7	42
472.	e	6	263	506.	d	7	421
473.	d	6	101	507.	b	51	387
474.	a	6	174	508.	c	51	373
475.	b	40	18	509.	a	28	3
476.	e	40	18	510.	b	28	11
477.	d	40	19	511.	b	28	18
478.	b	3	26	512.	b	28	57
479.	a	3	27	513.	e	42	42
480.	b	3	221	514.	e	42	45
481.	b	2	18	515.	b	21	364
482.	d	3	222	516.	d	21	364-365
483.	d	7	248	517.	d	42	98
484.	d	3	27	518.	d	51	244
485.	a	3	39	519.	e	51	302
486.	a	4	483	520.	c	51	326
487.	b	32	213	521.	e	51	326-327
488.	c	32	213	522.	d	51	329
489.	b	32	214	523.	d	3	67
490.	e	32	214	524.	a	3	70
491.	b	4	483				
492.	a	32	180				

Passing-point total: 53

■ Education and Counseling Answers

	Answer	Reference	Page Number		Answer	Reference	Page Number
525.	c	4	19	565.	b	7	688
526.	a	4	19	566.	c	4	449
527.	a	7	423	567.	c	4	453
528.	b	53	38	568.	d	4	453-454
529.	b	4	361-362	569.	c	4	458
530.	e	50	147	570.	d	10	44
531.	a	7	438	571.	e	36	5
532.	a	32	108-109	572.	d	10	45
533.	b	27	207	573.	c	10	11
534.	a	32	151	574.	d	53	155
535.	b	32	152	575.	b	10	45
536.	d	6	38	576.	a	10	45
537.	b	6	70	577.	b	10	24
538.	d	6	73	578.	c	10	24
539.	e	6	75	579.	d	10	21
540.	c	6	94	580.	e	10	33
541.	a	6	219	581.	d	10	171
542.	c	6	245	582.	e	36	112
543.	c	23	31	583.	d	36	115
544.	a	23	61	584.	c	39	2-3
545.	c	23	303	585.	a	52	68
546.	b	23	312	586.	d	52	74
547.	c	23	315	587.	a	52	209
548.	c	2	112	588.	c	52	244
549.	a	2	113	589.	d	52	274
550.	a	2	113	590.	e	52	276
551.	e	2	114	591.	b	52	363
552.	d	2	482-485	592.	a	52	23
553.	b	2	482-485	593.	c	28	57
554.	a	46	54	594.	c	28	66
555.	e	7	176	595.	d	28	66
556.	b	7	177	596.	d	28	11
557.	a	7	176	597.	a	53	179
558.	c	7	182	598.	d	53	39
559.	d	7	182	599.	c	53	56
560.	e	7	172-173	600.	e	53	65
561.	a	7	241				
562.	d	7	395				
563.	e	7	398				
564.	b	7	448				

Passing-point total: 53

Passing-point total
   for all sections: 420

B

APPENDIX

Answers to the Oral/ Practical Test Study Questions

The following checklist will help you be sure that you thoroughly cover all necessary points when demonstrating a response to questions on the oral/practical section of the exam. To use this checklist, have a partner read and show you the questions, which appear in chapter 7.

As you demonstrate the proper responses have your partner indicate, by placing a check mark in the appropriate box, whether you made the appropriate response that counts for points on the exam. At the end of each question is a passing-point total. Have your partner add together all yes answers and compare them to the passing-point total. The point totals are 70% of points possible for that question.

1. explains the increase in subcutaneous tissue temperatures
   ❏ Yes   ❏ No

   explains an increase in muscle temperature
   ❏ Yes   ❏ No

   explains that there is vasodilation
   ❏ Yes   ❏ No

   explains use for reduction of spasms and pain
   ❏ Yes   ❏ No

   explains that the hydroculator pack is efficient and inexpensive to use
   ❏ Yes   ❏ No

   explains that deep tissue is not significantly heated
   ❏ Yes   ❏ No

explains that heat transfer is inhibited by fat

❑ Yes   ❑ No

explains that the hydroculator pack is used for general relaxation or before other therapeutic modalities

❑ Yes   ❑ No

explains that the hydroculator pack is not to be used with loss of sensation

❑ Yes   ❑ No

explains that the hydroculator pack is not to be used within 48 hr of an acute injury

❑ Yes   ❑ No

explains that the hydroculator pack is not to be used with decreased circulation

❑ Yes   ❑ No

explains that the hydroculator pack is not to be used over the eyers, over the genitals, or over the abdomen during a pregnancy

❑ Yes   ❑ No

explains that the athlete should not lay directly on the pack

❑ Yes   ❑ No

explains and demonstrates removal and draining of the pack

❑ Yes   ❑ No

explains and demonstrates application of dry toweling

❑ Yes   ❑ No

explains and demonstrates positioning the athlete for treatment

❑ Yes   ❑ No

explains that there is a need to check the athlete for comfort

❑ Yes   ❑ No

explains that treatment time is 15 to 20 min

❑ Yes   ❑ No

explains and demonstrates the removal of toweling as the pack cools

❑ Yes   ❑ No

completes this task in 8 min or less

❑ Yes   ❑ No

Passing-point total: 14

2. foot position is relaxed (neither dorsiflexed nor plantarflexed)

❑ Yes ❑ No

applies tape adherent

❑ Yes ❑ No

applies strips that X across foot, covering the ball of the foot to the fifth metatarsal head

❑ Yes ❑ No

uses a minimum of three strips

❑ Yes ❑ No

tape overlays

❑ Yes ❑ No

tape is wrinkle free

❑ Yes ❑ No

tape covered and not binding once athlete applies pressure

❑ Yes ❑ No

completes this task in 5 min or less

❑ Yes ❑ No

Passing-point total: 6

3. positions athlete in a standing position with the injured knee in slight flexion

❑ Yes ❑ No

applies tape adherent

❑ Yes ❑ No

applies an anchor strip to the midthigh

❑ Yes ❑ No

applies an anchor strip to the midcalf

❑ Yes ❑ No

applies padding to the popliteal space

❑ Yes ❑ No

applies at least three vertical strips of tape across the posterior popliteal space from anchor to anchor

❑ Yes ❑ No

has athlete contract thigh while encircling the entire area

❑ Yes ❑ No

applies tape from distal to proximal
❏ Yes ❏ No

checks the athlete for circulation difficulties
❏ Yes ❏ No

tape is wrinkle free
❏ Yes ❏ No

completed taping prevents hyperextension
❏ Yes ❏ No

completes this task in 10 min or less
❏ Yes ❏ No

Passing-point total: 9

4. asks when the injury occurred
   ❏ Yes ❏ No

   asks how the injury occurred
   ❏ Yes ❏ No

   asks if there is a previous injury
   ❏ Yes ❏ No

   asks if any "cracking" or "snapping" occurred
   ❏ Yes ❏ No

   explains and demonstrates evaluation of foot for abnormalities (pes cavus, pes planus, hammer toes)
   ❏ Yes ❏ No

   explains and demonstrates visual evaluation of the ankle for swelling, discoloration, and deformity
   ❏ Yes ❏ No

   explains and demonstrates passive and active-resistive plantar flexion
   ❏ Yes ❏ No

   explains and demonstrates passive, active, and active-resistive dorsiflexion
   ❏ Yes ❏ No

   explains and demonstrates passive and active-resistive inversion
   ❏ Yes ❏ No

   explains and demonstrates passive and active-resistive eversion
   ❏ Yes ❏ No

explains and demonstrates palpation of the anterior aspect of the ankle

❏ Yes   ❏ No

explains and demonstrates palpation of the posterior aspect of the ankle

❏ Yes   ❏ No

explains and demonstrates palpation of the medial aspect of the ankle

❏ Yes   ❏ No

explains and demonstrates palpation of the lateral aspect of the ankle

❏ Yes   ❏ No

explains and demonstrates palpation at the base of the fifth metatarsal

❏ Yes   ❏ No

explains and demonstrates the anterior drawer test

❏ Yes   ❏ No

explains and demonstrates palpation of the dorsal pedal or posterior tibial pulse

❏ Yes   ❏ No

explains and demonstrates evaluation of dermatomes S1, L5, and L4 (lateral aspect, anterior aspect, and medial aspect)

❏ Yes   ❏ No

does all tests bilaterally

❏ Yes   ❏ No

explains and demonstrates evaluation of walking and running gait

❏ Yes   ❏ No

mentions referral to a physician

❏ Yes   ❏ No

completes this task in 10 min or less

❏ Yes   ❏ No

Passing-point total: 16

5. determines the position athlete will play

❏ Yes   ❏ No

explains and demonstrates measurement of chest size at the nipple line (with measuring tape or calipers)

❏ Yes   ❏ No

explains and demonstrates that the neck opening is adequate (no chaffing of the neck or looseness)

❑ Yes ❑ No

explains and demonstrates that the clavicle is covered

❑ Yes ❑ No

explains and demonstrates that the pads are centered on the athlete

❑ Yes ❑ No

explains and demonstrates snugness of the front laces

❑ Yes ❑ No

explains and demonstrates snugness of the side chest straps (Two finger widths can be placed under strap.)

❑ Yes ❑ No

explains and demonstrates that there is padding over the sternoclavicular joint

❑ Yes ❑ No

explains and demonstrates that the acromioclavicular joint is covered by padding (epaulets)

❑ Yes ❑ No

explains and demonstrates that the deltoid is completely covered by padding (The padding extends over the outside edge to the shoulder.)

❑ Yes ❑ No

explains and demonstrates that the shoulder pads do not shift with application of pressure

❑ Yes ❑ No

explains and demonstrates that the scapula is covered

❑ Yes ❑ No

explains and demonstrates that the athlete can raise the arms normally (No pinching about the neck occurs.)

❑ Yes ❑ No

explains and demonstrates that when the arms are raised that the pads still cover the areas of the sternum, clavicle, deltoid, and scapula

❑ Yes ❑ No

explains that the athlete has a normal, not forced, breathing pattern

❑ Yes ❑ No

explains and demonstrates that the athlete has full head and arm ranges of motion with a helmet and jersey

❏ Yes ❏ No

completes this task in 8 min or less

❏ Yes ❏ No

Passing-point total: 12

6. explains and demonstrates the NOCSAE seal

❏ Yes ❏ No

explains and demonstrates the spearing seal on the helmet

❏ Yes ❏ No

explains that the athlete should check the manufacturer's instructions about inspection and the application of waxes, paints, and stickers

❏ Yes ❏ No

explains and demonstrates checking the helmet for cracks and shell imperfections and distortions

❏ Yes ❏ No

explains and demonstrates inspecting all the helmet's hardware (Screws, snaps, and rivets are tightly in place and free of rust.)

❏ Yes ❏ No

explains and demonstrates that all padding is in good shape (without cracks, leaks, or tears)

❏ Yes ❏ No

explains and demonstrates that the face mask is correct for the helmet

❏ Yes ❏ No

explains and demonstrates that the face mask is covered with plastic and is not distorted or broken

❏ Yes ❏ No

explains and demonstrates that the helmet has parts

❏ Yes ❏ No

explains and demonstrates that the chin strap is not cracked or rough

❏ Yes ❏ No

explains and demonstrates inspection of air valves for leakage

❏ Yes ❏ No

explains and demonstrates inspection of the helmet for alterations (e.g., extra padding)

❏ Yes ❏ No

completes this task in 8 min or less

❏ Yes ❏ No

Passing-point total: 9

7. explains and demonstrates check for breathing rate and breathing difficulty

❏ Yes ❏ No

explains and demonstrates checking for pulse and determining pulse rate

❏ Yes ❏ No

asks when the injury occurred

❏ Yes ❏ No

asks how the injury occurred

❏ Yes ❏ No

asks about previous injuries

❏ Yes ❏ No

asks about tinnitus

❏ Yes ❏ No

asks if the athlete was unconscious; if so, for how long

❏ Yes ❏ No

asks the athlete about headache

❏ Yes ❏ No

asks the athlete about dizziness

❏ Yes ❏ No

explains and demonstrates tests of athlete's visual acuity (to reveal blurred vision, loss of peripheral vision, or loss of color vision)

❏ Yes ❏ No

explains and demonstrates inquiry about nausea or vomiting

❏ Yes ❏ No

explains and demonstrates evaluation for memory loss or confusion (e.g., what happened, what is the game score)

❏ Yes ❏ No

explains and demonstrates palpation of the skull (to reveal bleeding, depression, swelling, or discoloration)

❏ Yes ❏ No

explains and demonstrates checking for cerebrospinal fluid from the ear and nose

❏ Yes   ❏ No

explains and demonstrates check of pupil size

❏ Yes   ❏ No

explains and demonstrates checking for nystagmus

❏ Yes   ❏ No

explains the significance of a change in behavior that is out of the athlete's normal pattern

❏ Yes   ❏ No

explains and demonstrates Romberg's orientation (finger-nose test)

❏ Yes   ❏ No

explains and demonstrates Babinski's reflex test

❏ Yes   ❏ No

explains and demonstrates athlete's reaction time

❏ Yes   ❏ No

explains and demonstrates measuring blood pressure

❏ Yes   ❏ No

mentions referral to a physician

❏ Yes   ❏ No

completes this task in 10 min or less

❏ Yes   ❏ No

Passing-point total: 16

8. determines age of athlete

❏ Yes   ❏ No

pinches fat fold between finger and thumb

❏ Yes   ❏ No

explains and demonstrates pulling fat fold away from muscle

❏ Yes   ❏ No

explains and demonstrates having athlete tighten muscle

❏ Yes   ❏ No

applies skin-fold calipers to skin fold

❏ Yes   ❏ No

explains and demonstrates taking measurements at a minimum of three different sites (midtriceps, abdominal, and midaxillary)

❏ Yes ❏ No

explains and demonstrates taking measurements at each site

❏ Yes ❏ No

takes all measurements on the same side of the body

❏ Yes ❏ No

completes this task in 8 min or less

❏ Yes ❏ No

Passing-point total: 6

9. explains that the sleeping surface should be firm

❏ Yes ❏ No

explains that sleeping on the abdomen should be avoided

❏ Yes ❏ No

explains and demonstrates sleeping on one's side

❏ Yes ❏ No

explains and demonstrates sleeping on one's back (using a pillow under the knees)

❏ Yes ❏ No

explains that arms should remain at the side when sleeping

❏ Yes ❏ No

explains and demonstrates keeping knees higher than hips when sitting

❏ Yes ❏ No

explains avoiding soft chairs

❏ Yes ❏ No

explains and demonstrates elimination of the hollow in the back while sitting

❏ Yes ❏ No

explains avoidance of sitting for long periods of time

❏ Yes ❏ No

explains and demonstrates shifting weight while standing

❏ Yes ❏ No

explains and demonstrates standing with a flattened back and knees relaxed

❑ Yes   ❑ No

explains and demonstrates bending the knees when lifting

❑ Yes   ❑ No

explains and demonstrates tightening the buttocks and abdomen when lifting

❑ Yes   ❑ No

explains and demonstrates keeping the head up when lifting

❑ Yes   ❑ No

completes this task in 10 min or less

❑ Yes   ❑ No

Passing-point total: 11

10. mentions position of the athlete as sign of abdominal injury (knees flexed to chest)

❑ Yes   ❑ No

explains and demonstrates placing the athlete in a supine position

❑ Yes   ❑ No

explains and demonstrates palpation of all four quadrants

❑ Yes   ❑ No

asks when the injury happened

❑ Yes   ❑ No

asks how the injury happened

❑ Yes   ❑ No

asks where the pain is located

❑ Yes   ❑ No

asks if there was a previous injury

❑ Yes   ❑ No

explains and demonstrates measuring blood pressure

❑ Yes   ❑ No

mentions signs of shock (anxiety, decreased blood pressure, pale skin tone, etc.)

❑ Yes   ❑ No

mentions nausea or vomiting

❑ Yes   ❑ No

mentions looking for bleeding, distention, or wounds
❑ Yes   ❑ No

mentions referral to a physician
❑ Yes   ❑ No

explains and demonstrates evaluation of Kehr's sign
❑ Yes   ❑ No

explains and demonstrates palpation of pelvis
❑ Yes   ❑ No

mentions significance of rigidity, rebound pain, or pain
❑ Yes   ❑ No

explains and demonstrates auscultation of abdomen (upper left-upper right, lower left-lower right) for bowel sounds
❑ Yes   ❑ No

completes this task in 10 min or less
❑ Yes   ❑ No

Passing-point total: 11

11. checks for unresponsiveness (shakes or shouts)
❑ Yes   ❑ No

calls for help
❑ Yes   ❑ No

opens airway
❑ Yes   ❑ No

listens for breathing (5 s)
❑ Yes   ❑ No

gives two slow, full breaths
❑ Yes   ❑ No

reopens airway
❑ Yes   ❑ No

gives two more slow, full breaths
❑ Yes   ❑ No

tells someone to call EMS (due to airway obstruction)
❑ Yes   ❑ No

gives up to five abdominal thrusts
❑ Yes   ❑ No

uses crossed finger technique to open airway

❏ Yes   ❏ No

finger sweeps (tell candidate an object from the throat is removed from the throat)

❏ Yes   ❏ No

checks for breathing (tell candidate athlete is breathing)

❏ Yes   ❏ No

completes this task in 5 min or less

❏ Yes   ❏ No

Passing-point total: 9

12. asks about pain

❏ Yes   ❏ No

explains and demonstrates evaluation for swelling

❏ Yes   ❏ No

explains and demonstrates ranges of motion (flexion, extension, lateral flexion, and rotation)

❏ Yes   ❏ No

explains and demonstrates passive ranges of motion (flexion, extension, lateral flexion, and rotation)

❏ Yes   ❏ No

explains and demonstrates active range of motion (flexion, extension, lateral flexion, and rotation)

❏ Yes   ❏ No

explains and demonstrates isometric strengthening (flexion, extension, lateral flexion, and rotation)

❏ Yes   ❏ No

explains and demonstrates progressive resistive strengthening (flexion, extension, lateral flexion, and rotation) using helmet weight, manual resistance, rubber tubing, weights, and machines

❏ Yes   ❏ No

explains and demonstrates shoulder shrugs with resistance

❏ Yes   ❏ No

explains and demonstrates full range of motion

❏ Yes   ❏ No

explains and demonstrates bilateral strength at 90%

❏ Yes ❏ No

mentions absence of pain and absence of swelling

❏ Yes ❏ No

mentions that aerobic and anaerobic capacities have been dealt with

❏ Yes ❏ No

mentions a physician's release

❏ Yes ❏ No

completes this task in 10 min or less

❏ Yes ❏ No

Passing-point total: 10

13. asks about pain

❏ Yes ❏ No

explains and demonstrates evaluation for swelling

❏ Yes ❏ No

explains and demonstrates range of motion

❏ Yes ❏ No

explains isometric exercises in all planes (shoulder—internal rotation, external rotation, adduction, abduction, flexion, extension, retraction, and elevation; elbow—flexion and extension)

❏ Yes ❏ No

explains and demonstrates range of motion (wall climbing, Codman's pendulum, shoulder wheel)

❏ Yes ❏ No

explains and demonstrates isotonic exercise with light resistance (shoulder flexion, shoulder extension, shoulder abduction, shoulder adduction, shoulder elevation, internal rotation, and shoulder retraction)

❏ Yes ❏ No

explains and demonstrates progressive resistive exercises (internal rotation, external rotation, shoulder flexion, shoulder extension, shoulder elevation, shoulder adduction, shoulder abduction, and shoulder retraction)

❏ Yes ❏ No

explains and demonstrates proprioceptive neuromuscular facilitation patterns

❏ Yes   ❏ No

explains and demonstrates progressive resistive exercise (empty can and Hughston exercise)

❏ Yes   ❏ No

mentions the need for caution in external rotation and abduction

❏ Yes   ❏ No

explains and demonstrates 90% strength as compared to the other side

❏ Yes   ❏ No

seeks physician clearance for return to competition

❏ Yes   ❏ No

explains absence of pain and swelling and presence of full range of motion

❏ Yes   ❏ No

discusses possible bracing/tape

❏ Yes   ❏ No

explains need to maintain strength

❏ Yes   ❏ No

completes this task in 10 min or less

❏ Yes   ❏ No

Passing-point total: 11

14. positions the athlete in a prone position

    ❏ Yes   ❏ No

    places the foot in a relaxed plantarflexed position

    ❏ Yes   ❏ No

    applies tape adherent

    ❏ Yes   ❏ No

    applies anchor to midcalf and metatarsal arch

    ❏ Yes   ❏ No

    applies at least two strips of tape from metatarsal arch to midcalf

    ❏ Yes   ❏ No

    overlaps longitudinal tape strips

    ❏ Yes   ❏ No

encircles longitudinal tape from distal to proximal

❏ Yes ❏ No

tape is wrinkle free

❏ Yes ❏ No

completes this task in 5 min or less

❏ Yes ❏ No

Passing-point total: 6

15. explains and demonstrates protecting athlete from injury by moving objects out of the way

❏ Yes ❏ No

explains and demonstrates loosening of clothing

❏ Yes ❏ No

explains and demonstrates timing of seizure length

❏ Yes ❏ No

explains and demonstrates checking the mouth for vomitus, saliva, or mucus

❏ Yes ❏ No

explains and demonstrates turning the athlete on the side

❏ Yes ❏ No

explains and demonstrates assessing the airway and breathing

❏ Yes ❏ No

mentions mouth-to-mouth resuscitation if necessary

❏ Yes ❏ No

mentions evaluating the rest of the body for injury

❏ Yes ❏ No

mentions referral to a physician

❏ Yes ❏ No

completes this task in 10 min or less

❏ Yes ❏ No

Passing-point total: 7

16. explains and demonstrates range of motion

❏ Yes ❏ No

explains and demonstrates assessment for swelling
❏ Yes ❏ No

explains and demonstrates measurement for quadriceps for atrophy
❏ Yes ❏ No

explains and demonstrates checking the scar for mobility
❏ Yes ❏ No

explains and demonstrates checking patella mobility
❏ Yes ❏ No

asks the athlete about pain
❏ Yes ❏ No

explains and demonstrates passive range of motion
❏ Yes ❏ No

explains and demonstrates active range of motion with flexion to 20 degrees
❏ Yes ❏ No

explains and demonstrates cocontraction
❏ Yes ❏ No

explains and demonstrates ankle pumps
❏ Yes ❏ No

explains and demonstrates patellar mobilization
❏ Yes ❏ No

explains that terminal extension is avoided in the early stages of rehabilitation
❏ Yes ❏ No

explains and demonstrates straight-leg raises four ways
❏ Yes ❏ No

explains and demonstrates terminal extension exercises (bike, etc.)
❏ Yes ❏ No

explains and demonstrates proprioceptive neuromuscular facilitation patterns
❏ Yes ❏ No

explains and demonstrates hip abductors, hip flexors, and gastrocnemius with a form of resistance
❏ Yes ❏ No

explains and demonstrates progressive resistive exercises with quadriceps (knee extension exercises)

❏ Yes   ❏ No

explains and demonstrates progressive resistive exercises with hamstring (knee flexion exercises)

❏ Yes   ❏ No

explains and demonstrates 90% strength of nonaffected knee

❏ Yes   ❏ No

explains and demonstrates tests of athlete's ability to do sport-specific skills

❏ Yes   ❏ No

explains and demonstrates hamstring to quadriceps ratio of 70% or more (when compared to nonaffected knee)

❏ Yes   ❏ No

explains the absence of pain

❏ Yes   ❏ No

explains and demonstrates the absence of swelling

❏ Yes   ❏ No

mentions medical approval

❏ Yes   ❏ No

Passing-point total: 17

17. asks how the injury happened

    ❏ Yes   ❏ No

    asks when the injury happened

    ❏ Yes   ❏ No

    asks if the knee was previously injured

    ❏ Yes   ❏ No

    asks if there was a pop, snap, crack, slip, or if the knee gave

    ❏ Yes   ❏ No

    asks if the knee has pain

    ❏ Yes   ❏ No

    asks if the foot was planted at the time of injury

    ❏ Yes   ❏ No

explains and demonstrates evaluation of the knee for abnormalities (genu valgum, genu varum, or genu recurvatum)

❑ Yes ❑ No

explains and demonstrates evaluation of knee for swelling, discoloration, and deformity

❑ Yes ❑ No

explains and demonstrates medial aspect (medial joint line, pes anserinus, patellar tendon, medial meniscus, medial collateral ligament)

❑ Yes ❑ No

explains and demonstrates lateral aspect (lateral joint line, head of fibula, lateral collateral ligament, lateral meniscus)

❑ Yes ❑ No

explains and demonstrates anterior aspect (quadriceps, patella, tibial tubercle)

❑ Yes ❑ No

explains and demonstrates posterior aspect (hamstrings, popliteal space)

❑ Yes ❑ No

explains and demonstrates active, active-resistive, and passive flexion

❑ Yes ❑ No

explains and demonstrates active, active-resistive, and passive extension

❑ Yes ❑ No

explains and demonstrates active, active-resistive, and passive adduction

❑ Yes ❑ No

explains and demonstrates active, active-resistive, and passive abduction

❑ Yes ❑ No

explains and demonstrates active, active-resistive, and passive internal rotation

❑ Yes ❑ No

explains and demonstrates active, active-resistive and passive external rotation

❑ Yes ❑ No

explains and demonstrates varus lateral (0 degrees and 30 degrees)
❑ Yes   ❑ No

explains and demonstrates valgus medial (0 degrees and 30 degrees)
❑ Yes   ❑ No

explains and demonstrates test for anterior cruciate injury (drawer test, Lachman's test, crossover test)
❑ Yes   ❑ No

explains and demonstrates tests for meniscus injury (McMurray test, Appleys compression)
❑ Yes   ❑ No

explains and demonstrates tests for patellar injury (apprehension test and patellar compression)
❑ Yes   ❑ No

explains and demonstrates Obers test (iliotibial band tightness)
❑ Yes   ❑ No

explains and demonstrates determining of the Q angle
❑ Yes   ❑ No

explains and demonstrates neurological test of dermatome L3 (anterior aspect of femur)
❑ Yes   ❑ No

explains and demonstrates neurological test of dermatome L4 (medial aspect of knee and tibia)
❑ Yes   ❑ No

explains and demonstrates neurological test of dermatome L5 (lateral aspect of knee and tibia)
❑ Yes   ❑ No

explains and demonstrates neurological test of dermatome S2 (posterior aspect of knee)
❑ Yes   ❑ No

explains and demonstrates neurological test patellar reflex (dermatomes L2, L3, and L4)
❑ Yes   ❑ No

does all tests bilaterally
❑ Yes   ❑ No

mentions referral to a physician
❑ Yes   ❑ No

completes this task in 10 min or less

❏ Yes　❏ No

Passing-point total: 23

18. asks how the injury happened

   ❏ Yes　❏ No

   asks when the injury happened

   ❏ Yes　❏ No

   asks about previous injuries to the back

   ❏ Yes　❏ No

   asks if the athlete heard or felt a pop, snap, crack, slip, or give

   ❏ Yes　❏ No

   asks if the athlete has pain in the back

   ❏ Yes　❏ No

   explains and demonstrates the evaluation of discoloration, deformity, or swelling

   ❏ Yes　❏ No

   explains and demonstrates hip alignment (anterior and posterior superior iliac spines)

   ❏ Yes　❏ No

   explains and demonstrates observation of back abnormalities (flat back, scoliosis, lordosis)

   ❏ Yes　❏ No

   explains and demonstrates palpation of spine and spinal muscles

   ❏ Yes　❏ No

   explains and demonstrates active, active-resistive, and passive flexion

   ❏ Yes　❏ No

   explains and demonstrates active, active-resistive, and passive extension

   ❏ Yes　❏ No

   explains and demonstrates active, active-resistive, and passive lateral flexion

   ❏ Yes　❏ No

explains and demonstrates active, active-resistive, and passive rotation

❏ Yes ❏ No

explains and demonstrates sciatic nerve pain (straight-leg raising test, bowstring test, Lasègue's sign)

❏ Yes ❏ No

explains and demonstrates sacroiliac joint problem (pelvic rock, Gaenslen's sign, Fabere test)

❏ Yes ❏ No

explains and demonstrates measurement of leg length

❏ Yes ❏ No

explains and demonstrates Babinski's reflex

❏ Yes ❏ No

explains and demonstrates neurological test of dermatome L1 (upper anterior thigh)

❏ Yes ❏ No

explains and demonstrates neurological test of dermatome L2 (middle anterior thigh)

❏ Yes ❏ No

explains and demonstrates neurological test of dermatome L3 (lower anterior thigh)

❏ Yes ❏ No

explains and demonstrates neurological test of dermatome L4 (medial leg and foot and patellar reflex)

❏ Yes ❏ No

explains and demonstrates neurological test of dermatome L5 (anterior foot)

❏ Yes ❏ No

explains and demonstrates neurological test of dermatome S1 (lateral foot and leg Achilles reflex)

❏ Yes ❏ No

explains and demonstrates all test bilaterally

❏ Yes ❏ No

mentions referral to a physician

❏ Yes ❏ No

completes this task in 10 min or less

❏ Yes   ❏ No

Passing-point total: 18

19. asks how the injury happened

    ❏ Yes   ❏ No

    asks when the injury happened

    ❏ Yes   ❏ No

    asks the athlete about a previous injury

    ❏ Yes   ❏ No

    asks the athlete about a pop, snap, crack, slip, or give

    ❏ Yes   ❏ No

    asks about pain in the wrist or hand

    ❏ Yes   ❏ No

    explains and demonstrates evaluation for swelling, discoloration, and deformity

    ❏ Yes   ❏ No

    explains and demonstrates palpation of bony area of the forearm (radial styloid process, ulnar styloid process, radius, and ulna)

    ❏ Yes   ❏ No

    explains and demonstrates palpation of bony area of wrist (navicular [anatomical snuffbox] trapezium, capitate, lunate triquetrum, pisiform, hamate)

    ❏ Yes   ❏ No

    explains and demonstrates palpation of soft tissues of the palmar surface

    ❏ Yes   ❏ No

    explains and demonstrates palpation of soft tissues of the dorsal surface

    ❏ Yes   ❏ No

    explains and demonstrates active, active-resistive, and passive wrist flexion

    ❏ Yes   ❏ No

    explains and demonstrates active, active-resistive, and passive wrist extension

    ❏ Yes   ❏ No

explains and demonstrates active, active-resistive, and passive supination

❏ Yes   ❏ No

explains and demonstrates active, active-resistive, and passive pronation

❏ Yes   ❏ No

explains and demonstrates active, active-resistive, and passive radial deviation

❏ Yes   ❏ No

explains and demonstrates active, active-resistive, and passive ulnar deviation

❏ Yes   ❏ No

explains and demonstrates carpal tunnel testing (Tinel's sign, Phalen's test)

❏ Yes   ❏ No

explains and demonstrates checking radial and ulnar pulse

❏ Yes   ❏ No

explains and demonstrates Allen test (testing for arterial supply to fingers)

❏ Yes   ❏ No

explains and demonstrates neurological test of dermatome C6 (radial nerve—thumb side of hand, dorsal side through the third phalange)

❏ Yes   ❏ No

explains and demonstrates neurological test of dermatome C7 (median nerve—palmar–thumb aspect of hand)

❏ Yes   ❏ No

explains and demonstrates neurological test of dermatome C8 (ulnar nerve—lateral aspect of hand, palmar and dorsal at third phalange)

❏ Yes   ❏ No

explains and demonstrates neurological test of dermatome T1 (medial aspect of elbow)

❏ Yes   ❏ No

explains and demonstrates all tests bilaterally

❏ Yes   ❏ No

mentions referral to physician

❏ Yes   ❏ No

completes this task in 10 min or less

❏ Yes   ❏ No

Passing-point total: 17

20.   applies tape adherent

❏ Yes   ❏ No

applies two anchors

❏ Yes   ❏ No

elbow is flexed at least 30 degrees

❏ Yes   ❏ No

tape is applied from midforearm to midbiceps (at least three strips are applied)

❏ Yes   ❏ No

tape is wrinkle free

❏ Yes   ❏ No

tape prevents full extension

❏ Yes   ❏ No

tape allows normal circulation to fingertips

❏ Yes   ❏ No

completes this task in 5 min or less

❏ Yes   ❏ No

Passing-point total: 6

21.   explains that electrical energy is converted by a crystal into vibration

❏ Yes   ❏ No

explains that the vibration has a thermal effect on tissues

❏ Yes   ❏ No

explains reduction of muscle spasm

❏ Yes   ❏ No

explains reduction of pain

❏ Yes   ❏ No

explains increase in blood flow

❏ Yes   ❏ No

explains increase in metabolism at the site

❏ Yes   ❏ No

explains indication for subacute and chronic conditions (e.g., bursitis, fibromyalgia, and myositis)

❏ Yes   ❏ No

explains contraindication of any acute condition

❏ Yes   ❏ No

explains contraindication of sensitive areas (e.g., heart, brain, spinal cord, and metal implants)

❏ Yes   ❏ No

explains and demonstrates application of gel

❏ Yes   ❏ No

explains and demonstrates overlapping motion of ultrasound head

❏ Yes   ❏ No

explains and demonstrates that the ultrasound head must remain in contact with the body part

❏ Yes   ❏ No

completes this task in 10 min or less

❏ Yes   ❏ No

Passing-point total: 9

22. (*Note*: The examiner is to indicate no need for a tourniquet if the applicant attempts to apply one.)

explains and demonstrates use of latex gloves for protection

❏ Yes   ❏ No

explains and demonstrates application of sterile gauze

❏ Yes   ❏ No

explains and demonstrates direct pressure

❏ Yes   ❏ No

explains and demonstrates elevation

❏ Yes   ❏ No

explains and demonstrates use of brachial pressure point

❏ Yes   ❏ No

explains and demonstrates application of a pressure bandage

❏ Yes   ❏ No

explains and demonstrates glove removal without touching the outsides of the gloves

❏ Yes   ❏ No

explains and demonstrates that soiled items are placed in a blood-borne-pathogen-safe container

❏ Yes   ❏ No

mentions referral to a physician

❏ Yes   ❏ No

completes this task in 8 min or less

❏ Yes   ❏ No

Passing-point total: 7

23. explains and demonstrates application of splints from fingertips to above the elbow

    ❏ Yes   ❏ No

    explains and demonstrates placement of gauze roll under the palm

    ❏ Yes   ❏ No

    explains and demonstrates checking the pulse before and after splint application

    ❏ Yes   ❏ No

    explains and demonstrates application of three strips of cloth to hold the splint in place (but not over the fracture site)

    ❏ Yes   ❏ No

    explains and demonstrates checking the fingertips

    ❏ Yes   ❏ No

    explains and demonstrates application of a sling

    ❏ Yes   ❏ No

    mentions referral to a physician

    ❏ Yes   ❏ No

    completes the task in 10 min or less

    ❏ Yes   ❏ No

    Passing-point total: 6

24. explains and demonstrates placing bolster under the athlete's lower legs

    ❏ Yes   ❏ No

    explains and demonstrates draping of the athlete

    ❏ Yes   ❏ No

explains and demonstrates telling the athlete to relax

❏ Yes   ❏ No

explains and demonstrates application of massage oil

❏ Yes   ❏ No

explains and demonstrates long stroking (effleurage)

❏ Yes   ❏ No

explains and demonstrates kneading (petrissage)

❏ Yes   ❏ No

explains and demonstrates friction

❏ Yes   ❏ No

explains and demonstrates tapotement (e.g., pinching, hacking, and cupping)

❏ Yes   ❏ No

completes this task in 10 min or less

❏ Yes   ❏ No

Passing-point total: 6

Passing-point total for all Oral/Practical questions: 262

C
APPENDIX

Answers to the Written Simulation Study Questions

When taking the written simulation, you will mark your answer or answers with a highlight pen, and you will receive immediate feedback on whether your response is correct or not. What follows is a list of the responses for each situation that appears in chapter 8. However, the highlighted response appears here in parentheses.

To fully benefit from this section, have a partner read aloud the feedback that would be highlighted as you select your responses from those provided. After each section there are notes to assist you in determining what you know and what are the priorities at this point in the question. Your partner can go over the "What you know" and "Priorities" once you have completed a question. These are for your benefit only. They do not appear on the actual certification examination.

Each response you select has a point total after it. You are attempting to select as many positive responses as you can. Some questions are weighted, either positively or negatively. In some instances an answer has a zero point total. This means the response is neither helpful nor harmful in this situation.

After each question is a passing-point total. To determine if you passed this question, have your partner add up all your points. Remember to subtract any negative points. Compare your total against the passing-point total. If your score is higher or equal, you passed. Otherwise you have some work to do. The passing-point total is 70% of total points possible.

■ Problem 1

A. 1. Apply ice to the head. (*inappropriate*) −1
   2. Return the athlete to competition. (*inappropriate*) −1

3. Write a note to excuse her from school tomorrow. (*inappropriate*) −1

4. Return the athlete to competition, but using a soccer helmet. (*inappropriate*) −1

5. Rest the athlete and periodically recheck blood pressure and level of consciousness. (*All vitals are in normal range, but athlete reports a headache.*) +4

Examiner (*Do not read to candidate.*)

What you know—A 14-year-old by implied consent allows you to treat. The athlete has a first-degree concussion caused by direct impact, with no deformities and no cervical spine injuries.

Priorities—a more in-depth evaluation or assessment

B.   6. Call an ambulance. (*It will arrive in 1/2 hour.*) +1

7. Continue to ice the area. (*inappropriate at this time*) −1

8. Monitor the athlete's airway, breathing, and circulation. (*Pulse is rapid.*) +1

9. Note the athlete's skin color. (*Athlete appears pale.*) +1

10. Monitor blood pressure. (*Pressure is dropping to 90/60.*) +1

11. Elevate the athlete's feet. (*Athlete dies. Go to the next problem.*) −14

12. Cover the athlete with a blanket. (*OK*) +1

13. Take the athlete's temperature. (*inappropriate*) −1

14. Check the athlete's pupils. (*normal response*) +1

15. Elevate the athlete's head. (*inappropriate*) −1

16. Turn the athlete on her side. (*inappropriate*) −1

17. Give the athlete aspirin. (*inappropriate*) −3

Examiner (*Do not read to candidate.*)

What you know—The athlete is having memory recall and recognition problems, and the head injury is progressively worsening.

Priorities—Get the athlete to medical attention as soon as possible in a safe manner, while not foregoing care of the athlete.

C.   18. Try to convince the athlete and her parents to wait for an ambulance. (*They are insistent.*) 0

19. Take a long time to reassess the athlete. (*inappropriate*) −1

20. Ignore the parents. (*They become enraged.*) −1

21. Have the parents sign a waiver. (*The parents refuse to sign anything.*) +2

22. Keep assessing the athlete's vital signs. (*The signs are worsening.*) +1

23. Release the athlete into the parents' care. (*appropriate*) 0

24. Have a witness to the situation. (*appropriate*) +2

25. Write an accident report. (*appropriate*) +2

Examiner (*Do not read to candidate.*)

What you know—The parents are taking a seriously injured athlete out of your care. The potential exists for serious injury or death of this student.
Priorities—Protect yourself from liability.

Passing-point total: 12
End of Problem 1

■ Problem 2

A. 1. Tape the knee and return the athlete to practice. (*inappropriate*) –1
2. Have the athlete walk around on the knee. (*inappropriate, athlete collapses*) –1
3. Have the athlete do a deep knee bend. (*inappropriate*) –1
4. Apply ice to the right knee. (*good choice*) +1
5. Apply a wet compression wrap to the right knee. (*appropriate*) +1
6. Have the athlete cold whirlpool the knee. (*There are better ways.*) 0
7. Have the athlete hop on one leg. (*inappropriate*) –1
8. Have the athlete lift weights. (*inappropriate*) –1

Examiner (*Do not read to candidate.*)
What you know—Evaluation reveals a lateral meniscus injury.
Priorities—Treat the lateral meniscus injury.

B. 9. Take a girth measurement of the thigh. (*Measurements are slightly enlarged.*) +1
10. Apply a dry compression wrap. (*The support helps.*) +2
11. Apply a knee immobilizer. (*The athlete feels better.*) +1
12. Call an ambulance. (*inappropriate*) –1
13. Write a note excusing the athlete from physical education class tomorrow. (*inappropriate*) –1
14. Secure, measure, and instruct the athlete in the use of crutches. (*helpful*) +2
15. Instruct the athlete to continue use of ice. (*helpful*) +1
16. Instruct the athlete to keep knee elevated. (*helpful*) +1
17. Instruct the athlete to massage the injured leg. (*inappropriate*) –2

Examiner (*Do not read to candidate.*)
What you know—Swelling is apparent about the lateral aspect of knee joint, and the athlete cannot weight bear.
Priorities—Control the swelling, and allow for ambulation of the athlete.

C. 18. Instruct the athlete to use ice treatments. (*This helps the athlete.*) +1
19. Instruct the athlete to use a warm whirlpool. (*Try again.*) –2
20. Instruct the athlete to use an analgesic balm. (*Try again.*) –1
21. Instruct the athlete in straight-leg raises. (*good*) +2
22. Instruct the athlete in cocontractions of thigh musculature. (*good*) +1

23. Call the physician and tell her she has made the wrong diagnosis. (*inappropriate*) −2

Examiner (*Do not read to candidate.*)
What you know—The physician diagnosis is a patellar subluxation, and athlete is to use crutches.
Priorities—control of swelling and strengthening as tolerated

Passing-point total: 10
End of Problem 2

■ Problem 3

A. 1. stretching before and after activity (*good choice*) +1
2. weight training to improve power (*inappropriate at this time*) −1
3. rest—no workout or activity (*inappropriate at this time*) −1
4. Build up long-distance running. (*good answer*) +1
5. weight training to improve strength (*yes*) +1
6. soccer practice (*inappropriate*) −1
7. interval training (*It is a good time.*) +1
8. limited ball-handling drills (*OK, but not too much.*) 0
9. Begin the athlete on anabolic steroids. (*inappropriate*) −1
10. Determine the target heart rate. (*appropriate*) 0
11. recreational soccer or other activity (*OK*) 0
12. flexibility program (*appropriate*) +1

Examiner (*Do not read to candidate.*)
What you know—Soccer is an endurance sport with components of anaerobic and aerobic fitness, and an off-season program is needed.
Priorities—Strengthening, endurance, and interval training are important at this point.

B. 13. intense development of skills (*Athlete becomes too tired and quits the team.*) −1
14. scrimmages of soccer (*Your athlete is injured and is out for a year.*) −1
15. upper and lower body weight training 3 days per week (*OK*) +1
16. regular games (*The NCAA fines your school for out-of-season games.*) 0
17. stretching before and after activity (*good*) +1
18. weight training to improve power (*yes*) +1
19. increasing dietary intake (*The athlete is now overweight.*) −1
20. Determine the target heart rate. (*It is now too late.*) 0
21. Begin heat acclimatization. (*yes*) +2
22. a maintenance program (*inappropriate at this time*) −1
23. rest—no workouts (*inappropriate at this time*) −1
24. a flexibility program (*appropriate*) +1

Examiner (*Do not read to candidate.*)
What you know—A soccer team needs a preseason conditioning program.
Priorities—preseason conditioning, tapering of strength, recognizing the need for power, maintaining gains from off-season program

C.
25. running intensity at high level twice per week (*appropriate*) +1
26. regular games (*of course*) 0
27. weight training to improve power, 3 days per week (*inappropriate at this time*) −1
28. weight training to improve strength, 3 days per week (*inappropriate at this time*) −1
29. maintenance program (*appropriate*) +1
30. intense skill drills (*appropriate*) +1
31. flexibility program (*appropriate*) +1
32. Begin amphetamine usage. (*inappropriate*) −1

Examiner (*Do not read to candidate.*)
What you know—The soccer team is now in season.
Priorities—maintaining endurance and specific sport skills

Passing point total: 11
End of Problem 3

■ Problem 4

A.
1. Give the athlete a high-protein diet to follow. (*inappropriate*) −1
2. Determine the athlete's activity level. (*appropriate*) +1
3. Recommend the use of massage to reduce weight. (*No weight loss occurs.*) 0
4. Restrict water intake to two glasses daily. (*The athlete feels poorly.*) −2
5. Determine percent body fat. (*The athlete has 32 percent body fat.*) +2
6. Recommend liposuction. (*inappropriate*) −1
7. Send the athlete to a physician for a physical. (*The physician gives permission for a diet plan.*) +2
8. Recommend the athlete eat slowly. (*inappropriate*) 0
9. Determine the athlete's dietary intake. (*It is 2,000 cal per day.*) +2
10. Recommend the athlete avoid situations where food is involved. (*helpful*) 0
11. Check athlete's height and weight. (*She is 5 ft, 9 in. and 175 lb*) +1
12. Recommend multiple vitamins. (*not necessary*) 0

Examiner (*Do not read to candidate.*)
What you know—A 17-year-old female athlete desires to lose 30 lb.
Priorities—Determine if there is a need for the athlete to lose weight.

B.
13. Recommend fasting 1 day per week. (*inappropriate*) −2
14. Have the athlete decrease caloric intake by 500 cal per day.(*The athlete loses one lb per week.*) +2

15. Have the athlete increase energy output by 500 cal per day. (*Good choice—the athlete loses 1 lb per week.*) +2
16. Recommend diet pills. (*The athlete is tired and cannot sleep.*) −1
17. Send the athlete to a physician for stomach stapling. (*The physician is outraged by your recommendation.*) 0
18. Recommend a liquid diet. (*The athlete becomes constipated.*) −1
19. Recommend only bland foods. (*The athlete does not adhere to the diet plan.*) 0
20. Encourage the athlete to lose 5 lb per week. (*inappropriate*) −1
21. Encourage the athlete to avoid television. (*not a chance*) 0
22. Recommend the use of saunas to reduce weight. (*inappropriate*) −1
23. Recommend the use of rubberized clothing to reduce weight. (*Athlete collapses, is rushed to hospital, and dies. Go to the next problem.*) −14
24. Recommend the athlete increase caffeine intake. (*The athlete cannot sleep and is agitated.*) −1
25. Have the athlete reduce calorie intake by 2,000 cal per day. (*The athlete dies. Go to the next problem.*) −14
26. Give the athlete a list of high-nutrient, dense foods. (*excellent*) +1
27. Recommend a single-food diet plan. (*The athlete does not follow the plan for long.*) 0
28. Recommend an alternative activity to eating. (*appropriate*) 0
29. Give the athlete a well-balanced diet plan to follow. (*excellent*) +1

Examiner (*Do not read to candidate.*)
What you know—The athlete is 30 lb overweight.
Priorities—Recommend a controlled way to lose weight.

C. 30. Determine current body weight. (*Weight is 130 lb.*) +1
31. Determine activity level. (*She exercises three hr a day.*) +1
32. Determine the athlete's dietary intake. (*appropriate*) +1
33. Ask about the athlete's menstrual period. (*She indicates she has missed her last three.*) +1
34. Ask about the athlete's use of laxatives or vomiting. (*The athlete does not use these.*) 0
35. Recommend a well-balanced diet plan. (*She refuses to eat it.*) 0
36. Recommend an increased activity plan. (*The athlete dies. Go to the next problem.*) −15
37. Recommend a particular laxative. (*inappropriate*) −3
38. Refer the athlete to a physician. (*The physician refers her to a psychiatrist.*) +1
39. Speak to the athlete's friends about her eating habits. (*They indicate she eats only small amounts.*) 0
40. Recommend a particular brand of diuretic. (*inappropriate*) −2
41. Ask the athlete about her perception of her body. (*She indicates she thinks she is "too fat."*) +1

42. Recommend a liquid diet. (*inappropriate*) −1
43. Refer the athlete to a psychiatrist. (*It is determined she is anorexic.*) +2
44. Recommend a high-calorie diet. (*The athlete refuses to eat it.*) 0
45. Inquire about the athlete's having constipation or diarrhea. (*She indicates no problems.*) +1
46. Tell the athlete she is bulimic. (*The athlete laughs and asks you if you are a doctor.*) 0
47. Ask about the athlete's dental problems. (*Her gums are bleeding more often.*) +1
48. Assess the athlete's hair and skin. (*Skin is dry and hair is brittle.*) +1
49. Indicate to the athlete that she is at appropriate body weight. (*The athlete leaves disgruntled and later dies of a cardiac arrest. Go to the next problem.*) −15
50. Evaluate the athlete for swollen glands about the neck. (*none*) 0
51. Give the athlete a high-fat, high-carbohydrate diet. (*inappropriate*) −1
52. Recommend a diet that is high in grains, fiber, and protein. (*The athlete refuses to eat it.*) −1
53. Say that you believe the athlete is a diabetic. (*incorrect*) −1
54. Say that the athlete is anorexic. (*The athlete asks to see your medical license.*) 0
55. Ask if the athlete has food binges. (*She does not.*) 0
56. Ask the athlete about fluctuations in weight. (*No fluctuations—she is just too fat.*) 0
57. Assess the athlete's mood. (*She indicates she is upset by being overweight.*) 0
58. Check the athlete's blood pressure. (*It is lower than at her physical last year.*) +1
59. Check the athlete's heart rate. (*It is lower than at her physical last year.*) +1
60. Inquire about the athlete's heart rate. (*The athlete indicates her heart beats very fast sometimes.*) +1
61. Have the athlete take calcium supplements. (*not helpful*) 0

Examiner (*Do not read to candidate.*)
What you know—The athlete has lost 15 lb more than was initially recommended by a physician, and her body fat is 19%.
Priorities—What is the current state of the athlete's health?

D. 62. anorexic (*correct*) +1
   63. bulimic (*incorrect*) −1
   64. diabetic (*incorrect*) −1
   65. a patient with an ulcer (*incorrect*) −1
   66. a patient with appropriate weight loss (*incorrect*) −1

67. a substance abuser (*incorrect*) –1
68. hypoglycemic (*incorrect*) –1

Examiner (*Do not read to candidate.*)
What you know—loss of weight and low body fat content
Priorities—assessment of illness

Passing-point total: 21
End of Problem 4

■ Problem 5

A. 1. Do a primary survey. (*The athlete is conscious, has a pulse, and is breathing without difficulty, but has pain when breathing.*) +2
2. Remove the athlete from the field. (*inappropriate at this time*) 0
3. Check the athlete for bleeding. (*no bleeding*) +1
4. Tell the coaches to check that all players are wearing mouth guards. (*inappropriate*) –1
5. Determine the athlete's level of consciousness. (*The athlete is conscious.*) +1
6. Determine if a goal was scored on the play. (*inappropriate*) –1
7. Ask the athlete what happened. (*The athlete indicates her torso contacted the goalpost.*) +1
8. Ask the athlete if there is pain. (*Ribs are painful, especially when breathing.*) +1
9. Determine the score of the game. (*inappropriate*) 0
10. Note the athlete's position as you approach. (*The athlete is sitting up.*) +1
11. Ask athlete if she felt or heard a snap. (*She indicates she did not.*) +1
12. Determine who pushed the athlete into the goalpost. (*inappropriate*) 0
13. Get rib protectors. (*OK*) +1
14. Determine if there was a penalty assessed on the play. (*inappropriate*) –1
15. Have a stretcher brought onto the field. (*not appropriate at this time*) –1
16. Do a secondary survey of the athlete bilaterally. (*The athlete indicates the left acromioclavicular joint is painful and crepitus is heard over the left eighth rib.*) +2
17. Have a student athletic trainer call for an ambulance. (*not necessary at this time*) 0
18. Have the athlete touch toes. (*inappropriate*) –1
19. Ask the athlete if breathing is painful on inhalation. (*She says it is.*) +1
20. Ask the athlete if breathing is painful on exhalation. (*She says it is.*) +1

21. Auscultate the chest for breath sounds. (*Both sides are equal.*) +1
22. Ask the athlete to lay down. (*not necessary*) 0
23. Apply ice bags. (*inappropriate at this time*) 0
24. Determine the athlete's blood pressure. (*136/82*) +1
25. Determine the athlete's breathing rate. (*24 breaths per min*) +1
26. Have the athlete do a couple sit-ups. (*inappropriate*) −1

Examiner (*Do not read to candidate.*)
What you know—A 15-year-old has been injured by a direct impact with a goalpost.
Priorities—Determine any immediately life-threatening injuries; determine seriousness of non-life-threatening injuries if there are no life-threatening injuries.

B. 27. Actively test range of motion in all directions. (*The injury prevents movement.*) 0
28. Monitor breathing. (*Breathing is painful, but normal.*) +1
29. Call an ambulance. (*Parents calm down.*) +1
30. Apply ice to the injured area. (*OK*) +1
31. Have the parents get away from the athlete. (*The parents are outraged.*) −1
32. Indicate that the athlete will require long-term immobilization. (*inappropriate*) 0
33. Strap the athlete's arm across the chest. (*slightly painful to the rib*) 0
34. Record the athlete's vital signs for ambulance personnel. (*136/ 82, breathing rate is 24 per min*) +1
35. Apply compression to the athlete's ribs. (*The athlete is in pain and can hardly breathe.*) −2
36. Apply a sling to the athlete's left arm. (*appropriate*) +1
37. Ask the athlete's parents what insurance they have. (*inappropriate*) −1
38. Tell the coach that the athlete is out for a couple games. (*inappropriate*) 0
39. Apply rib protectors and allow the athlete to return to the game. (*inappropriate*) −3

Examiner (*Do not read to candidate.*)
What you know—The athlete can walk, and her parents have requested an ambulance.
Priorities—Treat the athlete for injuries and call for an ambulance as requested by her parents.

C. 40. Measure the circumference of the athlete's chest with full inflation. (*inappropriate*) 0
41. Indicate the goals for the athlete's full recovery. (*The athlete is motivated to get going.*) +1

42. Begin the athlete on a stationary-bike exercise program. (*Great!*) +1
43. Have the athlete continue to use ice. (*She is more comfortable.*) +1
44. Have the athlete lift lower-body weights. (*Athlete's legs gain strength.*) +1
45. Begin Codman pendulum exercises. (*The athlete indicates these are too painful.*) −1
46. Begin isometrics. (*OK*) +1
47. Fit the athlete for rib protectors. (*inappropriate at this time*) 0
48. Have the athlete begin a forearm exercise program. (*good*) +1
49. Begin a flexibility program for the left shoulder. (*More swelling occurs.*) −1
50. Begin proprioceptive neuromuscular facilitation. (*The team physician is upset.*) −1
51. Recommend heat therapy. (*Swelling increases dramatically.*) −2

Examiner (*Do not read to candidate.*)
What you know—The athlete has a fracture of the eighth rib that requires no treatment and a shoulder separation that must be kept immobilized for 2 weeks.
Priorities—Keep the athlete as fit as possible.

D. 52. Check the athlete for brachial plexus response. (*inappropriate*) 0
53. Continue ice treatments after therapy. (*OK*) +1
54. Check the athlete's instability. (*The athlete has no instability.*) +1
55. Have the athlete do Codman's pendulum exercises. (*The athlete gains full range of motion.*) +1
56. Have the athlete begin a running program. (*She is tired, but happy to be running.*) +1
57. Allow the athlete to begin ball-handling drills. (*The team physician is upset.*) −1
58. Tell the field hockey coach when the athlete can return to play. (*3 to 6 weeks*) 0
59. Apply ultrasound for pain. (*not helpful*) 0
60. Have the athlete begin a progressive resistive-exercise program. (*OK*) +1
61. Have the athlete begin an upper-body exercise program. (*OK*) +1
62. Keep the athlete in a sling. (*inappropriate*) −1
63. Fit the athlete in a shoulder harness. (*inappropriate*) −1
64. Begin proprioceptive neuromuscular facilitation techniques. (*OK*) +1

Examiner (*Do not read to candidate.*)
What you know—You have permission to begin rehabilitation of the shoulder, the athlete is two weeks postinjury, and she plays field hockey.
Priorities—Check the condition of the shoulder and begin initial rehabilitation for range of motion and strengthening.

Passing-point total: 24
End of Problem 5

■ Problem 6

A. 1. Cover the injured eye and refer the athlete to a physician. (*The athlete indicates photophobia.*) +1
2. Have the athlete rub the eye. (*The eye becomes more irritated.*) −1
3. Flush the eye with water. (*The dirt moves to the lateral corner of the eye and out.*) +1
4. Use a handkerchief to wipe the dirt out. (*The dirt does not move.*) 0
5. Use a toothpick to get the dirt out. (*The athlete scratches his eye.*) −1
6. Test the eye with a fluorescein sodium stain. (*The AMA files a lawsuit against you for practicing medicine.*) −1
7. Apply antibiotic ointment to eye. (*inappropriate*) −1
8. Have the athlete blink. (*The eye waters and becomes irritated.*) −1
9. Check pupillary reflex with a penlight. (*inappropriate*) 0
10. Fold the eyelid back. (*Nothing is found under the eyelid.*) +1
11. Apply eye drops. (*not helpful*) 0
12. Apply a topical anesthetic. (*inappropriate*) −1
13. Check the eye with funduscope. (*inappropriate*) −1
14. Ask the athlete what happened. (*The athlete slid into second base and dirt flew in his eye.*) 0
15. Apply ice to the eye. (*not helpful*) −1

Examiner (*Do not read to candidate.*)
What you know—The athlete has dirt in the eye resulting from a headfirst slide, and the eye is watering.
Priorities—removal of dirt, if possible without harm to the eye, or referral to physician

B. 16. Reassure the parent that eye injuries are rare. (*The parent is outraged.*) −1
17. Recommend that the athlete wear a batting helmet with a face mask. (*not helpful*) 0
18. Have the athlete wear polycarbonate 39 goggles. (*good*) +1
19. Ask the athlete to close his eyes when sliding. (*The athlete forgets and gets dirt in his eye again.*) 0
20. Say nothing to the athlete. (*The parent finds out and is very upset.*) −1
21. Put a restriction on headfirst sliding. (*inappropriate*) 0
22. Have the athlete wear sunglasses. (*The glasses shatter into the eye.*) −1
23. Have the athlete wear a baseball hat. (*The hat flies off during running.*) 0

Examiner (*Do not read to candidate.*)

What you know—The athlete's eye is unharmed, but the parent is concerned about a reoccurrence.
Priorities—prevention of reoccurrence

Passing-point total: 3
End of Problem 6

■ Problem 7

A. 1. Put on goggles and a face mask. (*overly cautious*) 0
    2. Ask how long the athlete has had the rash. (*two days*) +1
    3. Touch the rash. (*not a good idea*) −1
    4. Put on rubber gloves. (*appropriate*) +1
    5. Ask if athlete knows where he got it. (*He says from another wrestler about 10 days ago.*) +1
    6. Contact the coach and determine how often mats are cleaned. (*not important at the time*) 0
    7. Take athlete's temperature. (*It is 102 °F*) +1
    8. Wash your hands. (*appropriate*) +1
    9. Disinfect the area where you evaluated the athlete. (*appropriate*) +1
    10. Determine the athlete's age. (*inappropriate*) 0

Examiner (*Do not read to candidate.*)
What you know—A high-school wrestler has a red blotchy rash all over his body.
Priorities—Decrease the chance of spreading the rash, determine the effect of the rash on the wrestler, and determine the origin of the rash.

B. 11. Cover the rash. (*The rash spreads.*) 0
    12. Return the athlete to practice. (*Every athlete on the team and in classes gets the rash.*) −3
    13. Refer the athlete to a physician. (*The physician indicates that the athlete has measles.*) +2
    14. Send the athlete home. (*Yes!*) +1
    15. Disinfect the entire training room. (*inappropriate*) 0

Examiner (*Do not read to candidate.*)
What you know—The athlete has a rash and is in need of treatment.
Priorities—Prevent the spread of the rash to others.

C. 16. No further action is necessary. (*60% of the school gets measles.*) −5
    17. Have someone disinfect the athlete's locker. (*not necessary*) 0
    18. Determine all meets the athlete attended. (*There were three.*) +1
    19. Determine all wrestlers the athlete competed against. (*There were eight.*) +1
    20. Send all wrestlers home. (*inappropriate at this time*) 0

21. Have the mats disinfected with bleach. (*This kills all organisms on the mats.*) +1
22. Check all the athletes' immunization records. (*a long process, but worthwhile*) +1
23. Report the case to the county health department's communicable disease office. (*It is gathering information on the spread of this disease.*) +1
24. Give the school 10 days off. (*The students jump for joy, but the parents are ready to strangle you!*) −1
25. Contact all schools the wrestling team competed against. (*appropriate*) +1
26. Contact the school's medical staff. (*They will watch for new cases.*) +1
27. Issue an educational sheet on measles. (*appropriate*) +1
28. Send home only those students who show similar signs. (*There are none.*) +1
29. Send home and exclude from school all unimmunized students. (*Until they bring immunization proof, they are to stay out.*) +1
30. Have the entire school disinfected. (*not necessary*) −1
31. Contact the local newspaper. (*The story is blown out of proportion.*) −1
32. Remind all students to cover their mouths. (*It is now too late.*) 0
33. Set up an immunization clinic. (*It is now too late.*) 0
34. Make sure athletes use cups rather than water bottles. (*It is now too late.*) 0

Examiner (*Do not read to candidate.*)
What you know—The rash is communicable.
Priorities—Prevent others from getting the rash, and identify those who have been exposed.

D. 35. Say he can return when the school nurse gives him the OK. (*inappropriate*) −1
   36. Say he can return when he is immunized. (*It is now too late.*) 0
   37. Say he can return as soon as the coach needs him. (*inappropriate*) −1
   38. Say he can return when a physician gives approval. (*excellent*) +1

Examiner (*Do not read to candidate.*)
What you know—The athlete is feeling better and would like to return to school.
Priorities—To ensure the safety of all students involved and to ensure that returning this athlete will not spread the rash.

Passing-point total: 14
End of Problem 7

■ Problem 8

A. 1. Call the athletes' parents. (*Inappropriate—uncover answer 10.*) −6
2. Remove the athlete's helmet. (*Inappropriate—uncover answer 10.*) −6
3. Determine if the athlete is conscious. (*He is unconscious.*) +1
4. Ask if anyone knows what happened. (*The athlete was hit in the chest making a tackle.*) +1
5. Carry the athlete off the field. (*Inappropriate—uncover answer 10.*) −6
6. Determine if the athlete is breathing. (*He is not breathing.*) +2
7. Roll the athlete supine while controlling the head and neck. (*OK*) +1
8. Determine if the athlete has a heartbeat. (*The athlete has no heartbeat.*) +2
9. Auscultate the athlete's chest. (*Inappropriate—uncover answer 10.*) −6
10. (*Correct responses for this section are 6, 7, and 8. Please highlight those now, then move to Section B*).

Examiner (*Do not read to candidate.*)
What you know—A defensive back is lying motionless on the field.
Priorities—Determine any immediately life-threatening injuries; determine seriousness of non-life-threatening injuries if there are no life-threatening injuries.

B. 11. Send a student athletic trainer to direct the ambulance. (*Good, this saves valuable time.*) +1
12. Have the procedure videotaped. (*helpful if a lawsuit ensues*) 0
13. Open the athlete's airway with a head tilt. (*The athlete is paralyzed.*) −1
14. Have a student athletic trainer call the ambulance. (*OK*) +1
15. Remove the athlete's face mask. (*Yes!*) +2
16. Begin CPR. (*excellent*) +3
17. Remove the athlete's well-fitted helmet. (*The athlete dies because of the delay in treatment. Go to Section C.*) −10
18. Backboard the athlete. (*inappropriate at this time*) −1
19. Begin mouth-to-mouth breathing. (*inappropriate*) −2
20. Cover the athlete with blanket. (*not necessary*) 0
21. Remove the athlete's mouth guard. (*OK*) +1
22. Remove the athlete's shoulder pads and neck roll. (*inappropriate*) −1
23. Open the athlete's airway with a jaw thrust. (*good*) +2

Examiner (*Do not read to candidate.*)
What you know—The athlete has no breathing and no heartbeat.
Priorities—Give CPR while advanced medical help is being summoned.

C. 24. Stop CPR long enough to get the athlete on a backboard. (*OK*) +2
25. Ask a school administrator to speak with the parents. (*inappropriate*) 0
26. Have the announcer make a statement about the athlete's condition. (*inappropriate*) −1
27. Ask that the game be forfeited. (*inappropriate*) 0
28. Determine the athlete's insurance coverage. (*inappropriate*) 0
29. Determine the hospital to be used. (*OK*) +1
30. Call the hospital about the athlete. Call the hospital about the athlete. (*Paramedics have already informed the hospital.*) 0
31. Allow paramedics to assume CPR. (*Excellent—the athlete's condition is unchanged.*) +3
32. Determine the other athlete involved. (*inappropriate at this time*) 0
33. Have the athlete's parents driven to the hospital. (*This is not helpful in the immediate situation.*) 0
34. Have the lights turned off so spectators do not get upset. (*Spectators already are upset.*) 0
35. Have coaches try to motivate the other athletes to play. (*inappropriate*) 0
36. Make sure you have all athletes' liability waivers. (*It is now too late.*) −1
37. Tell the other athletes the defensive back will be fine. (*inappropriate*) −1

Examiner (*Do not read to candidate.*)
What you know—A secondary survey reveals no other injuries, and the parents and an ambulance have arrived.
Priorities—Turn the care of this athlete over to the ambulance personnel for transport to hospital.

D. 38. Get a drink of alcohol to calm you down. (*inappropriate*) −1
39. Indicate the proper tackling technique to other athletes. (*inappropriate*) −1
40. Check the school's liability insurance. (*inappropriate*) −1
41. Call the coordinator of the grief support team. (*good*) +1
42. Debrief the athletic training staff about their feelings. (*OK*) +1
43. Purchase additional malpractice insurance. (*It is now too late.*) −1
44. Write a detailed report about the incident. (*excellent*) +1
45. Have all staff present write detailed reports about the incident. (*excellent*) +1
46. Review films of the athlete's injury. (*inappropriate at this time*) 0
47. In event of death of an athlete, go over the guidelines with athletic training staff. (*OK*) +1
48. Go to the hospital. (*not helpful*) −1

Examiner (*Do not read to candidate.*)
What you know—The athlete may die, based on his condition.
Priorities—Prepare for possible death of this athlete.

E. 49. Call the coordinator of the grief support team. (*The coordinator puts the appropriate plan into place.*) +2

50. Call the school's public relations office. (*Good, this office has put together a prepared statement.*) +1

51. Disconnect your telephone. (*inappropriate*) −1

52. Send a sympathy card and flowers to the athlete's family. (*These would be appreciated.*) 0

53. Provide counselors for the other athletes. (*very helpful*) +1

54. Call the football team together and inform them of the death. (*appropriate*) +1

55. Assist the athlete's family with transportation and lodging. (*They are grateful.*) 0

56. Have the registrar's office contact all students with same last name. (*Their parents are thankful.*) +1

57. Collect the athletes' belongings from the locker room. (*appropriate*) +1

58. Hide your own feelings. (*Inappropriate—others need to know how you feel.*) −1

59. Address players' concerns about continuing to play. (*appropriate*) +1

60. Contact the school's attorney about liability. (*inappropriate*) −1

61. Try to isolate yourself to avoid the football players. (*inappropriate*) −1

62. Obtain the athlete's equipment from the hospital. (*not necessary*) 0

63. Close the training room for the day. (*not necessary*) 0

64. Pretend nothing happened. (*inappropriate*) −1

65. Answer media questions. (*inappropriate*) −2

66. Glamorize the athlete's death. (*inappropriate*) −2

67. Contact the opposing team. (*They send condolences.*) 0

Examiner (*Do not read to candidate.*)
What you know—The athlete died.
Priorities—Put the grief action plan into effect.

Passing-point total: 24
End of Problem 8

■ Problem 9

A. 1. Ask teammates what happened. (*Why ask them? They do not know.*) −1

2. Apply ice. (*inappropriate at this time*) −1

3. Call an ambulance. (*inappropriate at this time*) −1

4. Ask the athlete what happened. (*He indicates he was hit in the right thigh by another player's knee.*) +1

5. Ask about a previous injury. (*He had a bruise to the same area a year ago.*) +1
6. Determine if the athlete is conscious. (*The athlete is conscious.*) +1
7. Palpate low back for point tenderness. (*inappropriate at this time*) −1
8. Ask the athlete about crepitus or popping. (*The athlete reports none.*) +1
9. Have the athlete try and walk. (*inappropriate, as he was carried in*) −1
10. Ask if the athlete has pain anywhere else other than where already noted. (*He does not.*) +1
11. Massage the athlete's thigh. (*Severe hemorrhage results.*) −2
12. Apply an analgesic balm. (*inappropriate*) −1
13. Ask the athlete about previous abdominal injury. (*Why?*) −1
14. Apply direct pressure over the wound. (*Where is the wound?*) −1

Examiner (*Do not read to candidate.*)
What you know—A rugby player is not able to weight bear.
Priorities—Determine any immediately life-threatening injuries, and determine seriousness of non-life-threatening injuries if there are no life-threatening injuries.

B. 15. Determine active range of motion in both of the athlete's lower extremities. (*These are 30 degrees to 60 degrees in the right and full range in the left.*) +1
16. Palpate the anterior superior iliac spine bilaterally. (*There is no pain and there are no deformities in either side.*) +1
17. Check pupillary reflex with a penlight. (*inappropriate*) −1
18. Place a hydroculator pack on the injury. (*inappropriate*) −1
19. Check the athlete's strength in both lower extremities. (*The left is normal, but the right is too painful to test strength.*) +1
20. Palpate the athlete's abdomen. (*inappropriate*) −1
21. Palpate both thighs for point tenderness and spasm. (*The right thigh is painful, with a 10-c mass.*) +2
22. Check the athlete's dorsal pedal pulses. (*They are equal.*) +1
23. Check the athlete's carotid pulse. (*inappropriate*) −1
24. Give mouth-to-mouth breathing. (*The athlete is angry.*) −2
25. Visually check both thighs for swelling or deformity. (*The right is larger.*) +1
26. Remove the athlete's mouth guard. (*The athlete was not wearing one.*) 0
27. Perform bilateral femoral grinding tests. (*not necessary*) −1
28. Test patellar reflex bilaterally. (*painful*) 0
29. Ask the athlete about nausea. (*not necessary*) −1
30. Ask the athlete to perform a leg squat. (*inappropriate*) −1
31. Ask the athlete to run. (*inappropriate*) −1
32. Ask the athlete to perform a sit-up. (*inappropriate*) −1

Examiner (*Do not read to candidate.*)
What you know—Initial evaluation is complete.
Priorities—Do a secondary evaluation to determine the scope of the injury.

C. 33. Perform Lachman's drawer test bilaterally. (*not necessary*) –1
    34. Perform active hip flexion of the athlete's right leg. (*The athlete has 20 degrees of flexion, but with pain.*) +1
    35. Perform McMurray test bilaterally. (*not necessary*) –1
    36. Continue mouth-to-mouth resuscitation. (*inappropriate*) –1
    37. Check the athlete's pulse every four cycles. (*not necessary*) –1
    38. Test both knees for hyperextension. (*inappropriate*) –1
    39. Perform an apprehension test on the athlete's right knee. (*inappropriate*) –1
    40. Stress test both knees for varus and valgus. (*not necessary*) –1
    41. Stress test both knees for varus and valgus at 20 degrees of flexion. (*not necessary*) –1
    42. Check the athlete for Kehr's sign. (*inappropriate*) –1
    43. Perform Yergason test bilaterally. (*inappropriate*) –1

Examiner (*Do not read to candidate.*)
What you know—Secondary evaluation is complete.
Priorities—specific testing of injury

D. 44. Anterior cruciate tear (*Incorrect—see answer 50.*) –2
    45. Posterior cruciate tear (*Incorrect—see answer 50.*) –2
    46. Abdominal injury (*Incorrect—see answer 50.*) –2
    47. Lateral collateral injury (*Incorrect—see answer 50.*) –2
    48. Femur fracture (*Incorrect—see answer 50.*) –2
    49. Thigh contusion (*correct*) +1
    50. Patellar subluxation (*Incorrect—see answer 50.*) –2
    51. Medial meniscus injury (*Incorrect—see answer 50.*) –2
    52. Respiratory arrest (*Incorrect—see answer 50.*) –2

Examiner (*Do not read to candidate.*)
What you know—The seriousness of injury should be apparent.
Priorities—impression of injury

E. 53. Use a neoprene brace. (*inappropriate*) –1
    54. Place the athlete's knee in a locked, hinged knee immobilizer bent at 60 degrees. (*good*) +1
    55. Instruct the athlete on crutches use. (*good*) +1
    56. Use a hydroculator pack. (*inappropriate*) –1
    57. Refer the athlete to a physician. (*OK*) +1
    58. Call an ambulance. (*not necessary*) –1
    59. Take the athlete's blood pressure. (*not necessary*) –1
    60. No treatment is necessary. (*incorrect*) –1
    61. Compression wrap the injury. (*good*) +1

Examiner (*Do not read to candidate.*)
What you know—The athlete has a thigh contusion and requires acute treatment.
Priorities—Treat the thigh contusion by maintaining range of motion and keeping swelling down.

F. 62. Measure the athlete's thigh circumference. (*It is 2 in. larger than the left.*) +1
    63. Check the athlete's active range of motion. (*It is 30 to 60 degrees of flexion.*) +1
    64. Apply ice several times a day. (*This is helpful.*) +1
    65. Use cocontraction of the thigh. (*too painful*) −1
    66. Have the athlete start an upper-body lifting program. (*appropriate*) +1
    67. Have the athlete do straight-leg raises of the injured thigh while immobilized. (*This is too painful.*) 0
    68. Have the athlete start a lifting program for uninjured leg. (*appropriate*) +1
    69. Massage the injured thigh. (*It swells more.*) −1
    70. Have the athlete do deep knee bends. (*The athlete collapses and hurts the leg more.*) −1
    71. Ultrasound the injured thigh. (*inappropriate*) −1
    72. Recommend that the athlete use crutches. (*good choice*) +1
    73. Apply electrical stimulation to the injury. (*appropriate*) +1
    74. Apply heat to the injury for the first few days. (*Swelling increases and so does the pain.*) −2

Examiner (*Do not read to candidate.*)
What you know—The athlete has an acute thigh contusion, and myositis ossificans has been evaluated by a physician.
Priorities—Establish first week's treatment plan.

G. 75. straight-leg raising—no weights (*appropriate*) +1
    76. ultrasound (*appropriate*) +1
    77. deep knee bends (*inappropriate*) −1
    78. light jogging (*inappropriate*) −1
    79. leg press (*inappropriate*) −1
    80. electrical stimulation (*appropriate*) +1
    81. massage of the injured thigh (*appropriate*) +1
    82. active range-of-motion exercises (*appropriate*) +1
    83. application of analgesic balm (*inappropriate*) −1
    84. cocontraction of the thigh (*good*) +1

Examiner (*Do not read to candidate.*)
What you know—The athlete is one week post–acute injury of the thigh, with previous myositis ossificans, and he is pain free.

Priorities—regaining range of motion and strengthening the limb, as long as the athlete stays pain free

H.   85. biking (*good*) +1
      86. leg press (*OK*) +1
      87. duck walking (*inappropriate*) −1
      88. sport-specific exercises (*good choice*) +1
      89. massage (*OK*) +1
      90. using hydroculator packs (*OK*) +1
      91. jogging (*The athlete is excited about running.*) +1
      92. progressive resistive quadriceps exercises (*OK*) +1
      93. isokinetics (*good*) +1

Examiner (*Do not read to candidate.*)
What you know—The athlete has myositis ossificans that is resolving, he is three weeks postinjury, and he has full range of motion.
Priorities—Increase the strength in the thigh and begin a sport-specific program.

I.   94. ability to duck walk (*inappropriate*) −1
      95. physician permission (*X ray shows myositis ossificans is still apparent, but the physician gives written permission for athlete's full return.*) +1
      96. The injured leg is at 90% of strength, compared to noninjured leg. (*OK*) +1
      97. The athlete is pain free. (*OK*) +1
      98. maintenance of the athlete's weight program (*not necessary*) 0
      99. The athlete has full range of motion. (*OK*) +1
      100. special padding (*good idea*) +1
      101. The coach needs the athlete. (*inappropriate*) −1
      102. The athlete is mentally prepared. (*OK*) +1
      103. The athlete uses an elastic compression bandage over the area. (*not necessary*) −1
      104. The athlete is able to perform sport-specific activities. (*OK*) +1

Examiner (*Do not read to candidate.*)
What you know—The rugby player is anxious to return.
Priorities—Establish criteria to return the athlete to competition.

Passing-point total: 32
End of Problem 9

■ Problem 10

A.   1. Ask the athlete what happened. (*He is unable to tell you because he is in so much pain.*) +1
      2. Determine the athlete's level of consciousness. (*He is fully conscious.*) +1

3. Put on skates to get across the ice. (*The athlete dies. Go to the next problem.*) −15

4. Check the athlete for bleeding. (*The athlete has no apparent bleeding.*) +1

5. Have other skaters drag the athlete over to you. (*The athlete dies. Go to the next problem.*) −15

6. Determine who hit the athlete. (*inappropriate*) −1

7. Ask the athlete to skate off the ice. (*inappropriate*) −1

8. Ask the athlete where the pain is. (*He grabs his throat.*) +1

9. Determine if the check was legal. (*inappropriate*) −1

10. Determine if the athlete is breathing. (*His breathing is labored, and he is gasping for air.*) +1

11. Determine if the athlete has a heart beat. (*inappropriate at this time*) −1

12. Determine the athlete's blood pressure. (*inappropriate at this time*) −1

13. Determine the athlete's skin color. (*inappropriate at this time*) −1

14. Check the athlete's body temperature. (*inappropriate at this time*) −1

15. Visually examine the head and neck. (*Throat has a hematoma and is deformed.*) +1

16. Remove the athlete's mouth guard. (*He still has labored breathing.*) +1

Examiner (*Do not read to candidate.*)
What you know—A hockey player has a direct-impact injury, he is conscious, and he is down on the ice.
Priorities—Determine any immediately life-threatening injuries, and determine seriousness of non-life-threatening injuries if there are no life-threatening injuries.

B. 17. Give the athlete ice. (*It helps reduce the pain.*) +1

18. Have the athlete skate off the ice. (*inappropriate*) −1

19. Check the athlete's pupil size and reflex. (*Both are normal.*) +1

20. Remove the athlete's helmet. (*inappropriate*) −1

21. Open the athlete's airway with a chin lift or jaw thrust. (*There is no change, and the athlete still has labored breathing.*) +1

22. Call for an ambulance. (*Estimated time of arrival is 5 min.*) +1

23. Insert an oral airway. (*The athlete gags and vomits.*) −1

24. Put a soft neck collar on the athlete. (*inappropriate*) −1

25. Give the athlete's asthma medication. (*inappropriate*) −1

26. Keep the athlete calm and encourage slow breathing. (*Absolutely!*) +1

27. Determine the athlete's breathing rate. (*30 breaths per min*) +1

28. Position the athlete supine. (*His condition worsens.*) −1

29. Position the athlete on the side. (*This gives some relief.*) +1

30. Stabilize the athlete's head and neck. (*appropriate*) +1

Examiner *(Do not read to candidate.)*
What you know—A hockey player with a direct-impact injury is conscious, but down on the ice.
Priorities—Comfort the athlete and get immediate medical attention.

C. 31. a fracture of larynx *(correct)* +1
    32. a head injury *(No—see number 31.)* −2
    33. cardiac arrest *(No—see number 31.)* −2
    34. a seizure *(No—see number 31.)* −2
    35. epiglottitis *(No—see number 31.)* −2
    36. hyperventilation *(No—see number 31.)* −2
    37. croup *(No—see number 31.)* −2
    38. an asthma attack *(No—see number 31.)* −2

Examiner *(Do not read to candidate.)*
What you know—The ambulance has arrived and taken the athlete.
Priorities—assessment of injury

Passing-point total: 13
End of Problem 10

■ Problem 11

A. 1. Note the position of Player A's body. *(She is sitting holding her ankle.)* +1
    2. Ask Player B to get up and walk. *(She collapses.)* −1
    3. Ask Player B if she injured her shoulder before. *(inappropriate)* −1
    4. Determine if Player A is conscious. *(She is.)* +1
    5. Send a student athletic trainer for ice. *(inappropriate)* −1
    6. Ask Player B if there is pain anywhere. *(She indicates midtibia pain.)* +1
    7. Determine if Player B is conscious. *(She is.)* +1
    8. Ask Player A what happened. *(She indicates their legs hit hard.)* +1
    9. Note the position of Player B's body. *(She is lying supine.)* +1
    10. Ask Player A to get up and walk. *(She collapses.)* −1
    11. Ask Player B what happened. *(She indicates a collision with Player A, and their legs hit.)* +1
    12. Call an ambulance. *(inappropriate)* −1
    13. Ask Player A if there is pain anywhere. *(Her ankle is sore.)* +1
    14. Apply ice to the injured areas. *(not appropriate at this time)* −1
    15. Position both athletes in a supine position. *(inappropriate)* −1
    16. Apply a sling to the shoulder of Player B. *(not necessary)* −1

Examiner *(Do not read to candidate.)*
What you know—Two athletes are injured from a direct impact.
Priorities—Determine any immediately life-threatening injuries and determine seriousness of non-life-threatening injuries if there are no life-threatening injuries. Determine which athlete has a more urgent need for care.

B. 17. Visually examine Player A's lower extremities. (*There are no problems.*) +1
18. Ask Player A if she heard a snap or pop. (*She didn't.*) +1
19. Check dorsal pedal pulse and sensation in both of Player A's feet. (*inappropriate*) −1
20. Palpate Player A's ankle. (*inappropriate*) −1
21. Ask Player A if she injured the ankle before. (*inappropriate at this time*) −1
22. Tell Player A to be more careful next time. (*inappropriate*) −1
23. Palpate Player B's leg. (*She writhes in pain.*) −1
24. Tell Player B to wear thicker shin guards next time. (*inappropriate*) −1
25. Ask Player B if she heard a snap or pop. (*She did.*) +1
26. Ask other players if they are tired. (*inappropriate*) −1
27. Check dorsal pedal pulse and sensation in both of Player B's feet. (*OK*) +1
28. Visually examine Player B's lower extremities for swelling, deformity, and bleeding. (*There is swelling with slight misalignment at midtibia.*) +1
29. Have Player B move her lower leg. (*inappropriate*) −1
30. Have Player A move her ankle. (*inappropriate at this time*) −1
31. Externally rotate and abduct Player B's shoulder. (*not necessary*) −1
32. Check range of motion bilaterally of Player B's shoulders. (*inappropriate*) −1
33. Examine Player B's shoulder for swelling or deformity. (*None is found.*) −1
34. Palpate the left acromioclavicular joint of Player B. (*There is no laxity.*) −1

Examiner (*Do not read to candidate.*)
What you know—Two athletes collided.
Priorities—Assess athletes' injuries to determine who is in the most urgent need of care.

C. 35. Give the athlete ice. (*Pain decreases.*)+1
36. Carry the athlete off on a stretcher. (*good choice*) +1
37. Visually examine Player B's lower extremities for swelling, deformity, and bleeding. (*It is now too late.*) −1
38. Adjust the crutches and show the athlete how to use them. (*not appropriate at this time*) −1
39. Have the athlete walk off the field. (*She ends up with a compound fracture.*) −3
40. Splint the athlete's leg. (*Appropriate—she feels more comfortable.*) +3
41. Clap for the athlete as she leaves the field. (*inappropriate*) −1
42. Place the athlete's arm in a sling. (*not necessary*) −1
43. Splint the athlete's humerus. (*not necessary*) −1

Examiner (*Do not read to candidate.*)
What you know—You need to give care to Player B first.
Priorities—Treat Player B.

D. 44. Palpate the ankle for deformity. (*There is no swelling, crepitus, or deformity.*) +1
   45. Bilaterally compare both ankles left to right. (*They look and feel the same.*) +1
   46. Splint the athlete's ankle. (*not necessary*) −1
   47. Have the athlete actively move the injured ankle. (*The athlete has full range of motion.*) +1
   48. Have the athlete carried off on a stretcher. (*not necessary*) −1
   49. Test the athlete's active-resistive range of motion. (*It is normal.*) +1
   50. Clap for the athlete as she leaves the field. (*inappropriate*) 0
   51. Call an ambulance to transport the athlete. (*inappropriate*) −1
   52. Apply an anterior drawer stress test. (*The test is negative.*) +1
   53. Manually carry the athlete from the field. (*not necessary*) −1
   54. Provide ambulatory aid off the field. (*appropriate*) +1

Examiner (*Do not read to candidate.*)
What you know—You need to determine more extensively the injuries to Player A.
Priorities—Evaluate Player A.

E. 55. four-way straight-leg raises ((*OK*) +1
   56. upper body workouts (*OK*) +1
   57. a swimming program (*The athlete cannot swim with a cast.*) −2
   58. a running program (*inappropriate*) −1
   59. strengthening for the unaffected leg (*appropriate*) +1
   60. riding the stationary bike (*No way!*) −1

Examiner (*Do not read to candidate.*)
What you know—The athlete is in a full-leg cast, with a greenstick fracture of the tibia.
Priorities—initial rehabilitation of the athlete while still in a cast

F. 61. Goniometer active range of motion measurement of the knee. (*appropriate*) +1
   62. Measure girth. (*good*) +1
   63. Goniometer passive range of motion measurement of the knee. (*appropriate*) +1
   64. Goniometer active range of motion measurement of the ankle. (*appropriate*) +1
   65. Goniometer measurement of ankle passively. (*appropriate*) +1
   66. Ask about pain. (*The athlete has none.*) +1
   67. Palpate fracture site. (*Nothing noticeable is found.*) +1
   68. Note how hairy the leg is. (*inappropriate*) −1

69. Note how the leg smells. (*inappropriate*) −1
70. Check the athlete's gait. (*appropriate*) +1
71. Note the general condition of the athlete's skin. (*It is dry and scaly.*) +1

Examiner (*Do not read to candidate.*)
What you know—The athlete is out of full-leg cast 3 months postinjury.
Priorities—Evaluate the tibia.

G. 72. Stretch the gastroc and soleus. (*appropriate*) +1
73. Do ball-handling drills. (*inappropriate*) −1
74. Stretch the quadriceps and hamstrings. (*appropriate*) +1
75. Keep the knee active through normal range of motion. (*Full range of motion is accomplished.*) +1
76. Do four-way straight-leg raises. (*appropriate*) +1
77. Use ice or a cold whirlpool after activity. (*appropriate*) +1
78. Do hip range-of-motion exercises. (*not necessary*) −1
79. Do ankle range-of-motion exercises. (*appropriate*) +1
80. Do toe raises with weight. (*inappropriate at this time*) −1
81. Do patellar mobilization. (*OK*) +1

Examiner (*Do not read to candidate.*)
What you know—It is 3 months since the intial tibia fracture, and the athlete's leg is out of the case.
Priorities—Rehabilitate lower leg, beginning with range of motion.

H. 82. active ankle plantarflexion with resistance (*OK*) +1
83. proprioceptive knee exercises (*appropriate*) +1
84. active ankle eversion with resistance (*OK*) +1
85. active ankle inversion with resistance (*appropriate*) +1
86. active knee flexion with resistance (*OK*) +1
87. toe touches (*inappropriate*) −1
88. jumping on the previously casted leg (*inappropriate*) −1
89. analgesic balm application (*inappropriate*) −1
90. active ankle dorsiflexion with resistance (*OK*) +1
91. proprioceptive ankle exercises (*appropriate*) +1
92. active knee extension with resistance (*OK*) +1
93. running (*no*) −1
94. swimming (*OK*) +1
95. biking (*OK*) +1

Examiner (*Do not read to candidate.*)
What you know—The athlete has regained full range of motion and is in need of more advanced rehabilitation.
Priorities—increased strengthening of lower extremities

Passing-point total: 36
End of Problem 11

■ Problem 12

A. 1. Ask the athlete if he has pain anyplace else. (*He does not.*) +1
    2. Activate your emergency plan. (*inappropriate*) −1
    3. Ask the athlete if anyone else was injured. (*inappropriate*) −1
    4. Ask the athlete what happened. (*Playing basketball, he stepped on someone's foot and inverted his right ankle.*) +1
    5. Put the athlete on crutches. (*inappropriate at this time*) −1
    6. Ask if the athlete has injured the ankle before. (*He has not.*) +1
    7. Apply ice. (*inappropriate at this time*) −1
    8. Ask what type of shoes the athlete was wearing. (*inappropriate*) −1
    9. Check the athlete's blood pressure. (*inappropriate at this time*) −1
   10. Check the athlete's temperature. (*inappropriate at this time*) −1
   11. Ask if the athlete continued to play after getting hurt. (*He did not.*) +1
   12. Visually inspect the injured area for swelling, bleeding, or deformity. (*Swelling is apparent over the anterior lateral aspect of the ankle.*) +1
   13. Send a student athletic trainer to the gymnasium to find a supervisor. (*inappropriate*) −1
   14. Check the athlete's level of consciousness. (*He is conscious, but you already knew that.*) −1
   15. Check the athlete's skin color. (*He has normal skin tone.*) +1
   16. Check the athlete's pupil reflex. (*inappropriate*) −1
   17. Palpate the athlete's right ankle. (*There is pain with swelling over the anterior lateral aspect of the ankle.*) +1
   18. Ask the athlete to plantarflex and dorsiflex the left ankle. (*The athlete has normal range of motion.*) +1
   19. Apply a pressure bandage to the injury. (*inappropriate at this time*) −1
   20. Manipulate the athlete's right ankle. (*inappropriate*) −1
   21. Palpate the athlete's left ankle. (*There is no problem.*) +1
   22. Have the athlete hop on the ankle. (*inappropriate*) −1
   23. Ask the athlete to plantarflex and dorsiflex the right ankle. (*The athlete has minimal range of motion.*) +1
   24. Ask the athlete to invert and evert the right ankle. (*Inversion is painful.*) +1
   25. Ask the athlete to invert and evert left ankle. (*The athlete has full range of motion.*) +1
   26. Manipulate the athlete's left ankle. (*inappropriate*) −1
   27. Use traction on the injured ankle. (*inappropriate*) −2

Examiner (*Do not read to candidate.*)
What you know—An athlete with an injured ankle cannot fully weight bear, and the athlete is conscious.
Priorities—initial assessment of this injury

B. 28. Test the right foot for anterior drawer. (*The test is negative.*) +1
    29. Give a heel-pound test. (*The test is negative.*) +1
    30. Place the athlete in warm whirlpool. (*inappropriate*) −1
    31. Give the heel-pound test on the right foot. (*The test is negative.*) +1
    32. Do a Thompson test on the right foot. (*The test is negative.*) +1
    33. Massage the injured ankle. (*inappropriate*) −1
    34. Give a heel-pound test on the left ankle. (*The test is negative.*) +1
    35. Test the left ankle for anterior drawer. (*The test is negative.*) +1
    36. Do a McMurray test bilaterally. (*not necessary*) −1
    37. Put the athlete in a splint. (*inappropriate*) −1
    38. Do a Thomas test bilaterally. (*inappropriate*) −1
    39. Do a Thomas test of the right foot. (*inappropriate*) −1
    40. Varus test the knees bilaterally. (*not necessary*) −1
    41. Do a Lachman's test bilaterally. (*not necessary*) −1

Examiner (*Do not read to candidate.*)
What you know—The athlete has an ankle injury.
Priorities—Do specific tests to determine the extent of the ankle injury.

C. 42. Spray ethyl chloride on the injury. (*inappropriate*) −1
    43. Elevate the lower extremity. (*appropriate*) +1
    44. Put the athlete on crutches. (*Yes!*) +1
    45. Have the athlete walk. (*inappropriate*) −1
    46. elastic compression of the ankle (*appropriate*) +1
    47. ultrasound (*inappropriate*) −1
    48. toe-raise exercise (*inappropriate*) −1
    49. Have the athlete exercise on a stationary bike. (*inappropriate*) −1
    50. Have the athlete use a warm whirlpool. (*inappropriate at this time*) −1
    51. massage (*inappropriate at this time*) −1
    52. ice (*appropriate*) +1

Examiner (*Do not read to candidate.*)
What you know—The athlete has an injury to the ankle that does not allow weight bearing.
Priorities—Treat the inability to weight bear and control swelling.

D. 53. Apply ice several times, but not longer than 20 min. (*This is an excellent idea.*) +1
    54. Use over-the-counter pain medication. (*This is useful.*) +1
    55. Increase calcium intake. (*inappropriate*) −1
    56. Apply analgesic balm. (*inappropriate*) −1
    57. Keep the lower extremity elevated. (*helpful*) +1
    58. Eat red meat. (*inappropriate*) −1
    59. Apply a heating pad at night. (*The ankle swells to twice its size.*) −2
    60. Walk on the ankle as much as possible. (*The ankle swells to twice its size.*) −1

61. See a physician. (*No fracture is found.*) +2
62. Use over-the-counter anti-inflammatory medication. (*appropriate*) +1

Examiner (*Do not read to candidate.*)
What you know—The injury is an acute ankle sprain that does not allow the athlete to weight bear.
Priorities—Keep the athlete pain free and ambulatory and keep the swelling down.

E. 63. Ice for an hour. (*Inappropriate—see answer 65.*) −2
    64. Use hydroculator packs. (*Inappropriate—see answer 65.*) −2
    65. Use an intermittent compression device. (*appropriate*) +1
    66. Use infrared therapy. (*Inappropriate—see answer 65.*) −2
    67. Use a biofeedback unit. (*Inappropriate—see answer 65.*) −2
    68. Use ultrasound. (*Inappropriate—see answer 65.*) −2
    69. Use a TENS unit. (*Inappropriate—see answer 65.*) −2
    70. Run on the ankle. (*Inappropriate—see answer 65.*) −2

Examiner (*Do not read to candidate.*)
What you know—The ankle has edema, which needs to be removed.
Priorities—Find a modality to remove the edema.

F. 71. Apply electrodes. (*inappropriate*) −4
    72. Place ankle horizontally to infrared unit. (*inappropriate*) −4
    73. Place ice on the injured body part. (*inappropriate*) −4
    74. Apply a pressure wrap over ice. (*inappropriate*) −4
    75. Place the ice pack in towels. (*inappropriate*) −4
    76. Instruct the athlete on distance and speed of runs. (*inappropriate*) −4
    77. Place the injured ankle in a compression sleeve. (*appropriate*) +3
    78. Instruct the athlete to contract the injured body part. (*inappropriate*) −4
    79. Set the unit to tentenization. (*inappropriate*) −4
    80. Set unit for W/cm². (*inappropriate*) −4
    81. Set the pressure to 65 mmHg. (*appropriate*) +2
    82. Move the ultrasonic head in an overlapping motion. (*inappropriate*) −4
    83. Place an ice pack on the injury for 15 min. (*inappropriate*) −4
    84. Set on-off sequence. (*appropriate*) +3

Examiner (*Do not read to candidate.*)
What you know—The proper modality to remove the edema is the intermittent compression device.
Priorities—Set up the intermittent compression device.

Passing-point total: 26
End of Problem 12

■ Problem 13

A. 1. Recommend the athlete see the coach for this analysis. (*inappropriate*) −1
    2. Recommend the athlete weight lift. (*inappropriate at this time*) −1
    3. Have a student athletic trainer write a physician referral. (*inappropriate*) −1
    4. Strength test the athlete's shoulder extensor. (*appropriate*) +1
    5. Strength test the athlete's shoulder flexors. (*appropriate*) +1
    6. Check the athlete's shoulder range of motion. (*The athlete has full range of motion.*) +1
    7. Strength test the athlete's shoulder rotator cuffs. (*These are weak.*) +1
    8. Strength test the athlete's abdominals. (*inappropriate*) −1
    9. Strength test the athlete's neck musculature. (*inappropriate*) −1
    10. Strength test the athlete's horizontal shoulder flexors. (*These are weak.*) +1
    11. Strength test the athlete's horizontal shoulder extensors. (*These are weak.*) +1
    12. Strength test the athlete's elbow extensors. (*appropriate*) +1
    13. Strength test the athlete's elbow flexors. (*appropriate*) +1
    14. Ask if the athlete's coefficient of friction has ever been measured. (*inappropriate*) −1
    15. Strength test the athlete's neck rotators. (*appropriate*) +1
    16. Strength test the athlete's toe flexors. (*inappropriate*) −1
    17. Strength test the athlete's toe extensor. (*inappropriate*) −1
    18. Have the athlete watch other athletes swim in the pool. (*not helpful*) −1
    19. Determine the athlete's arm length. (*inappropriate*) −1
    20. Strength test the athlete's hip adduction. (*inappropriate*) −1
    21. Strength test the athlete's hip abduction. (*inappropriate*) −1
    22. Strength test the athlete's knee extension. (*appropriate*) +1
    23. Strength test the athlete's hip extension. (*appropriate*) +1
    24. Strength test the athlete's knee flexion. (*This is weak.*) +1
    25. Strength test the athlete's back extensors. (*inappropriate*) −1
    26. Strength test the athlete's hip abductors. (*inappropriate*) −1
    27. Strength test the athlete's foot plantar flexors. (*appropriate*) +1
    28. Determine the length of the race the athlete will compete in. (*inappropriate at this time*) 0
    29. Strength test foot dorsiflexion. (*inappropriate*) −1
    30. Determine the athlete's stroke count. (*inappropriate*) −1

Examiner (*Do not read to candidate.*)
What you know—A freestyle swimmer is trying to improve times.
Priorities—Assess deficiencies in this athlete.

B.   31. toe raises with shoulder weight (*inappropriate*) −1
      32. shoulder shrugs with weights (*appropriate*) +1
      33. bench press (*appropriate*) +1
      34. military press (*inappropriate*) −1
      35. leg press (*inappropriate*) −1
      36. leg squats (*inappropriate*) −1
      37. barbell flies (*appropriate*) +1
      38. wrist barbell curls (*inappropriate*) −1
      39. four-way neck weights (*inappropriate*) −1
      40. running with leg weights (*inappropriate*) −1
      41. four-way straight leg raises (*inappropriate*) −1
      42. empty can exercises with light weights (*appropriate*) +1
      43. increasing the stroke count (*inappropriate*) −1
      44. decreasing breathing rate (*inappropriate*) −1
      45. doing more rotation in the stroke (*inappropriate*) −1
      46. using swim fins at practice (*inappropriate*) −1
      47. using a kickboard at practice (*inappropriate*) −1
      48. leg extention with weight (*inappropriate*) −1
      49. arm curls (*inappropriate*) −1
      50. hip sled (*inappropriate*) −1
      51. jumping rope (*inappropriate*) −1
      52. running in waist-deep water (*inappropriate*) −1
      53. practicing race dive form (*inappropriate*) −1

Examiner (*Do not read to candidate.*)
What you know—The athlete requires strengthening exercises.
Priorities—Strengthen areas that are weak.

Passing-point total: 11
End of Problem 13

■ Problem 14

A.   1. vasodilates blood vessels (*incorrect*) −1
      2. hardens tissues (*correct*) +1
      3. the same as negative polarity characteristics (*incorrect*) −1
      4. creates an alkaline reaction under the pad (*incorrect*) −1
      5. acts as a pain reliever (*correct*) +1
      6. irritates nerve (*incorrect*) −1
      7. increases spasms (*incorrect*) −1
      8. repels hydrogen ions (*correct*) +1
      9. Its most effective use is for acute conditions. (*incorrect*) −1
     10. Its most effective use is for chronic conditions. (*correct*) +1

Examiner (*Do not read to candidate.*)
What you know—Use high-voltage galvanic stimulation on an acute knee injury.
Priorities—Learn positive polarity characteristics.

B. 11. absorbs fat (*incorrect*) –1
12. absorbs blood clots (*incorrect*) –1
13. decreases hemorrhaging (*incorrect*) –1
14. softens tissues (*correct*) +1
15. vasoconstricts blood vessels (*correct*) +1
16. repels oxygen and acids (*correct*) +1

Examiner (*Do not read to candidate.*)
What you know—You are using high-voltage galvanic stimulation.
Priorities—Learn the negative polarity characteristics of high-voltage galvanic stimulation.

C. 17. Do not use with ectomorphs. (*incorrect*) –1
18. Do not use over muscle motor points. (*incorrect*) –1
19. Do not use over resolved hemorrhaging. (*incorrect*) –1
20. Do not use over carotid sinus. (*correct*) +1
21. Do not use with acute spasms. (*incorrect*) –1
22. Do not use over metal implants. (*incorrect*) –1
23. Do not use with a pregnant patient. (*correct*) +1
24. Do not use with muscle atrophy. (*incorrect*) –1
25. Do not use with pacemakers. (*correct*) +1

Examiner (*Do not read to candidate.*)
What you know—You are using high-voltage galvanic stimulation.
Priorities—learning contraindications of high-voltage galvanic stimulation

D. 26. The equipment is checked yearly for safety. (*appropriate*) +1
27. Cords are kept close to pipes. (*inappropriate*) –1
28. A ground-fault-interrupter plug is used. (*appropriate*) +1
29. A three-pronged cord is used. (*appropriate*) +1
30. Other people have used this unit without injury. (*inappropriate*) –1
31. A long cord is used. (*inappropriate*) –1
32. The athlete can turn off the machine. (*inappropriate*) –1
33. Many cords come out of the same wall. (*inappropriate*) –1

Examiner (*Do not read to candidate.*)
What you know—You are using high-voltage galvanic stimulation and the athlete is fearful of electrocution.
Priorities—Ensure safety of the athlete when this modality is in use and calm the athlete's fears.

E. 34. an 8-pulse-per-s switch rate (*appropriate*) +1
35. treatment three times per day (*inappropriate*) –1
36. Place the pad at the motor point of the muscle. (*appropriate*) +1
37. Use the stimulator in conjunction with a hydroculator pack. (*Edema increases.*) –2

38. 128 pulses per s switch rate (*inappropriate*) −1
39. a treatment time of 45 min (*inappropriate*) −1
40. intensity set to patient's tolerance (*appropriate*) +1
41. Use the negative lead at treatment site. (*appropriate*) +1
42. Use the stimulator in conjunction with ice at the same time. (*helpful*) +2
43. Place a dispersive pad at the injury site. (*inappropriate*) −1

Examiner (*Do not read to candidate.*)
What you know—You are using high-voltage galvanic stimulation on an acute knee sprain.
Priorities—Set up and use the modality.

Passing-point total: 13
End of Problem 14

■ Problem 15

A.
1. Recommend athletes drink plenty of water. (*appropriate*) +1
2. Recommend athletes work out in air conditioning. (*inappropriate*) −1
3. Recommend athletes follow a conditioning program. (*appropriate*) +1
4. Have athletes monitor their daily diets. (*inappropriate*) 0
5. Have athletes monitor their weight daily. (*inappropriate*) 0
6. Have athletes wear sweats on warm days. (*inappropriate*) −2
7. Have athletes monitor their body temperature. (*inappropriate*) −1
8. Have athletes take cold showers. (*inappropriate*) −1
9. Have athletes take salt tablets. (*inappropriate*) −1

Examiner (*Do not read to candidate.*)
What you know—A heat-illness program is needed for summer vacation to prevent heat injuries in the fall.
Priorities—initial acclimatization of athletes

B.
10. Set practice times for early mornings. (*appropriate*) +2
11. Get a physical examination of each athlete. (*appropriate*) +2
12. Have athletes take salt tablets. (*inappropriate*) 0
13. Test all athletes' physical conditioning. (*appropriate*) +1
14. Check all athletes' body temperature. (*inappropriate*) −1
15. Check all athletes' blood pressure. (*inappropriate*) −1

Examiner (*Do not read to candidate.*)
What you know—Athletes are back from summer vacation and will begin practicing in warm weather.
Priorities—Prevent heat injuries and assess each athlete's physical condition.

C. 16. Withhold water until the end of practice. (*inappropriate*) −2
17. Have a list of athletes' names and phone numbers. (*inappropriate*) −1
18. Have athletes use salt tablets before going to practice. (*inappropriate*) −1
19. Weigh all athletes after practice. (*inappropriate*) −1
20. Use graduated physical conditioning. (*appropriate*) +1
21. Watch overweight athletes. (*appropriate*) +1
22. Take sling psychrometer readings before practice. (*appropriate*) +2

Examiner (*Do not read to candidate.*)
What you know—On the first day of practice there is a need to prevent heat injuries.
Priorities—Prevent heat injuries.

Passing-point total: 8
End of Problem 15

■ Problem 16

A. 1. Grab a pair of crutches to take with you. (*inappropriate*) −1
2. Ask the athlete what happened. (*The athlete is unable to speak.*) +1
3. Determine if the athlete has been disqualified. (*inappropriate*) −1
4. Hold the athlete's head and neck still. (*inappropriate*) 0
5. Determine if the athlete has a pulse. (*Tachycardia is present.*) +2
6. Visually check the athlete's body position. (*He is lying on his side.*) +1
7. Go get a stethoscope to auscultate the athlete's chest. (*inappropriate at this time*) −1
8. Ask others what happened. (*The athlete was running and began to wheeze and just stopped.*) +1
9. Determine if the athlete is breathing. (*The athlete is wheezing on exhalation.*) +2
10. Determine the athlete's skin color. (*His skin is red and he is crying.*) +1
11. Ask the athlete about pain. (*The athlete is not in pain.*) +1
12. Ask if the athlete is allergic to anything. (*The athlete is not.*) +1

Examiner (*Do not read to candidate.*)
What you know—An athlete has collapsed on the cross-country course.
Priorities—Determine any immediately life-threatening injuries, and determine the seriousness of non-life-threatening injuries if there are no life-threatening injuries.

B. 13. Call for an ambulance. (*Arrival time is five min.*) +1
14. Put the athlete in a comfortable position. (*Sitting up is his choice.*) +1

15. Give the athlete CPR. (*You just killed athlete—go to the end of this problem.*) –7
16. Monitor the athlete's breathing rate. (*It is 18 breaths per min.*) +1
17. Encourage the athlete to breathe slowly. (*inappropriate*) –1
18. Give the athlete oxygen. (*helpful*) +2
19. Give the athlete abdominal thrusts. (*inappropriate*) –2
20. Give the athlete a tracheotomy. (*inappropriate*) –1
21. Have the athlete breathe into a paper bag. (*inappropriate*) –1
22. Give the athlete glucose. (*inappropriate*) –1
23. Place the athlete on the side. (*The athlete's condition worsens.*) –1
24. Move everything away from the athlete. (*inappropriate*) –1
25. Monitor the athlete's blood pressure. (*It is 135/85.*) +1

Examiner (*Do not read to candidate.*)
What you know—You have a collapsed cross-country runner.
Priorities—Treat this athlete's injury or illness.

C. 26. a collapsed lung (*Incorrect—see number 30.*) –2
27. an airway obstruction (*Incorrect—see number 30.*) –2
28. a bee sting (*Incorrect—see number 30.*) –2
29. insulin shock (*Incorrect—see number 30.*) –2
30. an asthma attack (*correct*) +1
31. hyperventilation (*Incorrect—see number 30.*) –2
32. a seizure (*Incorrect—see number 30.*) –2
33. a contusion of the larynx (*Incorrect—see number 30.*) –2
34. pneumonia (*Incorrect—see number 30.*) –2
35. a pulmonary embolism (*Incorrect—see number 30.*) –2
36. a heart attack (*Incorrect—see number 30.*) –2

Examiner (*Do not read to candidate.*)
What you know—You have a collapsed cross-country runner.
Priorities—Assess the injury.

Passing-point total: 12
End of Problem16
Passing-point total for all written simulation questions: 219

Bibliography

Many of the following publications have been recommended by the National Athletic Trainers Association Board of Certification. Some of these are difficult to find, because they are no longer in print. If you intend to use these references to study from, begin early. Some of the references listed here have been given in Appendix A as useful for further study.

1. American Academy of Ophthalmology. (1982). *The athlete's eye* (Ophthalmology in Sports). San Francisco: Author.
2. American Academy of Orthopaedic Surgeons. (1984). *Athletic training and sports medicine*. Chicago: Author.
3. American Academy of Orthopaedic Surgeons. (1991). *Athletic training and sports medicine* (2nd ed.). Park Ridge, IL: Author.
4. American Academy of Orthopedic Surgeons. (1987). *Emergency care and transportation of the sick and injured* (4th ed.). Chicago: Author.
5. American Academy of Orthopedic Surgeons. (1965). *Joint motion: Method of measuring and recording*. New York: Churchill Livingstone.
6. Arnheim, D. (1991). *Essentials of athletic training*. St. Louis: Times/ Mirror Mosby.
7. Arnheim, D. (1989). *Modern principles of athletic training* (7th ed.). St. Louis: Times/Mirror Mosby.
8. Bates, B. (1983). *A guide to physical examination*. Philadelphia: Lippincott.
9. Bautista, V. (1990). *Improve your grades*. Farmington Hills, MI: Bookhaus.
10. Bell, G.W. (Ed.) (1982). *Professional preparation in athletic training*. Champaign, IL: Human Kinetics. (out of print)
11. Bike Athletic Co. *How to properly fit a player with the Bike helmet system: Vol. 3*. Knoxville, TN: Author.
12. Bike Athletic Co. (1985). *Winners wear Bike*. Knoxville, TN: Author.

13. Bluefarb, S.M. (1978). *Dermatology.* Chicago: Scope.

14. Booher, J., & Thibodeau, G. (1989). *Athletic injury assessment* (2nd ed.). St. Louis: Mosby.

15. Browner, B.D., Jupiter, J., Levine, A.M., & Trafton, P.G. (1992). *Skeletal Trauma: Vol. II.* Philadelphia: Saunders.

16. Buttaravoli, P.M., & Stair, T.O. (1985). *Common simple emergencies.* Bowie, MD: Prentice Hall.

17. Daniels, L., & Worthingham, C. (1980). *Muscle testing techniques of manual examination* (4th ed.). Philadelphia: Saunders.

18. Drez, D. (Ed.) (1989). *Therapeutic modalities for sports injuries.* St. Louis: St. Louis Times Mirror/Mosby.

19. Fox, E., & Matthews, D.K. (1986). *Physiological basis of physical education and athletics.* Philadelphia: Saunders.

20. Grace, P. (1991). *Study guide for the NATA Board of Certification, Inc. Entry-Level Athletic Trainer Certification Examination.* Raleigh, NC: Columbia Assessment Services.

21. Griffin, J.E., & Karselis, T.C. (1982). *Physical agents for physical therapists* (2nd ed.). Springfield, IL: Charles C Thomas.

22. Hawes, G., & Hawes, L. (1981). *Hawes guide to successful study skills.* New York: New American Library.

23. Hegarty, V. (1988). *Decisions in nutrition.* St. Louis: St. Louis Times Mirror/Mosby.

24. Hoppenfeld, S. (1976). *Physical examination of the spine and extremities.* New York: Appleton-Century-Crofts.

25. Howley, E.T., & Franks, B.D. (1986). *Health/fitness instructor's handbook.* Champaign, IL: Human Kinetics.

26. Katch, F.I., and McArdle, W.D. (1983). *Nutrition, weight control, and exercise.* Philadelphia: Lea & Febiger.

27. Kendall, F., & Wadsworth, G. (1983). *Muscles: Testing and function* (3rd ed.). Baltimore: Williams & Wilkins.

28. Kibler, W.B. (1990). *The sports preparticipation fitness examination.* Champaign, IL: Human Kinetics.

29. Kissner, C., & Colby, L.A. (1985). *Therapeutic exercise: Foundations and techniques.* Philadelphia: Davis.

30. Knight, K. (1985). *Cryotherapy* (1st ed.). Chattanooga, TN: Chattanooga Corporation-Education Division. (out of print)

31. Knight, K.L. (1990). *Clinical experiences in athletic training.* Champaign, IL: Human Kinetics.

32. Kuland, D.N. (1988). *The injured athlete* (2nd ed.). Philadelphia: Lippincott.

33. Kuprian, W. (1982). *Physical therapy for sports.* Philadelphia: Saunders.

34. Michigan High School Athletic Association, Inc. (1985). *Football helmet inspection*. East Lansing, MI: Author.

35. Mottram, D.R. (1988). *Drugs in sport*. Champaign, IL: Human Kinetics.

36. National Athletic Trainers Association Board of Certification. (1990). *Role delineation validation study for the entry-level athletic trainers certification examination* (2nd ed.). Raleigh, NC: Columbia Assessment Services.

37. National Athletic Trainers Association Board of Certification. (1991). *Certification information for entry-level eligibility requirements, continuing education policies and disciplinary procedures*. Dallas: NATA BOC.

38. National Athletic Trainers Association Board of Certification. (1993, Spring). *Certification update*. Dallas: NATA.

39. National Athletic Trainers Association. (1993, November). Code of ethics. *N.A.T.A. News*, pp. 9-21.

40. O'Donoghue, D.H. (1984). *Treatment of injuries to athletes* (4th ed.). Philadelphia: Saunders.

41. Olson, J., & Hunter, G. (1983, January). Weight training safety guidelines. *Athletic Purchasing and Facilities*, **7**(1), 31.

42. Prentice, W. (1990). *Rehabilitation techniques in sports medicine*. St. Louis: Times Mirror/Mosby.

43. Prentice, W. (Ed.) (1990). *Therapeutic modalities in sports medicine*. St. Louis: Times Mirror/Mosby.

44. Ray, R., Hanlon, J., & VanHeest, G. (1989). Facilitating team grieving: A case study. *Journal of the National Athletic Trainers Association, Inc.*, **24**(1), 39-42.

45. Roy, S., & Irvin, R. (1983). *Sports medicine: Prevention, evaluation, management, and rehabilitation*. Englewood Cliffs, NJ: Prentice Hall.

46. Salter, R.B. (1970). *Textbook of disorders and injuries of the musculoskeletal system*. Baltimore: Williams & Wilkins.

47. Shriber, W.J. (1975). *A manual of electrotherapy* (4th ed.). Philadelphia: Lea & Febiger.

48. Thomas, C.L. (Ed.) (1985). *Taber's cyclopedic medical dictionary* (13th ed.). Philadelphia: Davis.

49. Torg, J. (1982). *Athletic injuries to the head, neck, and face*. Philadelphia: Lea & Febiger.

50. Torg, J., Vegso, J., & Torg, E. (1990). *Rehabilitation of athletic injuries* (2nd ed.). St. Louis: Mosby.

51. Voltmer, E.F., & Esslinger, A.A. (1979). *Organization and administration of physical education* (5th ed.). New York: Appleton-Century-Crofts.

52. Williams, M. (1988). *Nutrition for fitness and sport*. Dubuque, IA: Brown.

53. Williams, M. (1989). *Beyond training: How athletes enhance performance legally and illegally.* Champaign, IL: Human Kinetics.

54. Williams, P., & Warwick, R. (1976). *Gray's anatomy* (36th ed.). Philadelphia: Saunders.

55. Zairns, B.J., & Carson, W. (1985). *Injuries to the throwing arm.* Philadelphia: Saunders.

About the Author

Lorin Cartwright, MS, EMT, ATC, teaches health education and directs the athletic training program at Pioneer High School in Ann Arbor, Michigan. She also works as a health and physical education instructor at the city's Scarlett Middle School.

Since she became certified as an athletic trainer in 1980, Lorin has put her knowledge and experience to good use by helping numerous students study for and pass the National Athletic Trainers Association (NATA) certification exam. Not only has she served as an examiner for several NATA exams, which has given her insights into common errors students make on the test, but she also has taken numerous certification tests herself and learned firsthand about test-taking strategies and skills.

Lorin received an MS in education from the University of Michigan in 1981. She is a member of NATA and the Michigan Athletic Trainers Society. In addition to being a frequent speaker at NATA clinical symposiums, Lorin is the author of several articles on injury prevention. In 1994 she became the first woman, as well as the first high school athletic trainer, to be elected president of District IV of NATA. When she's not working, Lorin enjoys scuba diving, working with stained glass, and attending auctions.

More great athletic training resources

Management Strategies in Athletic Training

Richard Ray, EdD, ATC

1994 • Cloth • 272 pp
Item BRAY0582 • ISBN 0-87322-582-1
$32.00 ($42.95 Canadian)

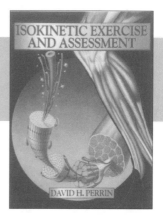

Isokinetic Exercise and Assessment

David H. Perrin, PhD, ATC

1993 • Cloth • 224 pp
Item BPER0464 • ISBN 0-87322-464-7
$29.00 ($38.95 Canadian)

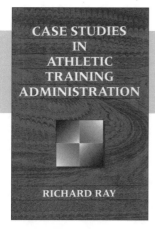

Case Studies in Athletic Training Administration

Richard Ray, EdD, ATC

1995 • Paper • 104 pp
Item BRAY0675 • ISBN 0-87322-675-5
$14.00 ($18.95 Canadian)

Facilitated Stretching

PNF Stretching Made Easy

Robert E. McAtee

1993 • Paper • 120 pp
Item BMCA0420 • ISBN 0-87322-420-5
$15.95 ($22.50 Canadian)

Prices subject to change.

Human Kinetics
The Information Leader in Physical Activity
2335

Place your order using the appropriate telephone number/address shown in the front of this book, or **call TOLL-FREE in the U.S. 1 800 747-4457.**